MW01027019

John Calvin

Sermons on the Saving Work of Christ

John Calvin

Selected and Translated
by Leroy Nixon

6749 Remington Cir
Pelham AL 35124

Solid Ground Christian Books
6749 Remington Circle
Pelham, AL 35124
205-443-0311
mike.sgcb@gmail.com
www.solid-ground-books.com

SERMONS ON THE SAVING WORK OF CHRIST

John Calvin (1509-1564)

Translated by Leroy Nixon in 1950

First Solid Ground edition is September 2011

Taken from edition published in 1950
by Eerdmans Publishing, Grand Rapids, MI

Cover design by Borgo Design
Contact them at borgogirl@bellsouth.net

ISBN- 978-159925-259-9

ACKNOWLEDGEMENTS

To the REV. EDWARD H. BISHOP, of New Brunswick, New Jersey, who nourished my interest in John Calvin.

To the REV. LOUIS H. BENES, editor of the *Church Herald*, for his kind permission to include in this volume some sermons, excerpts from which have already appeared in the *Church Herald*.

PREFACE

The reader of this volume of sermons should be aware (1) of one respect in which I, the translator, have endeavored to be true to John Calvin and (2) of another respect in which I have made no effort to be true to him.

(1) As for the style of the translations, I have tried to be as literal as possible. On the matter of vocabulary I have spent many hours with French-English and French dictionaries. For words not in any dictionary I consulted some graduate students from France working in the United States. As a last resort, I scanned many pages for the usage of certain words in order to arrive at their meaning by the process of induction. I have not skipped over any difficult words, as translators occasionally do. In the few instances where I have just guessed at the meaning of a word, I have indicated that fact in the footnotes.

Almost all of the sentence structure is as formed extemporaneously by Calvin. In only a very few instances did I transpose his word order. The punctuation is much like that indicated by Calvin's secretaries. I have made little effort to modernize it. In most of the sermons the paragraphs are the same as indicated by Calvin's secretaries and as indicated by Calvin's use of certain connective words.

Someone may complain that the style is not very literary. The answer is that Calvin's sermon style was never meant to be literary. He was not reading essays or delivering orations. Rather, he was extemporaneously expounding the Word of God under the guidance of the Holy Spirit. I made a few experiments in applying literary polish to these translations. The result was a distinct loss of the spirit of the man. Quickly I returned to the method of literal translation. It seems to be the best way to be true to Calvin.

(2) As for the selection of the sermons to be included, the choice was purely arbitrary. From about one thousand sermons available in the original French I chose twenty according to my own interests. It will be noted that they follow roughly the Christian year. This is my own device. Calvin would never have done such a thing.

It was Calvin's method to preach consecutively through a whole book of the Bible. For example, without any regard for the Christian year, Calvin preached two hundred consecutive sermons on the book of Deuteronomy. Once he preached a special sermon for Christmas Day, which I have included in this volume. On Easter Day, 1559, and on Easter Day, 1560, he preached a special sermon, which I have included in this volume. Otherwise, as far as the records go, Calvin ignored the Christian year as completely as possible.

The reader will miss something if he or she merely reads this volume of sermons silently as if reading any other book. These sermons should be read aloud. A dozen or more consecrated Christians should gather one evening a week for six months, beginning in December. The leader of the group should read slowly and thoughtfully.

As these sermons were originally instruments in meeting the heart-hunger of the refugees who congregated in Geneva, so today they will meet many a deep personal need. As one listens to these sermons being read aloud, he feels that he sits at the feet of one who through the power of God has overcome great personal handicaps. What we need in our Christian faith today is the personal note. Calvin puts the saving work of Jesus Christ in such a way that you will begin to get new nerve as His saving power surges through your soul.

LEROY NIXON

THE PARSONAGE
QUEENSBORO HILL COMMUNITY CHURCH
Flushing, New York

CONTENTS

Sermon Number	Sermon Title	Page
1.	The Deity of Jesus Christ	13
2.	The Nativity of Jesus Christ	35
	THE PASSION AND RESURRECTION OF CHRIST	
3.	First Sermon on the Passion of Our Lord Jesus Christ	51
4.	Second Sermon on the Passion of Our Lord Jesus Christ	66
5.	Third Sermon on the Passion of Our Lord Jesus Christ	82
6.	Fourth Sermon on the Passion of Our Lord Jesus Christ	99
7.	Fifth Sermon on the Passion of Our Lord Jesus Christ	117
8.	Sixth Sermon on the Passion of Our Lord Jesus Christ	134
9.	Seventh Sermon on the Passion of Our Lord Jesus Christ	150
10.	Eighth Sermon on the Passion of Our Lord Jesus Christ	167
11.	The Resurrection of Jesus Christ	184
	THE ASCENSION OF CHRIST	
12.	First Sermon on the Ascension of Our Lord Jesus Christ	197
13.	Second Sermon on the Ascension of Our Lord Jesus Christ	210
14.	Third Sermon on the Ascension of Our Lord Jesus Christ	221
15.	Fourth Sermon on the Ascension of Our Lord Jesus Christ	232
	PENTECOST AND THE RETURN OF CHRIST	
16.	First Sermon on Pentecost	243
17.	Third Sermon on Pentecost	258
18.	Fourth Sermon on Pentecost	269
19.	Fifth Sermon on Pentecost	279
20.	On the Final Advent of Our Lord Jesus Christ	290

Sermons on the Saving Work of Christ

SERMON 1

The Deity[1] of Jesus Christ *

In the beginning was the Word[2]*, and the Word was with God, and the Word was God. He was in the beginning with God. All things were made by him, and without him nothing was made that was made. In him was life, and the life was the light of men. The light shines in darkness, and the darkness comprehended it not.*—JOHN 1:1-5

THE WORD[3] "Gospel" declares how God loved us when He sent our Lord Jesus Christ into the world. We must note this well. For it is important to know how Holy Scripture uses words.[3] Surely we need not stop simply at words,[3] but we cannot understand the teaching of God unless we know what procedure, style and language He uses. We have to note this word,[3] all the more since it is such a common practice to refer to Holy Scripture as the Law and the Gospel. Those who speak thus intend that all the promises contained in the Old Testament should be referred to the word[3] "Gospel." Surely their intention is good, but Holy Scripture does not speak thus of itself. We should be careful and out of reverence for the Spirit of God retain the manner of speaking which He uses to instruct us.[4]

The word[3] "Gospel" indicates that God in sending our Lord Jesus Christ His Son declares Himself Father to all the world. St. Paul writes to the Ephesians that Jesus Christ came to evangelize those who were near and those who were far from God. Those near were the Jews, who were already allied with

1 The editors of the *Corpus Reformatorum* use "divinité," but "divinity" in modern English is ambiguous. Hence, "deity."
2 HO LOGOS (Greek), *sermo* (Latin), *la parole* (French).
3 TO RHEMA (Gr.), *verbum* (Lat.), *le mot* (Fr.).
4 Calvin in his exegesis was very faithful to the principle that all parts of the Old Testament are not necessarily fulfilled in the "Gospel." Read his commentary upon Genesis 3:15.
* From: *Corpus Reformatorum, Calvini Opera*, vol. 47, pp. 465-484.

God. Those far were the pagans who were aloof from His Church. When we have looked at it in the light of all Scripture we shall find that this word "Gospel" has no other meaning.

That is why this word[3] is the title of the four written histories[5] of how our Lord Jesus Christ came into the world, He went about,[6] He died, He rose again, He ascended into heaven. That, I say, comes under the title "Gospel." And why all that? Because the substance of the Gospel is comprehended in the Person of the Son of God, as I have already said. The Ancient Fathers[7] surely had the promises of salvation. They were well assured that God would be their Father. But they did not have the Guarantee[8] for the love of God and for their adoption. For when Jesus Christ came into the world, God signed and sealed His fatherly love. We have received full testimony of life, the substance of which (as I have already said) we have in Jesus Christ. That is why St. Paul says that all the promises of God are in Him, Yea and Amen. For God then ratified all that He had previously said and had promised to men.

So not without cause those four histories have been named "Gospel," where it is declared to us how the Son of God was sent, He took human flesh, and He went about with men in this life. All that is comprehended under the name "Gospel," because it declares to us how God perfected and accomplished everything which was required for the salvation of men, and it was all done in the Person of His Son.

St. Paul can well speak of his gospel,[9] but how so? It is not that he has written a Gospel history, but that his teaching conformed to all that is herein contained. Thus, following what I have already said, when the Gospel is proclaimed[10] to us, it is a manifestation of Jesus Christ, so that in Him we may know that all things are perfected[11] and that we have the truth of

5 Or stories, except that some people think a story is usually not true.
6 Fr. *conversé,* used in the old Latin sense.
7 Old Testament Jewish fathers, or Patriarchs. Calvin in speaking to the common people would not have used a word like "Patriarchs," but rather its colloquial equivalent.
8 Fr. *le gage* is a metaphor from the medieval pawnbrokers. It refers to the article one leaves "in hock."
9 Romans 2:16.
10 Fr. *announcé.*
11 Or completed.

that which had been promised from all time. But for all that the Epistles of St. Paul are not named "Gospel." And why not? Because there we have not a continuous history which shows us how God sent His Son, how He[12] willed that assuming our nature He[13] might have true brotherhood with us, how He[14] died, was raised, and ascended into heaven. These things, I say, are not deduced from a single, continuous thread in Saint Paul. It is very certain that the teaching which is contained in his Epistles is conformed to the teaching of the Gospel. But for all that the word[3] is especially ascribed to these four histories, for the reason that I have already alleged.

Now when we say that the substance of the Gospel is comprehended in the Person of the Son of God, that is not only to say that Jesus Christ has come into the world, but that we may know also His office, the charge committed to Him by God His Father, and His power.

Let us note the difference between the Gospel according to St. John and the other three. The four Gospel-writers are entirely agreed in that they declare[15] how the Son of God appeared in the world, that He has been made true man, like us in all things except sin. Next they describe[15] how He died, He rose again, and He ascended into heaven. Briefly, all that was committed to Him to draw us to God His Father is there declared.

But there are two things which are peculiar to Saint John. One is that he pays more attention to the teaching of Jesus Christ than do the others. Likewise, he declares to us with greater liveliness His virtue[16] and His power. Surely the others relate well the teaching of Jesus Christ, but more briefly. Little summaries in the others appear as long declarations in Saint John. For example, in chapter 6 we see what is said of the miracle He did in the desert, when He fed such a multitude. From that Saint John leads up to the proposition that

12 God.
13 God in Christ.
14 Christ.
15 Fr. *announcent,* thinking of them primarily as writers.
16 Fr. *vertu* is hardly equivalent to English "virtue." Calvin had in mind the Latin sense, which also includes power.

Jesus Christ is the Bread of Life Eternal. We see this teaching of Jesus Christ which is expounded at length by Saint John, and with a greater deduction than is made by the other Gospel-writers, and which was even omitted by them. So it is throughout. For after he has mentioned certain miracles and stories[17] he always comes back to the teaching and finds occasion to put in material treating on the virtue of our Lord Jesus Christ. From chapter 12 to the narrative[17] of the Passion he treats only of that teaching.

We see now the difference between the Gospel according to Saint John and the other three. To say it better, the Gospel according to Saint John is to us, as it were, the key by which we enter into an understanding of the others. For if we read Saint Matthew, Saint Mark, and Saint Luke we shall not know so well why Jesus Christ was sent into the world as when we shall have read Saint John. Having read Saint John, we shall know then how what our Lord Jesus Christ has done benefits us, that He took human flesh, that He died and rose again. We shall learn, I say, the purpose and the substance of all those things in reading this Gospel. That is why he does not linger over the story, as we shall see by the order which he follows. Surely these things ought to be considered more at length, but since there is much substance to the text we have to expound, I mention things as briefly as I can.

Let us be content, then, with what I have mentioned in summary of the office of Jesus Christ, namely, that Saint John declares to us how He was sent by God His Father to perfect the salvation of men. He declares how He took human flesh, how He died and rose again, how He is the Guarantee[18] for

17 Fr. *histoires.*

18 Again the Fr. *le gage.* Cf. note 8 above. Also cf. TON ARRHABON in 2 Cor. 1:22, 5:5, Eph. 1:14. Neither "earnest" as in King James nor "guarantee" as in Revised Standard version quite expresses the idea. Perhaps in this age of installment buying we should say that Jesus Christ is God's Down Payment through Whom we know that more installments of His love will follow if we accept His Down Payment, but this metaphor must not be pressed. Also, cf. Latin *pignus* in Vulgate in passages cited, which means literally a pledge, gage, pawn, security, guarantee, and figuratively a token, assurance, proof. The thought behind this Latin word is that surely God would not make such a payment as the sacrifice of His only begotten Son to secure our response to His love and then not continue to pour out His love toward us.

the love of God, that He is the Soul of our redemption, and that in Him the promises of God are ratified. We must note (as I have already said) that St. John discusses things more briefly than the other three. But he stops longer over the substance to show us the teaching of Jesus Christ, the charge committed to Him by God His Father, briefly, His virtue, His power, and His goodness toward us. The word "Gospel" itself means "good news." But this word ought to be so sacred that we hate[19] the things of this world and that we may know that all our welfare, happiness,[20] joy and glory are in Jesus Christ. When we pronounce the word "Gospel," which is to say "Good News," may we learn not to enjoy without restraint[21] things of this world, which are perishable[22] and vain. Let us not take pleasure in[23] entertainments, sensualities, or anything of that sort, but let us rejoice[23] that Jesus Christ was sent to us, that God gave Himself to us in His Person,[24] that Jesus Christ came to be our means of reconciliation between God and ourselves, that God accepts us as His children, apart from Whom we would be lost and damned. That is why this word should be sacred to us so as to make us prize this priceless gift which is brought to us by our Lord Jesus Christ.

It is said especially that this Gospel is *according to* St. John, so that we may know that it is not of a mortal man but that Saint John is only the minister of it. From whom, then, shall we say we have the Gospel? From Saint John or from Jesus Christ? It is from Jesus Christ. Even Jesus Christ uses this manner of speaking when He says the doctrine is not His own but He preaches it upon the authority of God His Father, from Whom it proceeds. That is so that we may hold all the more reverence for this doctrine and that we may not receive it as a

19 Fr. *faire hayr* is an alliterative intensive, for which there is no exact equivalent in modern English.
20 Fr. *felicité* is perhaps "bliss" here.
21 Fr. *outre measure.*
22 Fr. *caduque* is an onomatopoetic word, the meaning of which varies all the way from a mild frailty to downright rottenness, according to the manner in which the word is said.
23 Fr. *réjouir* and *s'éjouir*. The second intensive suggests that, of course, the former so-called enjoyments are not to be compared with the great joy we have in Jesus Christ.
24 Christ's Person.

common thing, but as the pure truth of God which has been proclaimed by His Only Son. Saint John, then, was surely the instrument and organ of God, as a pen will write in the hand of a man, but we must not receive the Gospel which was written by him as from a mortal man.

We come now to the text. *The Word,* says he, *was in the beginning.* The intention of St. John is to show us that, as the Son of God did not begin to exist when He appeared to the world, so also He did not begin only when His virtue was spread everywhere. For He already was, from all time and before all time. Already His virtue resided in Him and was not taken from elsewhere, but there was a virtue which was in the Word of God at the beginning. But finally it was manifested. We know it now since Jesus Christ was sent into the world. St. John, then, here wishes to show that when Jesus Christ came into the world, it was our Eternal God Who came, Who redeemed us to Himself.

But to still better understand the whole, we must note item by item the things said here. *The Word was in the beginning.* There is no doubt that he here calls the Son of God *the Word.* The reason is that it is the wisdom which always was in God, that is His counsel and His virtue. Surely we have not expounded things here according as their seriousness requires. I say it even of those things propounded by St. John. For although the Spirit of God has spoken by his mouth, yet he has not yet declared things in their grandeur and majesty. It is not a derogatory remark about the Spirit of God when we say that He did not manifest entirely and in perfection the things here indicated. For the Holy Spirit accommodates Himself to our weakness. In fact, if we heard God speaking to us in His Majesty, it would be useless to us, since we would understand nothing. So, since we are carnal, He must stutter. Otherwise we would not understand Him. By that, then, we see that we must understand that God made Himself little to declare Himself to us. And if it were not so, how would it be possible to express anything of the Majesty of God by speaking the language of men? Would it not be too great a step to take? St. John, then, although he is an instrument of the Holy Spirit, does not speak of these things in their grandeur. Nevertheless, he speaks a language which is, as it were, unknown to us. Yet one must conclude that the secrets here contained are not declared so openly that we can comprehend them as we comprehend the things of this world. Let us in simplicity be content with what is here shown us. For our Lord knew what would be sufficient for our good. He accommodated Himself to us and to our weakness in such a way that He has neither forgotten nor left behind anything which might be good and profitable to us.

So let us learn to cling to the purity and simplicity of His teaching, as we see how the world in this matter has been deceived by foolish imagination, vain speculations, and diabolical audacity. For when it came to a question of treating these things men have gone beyond their depth as they have wished, beyond the revelation and doctrine, with curiosity and audacity, to inquire into the eternal essence of God, as one might hear in the Papacy, as if one were disputing about a flock of goats, and I do not know what all. They have no more reverence for God than for a beast. We need not seek better testimony against the teaching of the Sophists of the Sorbonne in order to know that the devil reigns there and always has reigned there. I say again even if their teaching were not actually false, when one sees that they have so little respect for the majesty of God, one must surely say that it is a diabolical teaching which is today practiced by the Sophists and Sorbonnists in all the colleges of the Pope. So then, (as I have said) let us be content with this simplicity which is shown us by the Holy Spirit. For He treats of what is good and useful for our salvation. As I have already declared, He has here brought out what was suitable for us to know.

Let us come now to this word "Word."[25] When St. John calls Jesus Christ "the Word," it is as if he said, "The eternal plan of God, or the wisdom which resides in Him." However, we must note that God is not like men. When we have a plan, it can change. But not so with God. For whatever is in God's mind is unchangeable. Besides, a plan which we have does not

25 Fr. *ce mot de Parole.*

necessarily represent our essential nature. But God's plan is really God. For God is not like a veil which casts a shadow, as in the figure of speech St. James uses. We are like a shadow that flits about and we cannot remain firm. Now nothing like that exists in God, so that whatever is in Him is of His essence and eternity. That is why St. John declares that this Word is really God.

But as for the expression[26] (as I have already said) we must not imagine a plan or a wisdom in God like the word[27] of men. Surely we can make some comparison with ourselves, but we must always consider the long distance which is between us and God. For if the heavens are high above the earth, we must know that God is still higher above us. There is no proportion. So, when we deduce some figure of speech from our lives as creatures, we must always note this great distance which is between God and us.

One may well say that in the soul of men there is an intelligence which is so joined to the soul that the soul cannot exist without intelligence. There is also the will. I do not mean one desire now and another desire then, but the faculty (as they say) of willing which man has in himself. For man is not like a stone or a log without sense and without reason, but he has this peculiar nature[28] stamped upon him of willing this and that. So, then, we can certainly accept such figures of speech. However, we must remember that we are here speaking of things so high that all human sensibilities must be thrown down and that we must treat them in humility, applying them in their true sense, that we must not be too curious, that we must not have that foolish imagination which has until now prevailed in the world but that we must come to the school of God to listen to what He has to tell us and to flee every proposition of men which is contrary to what is released to us by the Holy Spirit.

However, we must also note that some, being driven by the devil, have perverted the sense of this doctrine, saying that this

26 Fr. *le mot.*
27 Fr. *la parole.*
28 Fr., *propriété,* used in the sense of its Latin source.

Word was not, apart from some plan and deliberation which God had made to redeem mankind in the person of Jesus Christ (Who was an idea, as they say, as when a man has resolved to do a piece of work which he has conceived in his mind). They do not allow eternity of essence to the Son of God in speaking thus. Now we have already seen, and we shall see still more fully, how Saint John calls Jesus Christ the Word of God to show His Deity, as I have already said. And may this be a visible testimony from God Himself. For he says that this Word was in the beginning. So He must have been eternal. To be sure, one might reply on the contrary that Moses says that in the beginning God created heaven and earth and now Saint John says that this Word was in the beginning. So it seems that, if heaven and earth and other creatures were in the beginning, one cannot prove the eternity of Jesus Christ by saying the Word was in the beginning. But the answer is easy, namely: that when Moses deals with this beginning, we must be advised how he speaks, that is, of heaven, of earth, and of other things which have a beginning.

Let us consider now what Saint John says. *"In the beginning"* (says he) "was the Word." And where was this beginning? *In God.* And what is the beginning of God? There is none. Otherwise God would have to be a creature of our imagination. Thus when mention is made of the beginning of God, we must conclude that it is a beginning which has no time element in it. It is well, then, to compare the passage of Moses where it says that God created everything in the beginning and this passage which says, "The Word was in the beginning." For Moses deals with creatures which began to be at a certain time. Here St.. John speaks only of God, who cannot be without His eternity. We must, then, conclude that this beginning has no beginning. So we see that Jesus Christ always was. That is how Saint John said that Jesus Christ is our eternal God, Who appeared to us in the flesh, as also Saint Paul speaks of it.

Next he adds, "this Word was with God," as if he said that we must separate the Word from all creatures. That is the intention of the Gospel-writer. We must not (says he) imagine that this Word has had something like creatures. We must withdraw from the world. We must ascend above earth and heaven when we think of this Word. One might perhaps ask, "Before there was heaven or earth was it possible that this Word was in the beginning?" Saint John, then, in answer separates this Word from all creatures. He might have said, "When I speak to you of this Word, you must come to God, for He is in God." Let us regard Him, then, as an Eternity Who belongs neither to creatures, nor to heaven nor to earth, nor to anything which may exist.

Nevertheless, the Gospel here makes a distinction between God and His Word. What is this distinction? It is not a distinction of essence. For he always means that this Word is God. And we must conclude, since we have only one God, and there is only one simple essence in Him, that Jesus Christ, this Eternal Word here spoken of, was not different from God His Father. Yet there is always some distinction. What is it?

Now because we cannot comprehend what is so high above all our intelligence and reason, ancient Teachers have used the word "Persons." They said that in God there were three persons, not as if we speak in ordinary language calling three men three persons, or as in the Papacy they even have the audacity to paint three grotesque pictures, and behold the Trinity! But the word "Persons" in this connection is to express the properties which are of the essence of God. The word "Substance" or (as the Greeks say) "Hypostasis" is still more suitable since it is from Holy Scripture. The Apostle uses it in the first chapter of the Letter to the Hebrews when he says that Jesus Christ is the living image, and the splendor of the glory, the image of the substance of God His Father. When he speaks there of the substance of God, he does not mean the essence. He speaks of this property which belongs to the Father: namely, that He is the Source of all things.

Now let us look at these three Hypostases, as they are called. Let us see how they agree, as much as God teaches us, as I have already said. For we must not exceed these limits, and let us pay as much attention to that as will be required for the exposition of this passage. When one speaks of God, surely men themselves are confused and do not know how to imagine Him without being led astray in their imaginations, as says Saint Paul. So it comes that they were given to too much pride for their prudence and wisdom. Yet God punishes them in such a way that they find themselves in such horrible labyrinths that they cannot get out. But when we allow God to lead us to Himself by Holy Scripture, we shall know how much God will be our Helper.[29] For we shall come to the Father as to the source of all things. Then we shall not be able to conceive of the Father without His Counsel and Eternal Wisdom. Then there will be a virtue which resides in Him which we shall also sense clearly. That is how we shall find these three properties in the essence of God.

This is what Saint John meant by the expression *"The Word was with God."* If there were not any distinction, he would not speak thus. For it would be speaking improperly to say, "God was with Himself." So we know that this Word has some distinction from the Heavenly Father. For this Word was begotten before time, even though God always had His plan and His wisdom. However, we must not imagine any beginning. For we must not say that God was without judgment, without plan, and wisdom. So, we must not put apart and separate from God the Property of this Word by saying that we judge that there was some time when He[30] was not with Him.[31] For this would make Him an idol. But as I have said, the Three are only One, and yet we must distinguish Them, since there is a definite distinction, as is here shown. However, it reminds us of a sentence of an ancient teacher, which is well worthy to be remembered, because it is excellent.

"I cannot," says he, "think upon these three properties which are shown me in God unless immediately my mind reduces them to one. On the other hand, it is impossible for me to know one only God unless I regard all the three properties, and I see them distinguished by my sense according to the clarity that is given me in Holy Scripture." That is how believers will

29 Fr., *mestier,* used in the sense of the Latin *minister.*
30 *la Parole.*
31 *le Dieu.*

know God. Knowing the Father, they will know His wisdom, which is this Word which is here spoken of. They will come more and more to this power which we have discussed. When they have known these three things, they will no longer go astray either this way or that way, but they will come to this sole essence—to know that there is only one God, even only one God who has so created the world that He has omitted nothing of all that was required to accomplish our redemption. That is what we must note with respect to what is said, that this Word was with God. That is, the Gospel-writer wished to separate Jesus Christ from all creatures. However, he showed us the distinction between Him and the Father.

Now he adds *"This Word was God"* to express still better what he wished to indicate, that Jesus Christ is not a created thing Who had a beginning, but He is our true God. This passage has been poorly understood by some. Someone has foolishly translated it, saying, "God is the Word." For if we said that God was the Word, the Father would no longer be God and the Holy Spirit would no longer be God. But St. John wished on the contrary to say that the Word is God, as if he said that Jesus Christ is, with respect to His Deity, of one same essence with the Father. Thus he does not exclude the Father from the Deity, but he shows that there is only one essence in God. Although there was a distinction of God from His Word, yet we must always come back to this simple proposition, that They are one God Whom we must adore. To be sure, ancient heretics have worked hard to pervert this passage so as not to be constrained to confess that Jesus Christ was our true God. But we see here that St. John speaks so clearly of the eternity of this Word that there is no place for shuffling or subterfuge.

Next he adds, *"This Word was in the beginning with God."* He had not said these two words together. He had said, "This Word was in the beginning" and "He was with God." Now he joins the two together. That is why we must so contemplate Jesus Christ that we do not estimate that He is not true God and of the same essence with the Father. He has, to be sure, been created with respect to His human nature, but we must go further to know Him as our eternal God, Who is in such a manner our God that He is the wisdom of His Father which has been with God from all time. That, then, is the summary of it. Now when we remember this exposition (as it is simply expressed) it will suffice to instruct us for our salvation. Surely it is all we need to know about it.

For if we come here to dispute foolishly it will happen to us (as I have already said) as it happened to the Papists. Besides, let us note that it is a foolish study to work hard to confirm what the Gospel-writer here says by the teaching of ancient Philosophers. There are people who try to do that. To be sure, in Plato one will find that there was an intelligence in God. For when he speaks of God, he says that God always had His intelligence in Himself. Almost all the other Philosophers speak in this way. Now those who are so curious as to wish thus to make the Philosophers agree with Holy Scripture think they do great service to the Christian Church when they can say that the Gospel-writers have not been the only ones who have spoken thus and that even the pagans have well known such things. It is very apropos! As though one put a veil before clear vision. Behold God Who makes Himself clear to us by the doctrine of His Gospel, and we are going to put a veil before it by saying, "Look at this! Your clearness will be still more clear."

It is very certain that God willed that these same things might be known by pagan Philosophers to render them so much more inexcusable before His Majesty. But that is not to say that His doctrine ought to be confirmed by what they have said. For the fact is that, although the more they thought they were approaching God, the further away they were straying. So is fulfilled this sentence which Saint Paul pronounces against all mankind. All those who wished to be too clever, who did not seek God in such reverence and humility as they ought, have fallen into the depth of error. And it is a just punishment from God if we come thus to pollute His doctrine, classing it among the foolish inventions of men.

Now let us pass on. The Gospel-writer says, *"All things were made by Him,* and without Him nothing was made of all that which was made." After he has assured us of the eternal essence of the Word of God, he adds a confirmation to show us His eternal Deity, so that we may be more certain of everything. "All things," says he, "were made by Him." The essence of God is known by us, not only by what we can comprehend of Him, but also when He declared Himself to us by His creation. For when Scripture deals with it, then and there it is made visible. Not only visible, but Saint Paul goes still further, saying that, although we are blind, we can feel it by the hand. Thus when our eyes will have closed, we can know this power of God. And how so? Since it is inside us. In whom do we live and move and have our substance? In God, Who has breathed life into us, and by Whom we subsist. That is what Saint John shows us by saying that all things were made by Him.

So, we know that the Word of God has been from the beginning, Who is our God. And how do we know that? Certainly we could not reach so high. And yet God has descended to us, even God with His Word, in such a way that we can know Him,[32] although our senses do not extend so far and we cannot ascend above the clouds, we are constrained to know that this Word is really God. How so? Because all things were made by Him. So it is in Him that all things have been. The Apostle to the Hebrews puts it, "Let us confess that the Word of God is eternal." Why so? Because by this Word all things were made. Saint Paul also says in the 17th chapter of Acts that God did not manifest Himself without ample testimony in order that we may be able to see Him in all His creation. Thus, since all things were made by His Word, we must know that He is our eternal God. There are some heretics who imagine that the Word of God had a beginning at the creation of the world, because the Word was never spoken of until the world was created. As Moses says, "God said, 'Let there be light,' and there was light," etc. They wish to infer by that that the Word began then. Really? On the contrary, we must rather conclude from that that the Word is eternal. For if a man begins to do something, that does not say that he did not pre-

32 God.

viously exist. If that is the case with respect to creatures, is it not even more true with respect to God?

So then, although the Word of God did not pour out His power before the creation of the world, that does not say that He did not exist before. That is what Saint John means by this manner of speaking, that is, when he says, "All things were made by this Word." Besides, let us note that when mention is made of God the Father and of His Word, we say then that all things are made by[33] God and through[33] His Word, and this word "Word"[34] is attributed only to Jesus Christ. To be sure, when we are speaking simply of God without distinction of Persons, we may well say that all things are by and through God.[35] But when there is some distinction as in this passage, this is the property that belongs to Jesus Christ, that "all things are made through Him." This is the distinction of Persons that I have mentioned: that all things are from God the Father, but Jesus Christ is the means.

That is what Saint John intended. It is as if he said, "God through His Word made all things." God, then, declares that He is the source of them, and all things had to be made by Him, through the means and in the power of His Word. *And without Him*[36] *nothing was made of that which was made.* Saint John thus repeats this sentence, not only on account of his manner of saying the same thing in two different ways, but because of the ingratitude of men. For although one tells them that all things are made by God through His Word[37] they do not apprehend[38] it. We see that the creatures of God do not touch us to the quick[39]; and that we are so stupid and

33. *de Dieu et par sa Parole.*

34 Fr., *ce mot de Par.* I doubt whether Calvin means to distinguish between *Par* and *Parole. Parler* and *Parole* are both derived from the Latin *parabolare.*

35 Fr., *de par Dieu.* Calvin in his mind is doing a little playing on the stem *par,* although the preposition *par* is derived from Latin *per.*

36 Fr., *sans icelle* (feminine). *La Parole* is evidently not personalized in the pronouns, although *La Parole* itself is capitalized. It would, of course, be awkward to say in English without *Her* nothing was made.

37 Fr., *par sa Parole.*

38 "Apprehend," like "comprehend" in the King James Version, is deliberately ambiguous. It says: (1) They do not understand it. (2) Even if they do understand it, they do not grab hold of it quickly.

39 Or, they do not charge us with life.

so gross in our senses that we cannot comprehend[40] things as they are proposed to us.

Saint John, then, to better express it to us, adds, "Without Him nothing was made of that which was made." As if he said, "And how unhappy[41] we are if we do not receive this eternal Word of God, since through Him we were created. That is, that the world was made, the heaven, the stars, and the earth which produces our nourishment. Briefly, all good things have been given to us by means of this Word. Thus, then, when we see that our life proceeds from Him, we must cling only to Him and reject everything that one may propose to us to the contrary. There is a double exposition, according to the position of the words. Not that they are changed, but they are treated differently. Some read thus, "Through this Word all things were made, and without Him nothing was made," and they finish the sentence there. Then they add, "All that was made was life in Him." But that declaration is not proper. To be sure, the sense that they put into it is a very good one. For they have the same exposition as we have. But it is a strange way of speaking. For it is not said of creatures that they are life, but that is attributed to God. As says Saint Paul to the Romans, "The Spirit is life, because of the freedom which was given to us through Jesus Christ." In brief, when we look all through Holy Scripture, never is it said that we are life in ourselves, but that God Himself alone has life, not only spiritual life, but the life from which all things have their being, and by which we live, and that we have life and breath in Him, as I have already shown from the passage from St. Paul.

So, we see the truth of this sentence, that nothing of all that was made was made without the Word of God. This is the order of reading which has been found in all the more ancient Greek teachers and other expositors. There was none who did not thus expound it. However, we have to note that the Manicheans wished to pervert this passage (saying, "All that was made in Him was life") to prove their foolish opinions, that all creatures are living—rocks, trees, wheat,

---

41 Fr., ***malheureux***, the opposite of ***bien-heureux*** of the Beatitudes.
40 Double meaning again, like "apprehend."

barley. All that, according to their imagination, was living, so that they did not dare to eat bread unless they were previously sanctified by God. And why not? "It must be God who eats this thing," they said. The devil possessed them, and yet they brought forward passages of Scripture, and abused them to prove their foolish speculations. I certainly wanted to mention this in passing to show that the devil has always tried to pervert Holy Scripture. Be that as it may, if we are seeking the truth of God we shall find it pure and simple. The devil will never be able to contrive[42] anything against it to turn us away from it, since it is shown before our eyes, and it will be our own fault if we do not see it in its purity just as God has revealed it to us.

Let us come now to the natural sense. After Saint John said, "Nothing was made of that which was made, without this Word," he adds, *"In Him is life."* Here he wishes to indicate two different things. That is, that as everything was once created by the power of the Word of God, also all things remain and are preserved by this power and by this same means. There are two things we must properly consider. One, that we have beginning and life through this Word. The other, that we are sustained through Him—and not only we, but all the world. Not only was the world in the beginning created through this Word, but also it would no longer exist unless it were preserved in this same condition and by this same means. Therefore (as I have said), let us remember well these two things here pointed out by Saint John.

In the first place, then, he declares to us that nothing of that which was made, was made without this Word. How so? Does he wish to except anything that was not made? It seems that he wishes to say that the Angels were not created. No, no. It is not that, but he wishes to show that we have nothing which does not depend upon God and which has not its being in Him. Surely the Angels have a very noble nature. Nevertheless they exist through this Word, and are established in Him. Otherwise they could not endure. As also there is noth-

42 Fr., *machiner.*

ing in the world which is not preserved through this same Word.

Here we are admonished of what poverty there would be in us unless God sustained us by His grace. That is why the Psalmist says that as soon as God withdraws His Spirit from us, there we are as dust, and entirely vanished. To be sure, he speaks there of creatures and things corporal. But we also see that all the rest also is surely sustained through the power of this Word. Although we must subsist through the Word of God, we must note that by means of Him we began to have life. And who declares it to us? The Gospel-writer. It is after all what the Apostle says in the first chapter of Hebrews. "The Son of God is the splendor of the glory or the image of the substance of God His Father and He[43] sustains all things by His[43] word."[44] He uses there the word "Word,"[45] but with such a meaning that he intends not only the power of the Son of God, but also an admirable arrangement and a well-defined order which He has put into created things, since He is the Wisdom of God. And we can behold Him in all creatures, because he sustains all things through His virtue and power.[46] That, then, is how we have life and movement, and after having fed[47] upon it today, we continue, that is, as long as God preserves us. For on our own power alone we might have perished any minute, unless the Word of God maintained us. That is the sense in which the Gospel-writer says "This Word was life." Not only were all things made by Him, but they must be established upon Him and He maintains them in their being.

Next he adds, "The life was the light of men." And why does he add this? For two reasons. The first is that after we have known the power of God and the virtue of His Word everywhere above and below, we must consider our relationship to it all. For it is surely reasonable that what touches us more

---

43 The Son.

44 *parole,* not capitalized. The "word" or "wisdom" of the Son, as He is the "Word" or "Wisdom" of the Father.

45 Fr., *du mot de Parole.*

46 Fr., *sa vertu et puissance; puissance* is always translated "power;" *vertu* sometimes indicates "virtue" and sometimes "power" and sometimes both at once.

47 Fr., *vescu,* lived.

closely we contemplate with greater diligence. How so? I ought to know the goodness of God in His preserving horses and oxen. So David tells us, saying that He gives nourishment to every beast. I see on the other hand the earth which by the commandment of God produces her fruits. If I look, then, at the beasts, I ought to know the goodness of God, which is shown even toward donkeys and dogs, but much more toward me. God comes even in that to make me feel His virtue. He gives me the bread by which I am nourished. And must I not be deeply moved by so many benefits? It is certain. For also when one considers the works of God he speaks especially of men, for God declares His virtue more greatly and more excellently in us than in other creatures.

God, then, surely wishes to be magnified both in heaven and on earth, and in all His works which we see, but much more in man, because He has stamped His image upon us more than upon all other creatures. For He has not said of the sun, of the stars, nor of any other creature however excellent it may be, "I will to make here a masterpiece who is to be in My image and likeness." So, then, the Gospel-writer, having spoken of the virtue of the Word of God, which extends to all creatures, comes to men. By that he shows that if men contemplate the goodness of God by everything they behold, surely they must consider it in their own persons. Although God has done us the honor to be magnified in us so that even the pagans have called man a little world,[48] because one sees in him a masterpiece which surmounts all others. There is good reason for us to know in him the virtue and the power of God. To be sure, we can contemplate God in all His creatures, but when He manifests Himself in man, then we see Him, as it were, by the face. When we consider Him in other creatures we see Him obscurely and, as it were, by the back So, although it may be said that God is made visible in other creatures, in them we see, as it were, only His feet, His hands, and His back. But in man we see, as it were, His face. Not that it should be His face so that we contemplate Him in perfection.

48 The philosophic term is "microcosm." Calvin does not usually use Greek in such cases, but rather colloquial French.

I do not mean that. For I do not speak of things divine, but only of what God wishes to be known in this world above and below.

That, then, is the sum of what St. John says, that "the life was the light of men." As if he said, "Certainly there is a life which was poured out upon all creatures. And what life? As all things are made and preserved through the Word of God. However, there is something more excellent in man, that is, soul, intelligence, and reason. For a man will not be insensible like a stone. He will not be without sense and reason as the beasts. But he has a more excellent life, to contemplate the things which are beyond the world.

Now he adds consequently, *"The light shines in the darkness, and the darkness comprehended it not."* He mentions this especially, because the light[49] which God put in man is almost entirely extinguished. In fact, if we judge according to what we can now see in mortal men, we shall not estimate very highly the grace of God. For although man has been created in the image of God, he has been disfigured by sin. What, then, do we see in men? We see there an image of God which is wholly deformed and spoiled, since the devil has soiled it by sin. But although men following what Satan suggested have extinguished the brightness[50] of God, however, the devil has not been able to do so much by his craftiness that this brightness of God did not still shine in the midst of darkness. That is what Saint John wishes to show. As if he said, "It is true, my little ones, that if what was originally given to men had remained in them, we would now see only the glory of God shining everywhere, instead of what we do see—that His image is so disfigured. Still it is true, however, that we may yet perceive some brightness of God left there and some spark of His light.

That is what the Gospel-writer wished to indicate. I omit other things, because time does not permit us to speak of them further, and already I have spoken too long. Nevertheless, we

49 Or clear intelligence.
50 Or clear light.

must note that men have enough light[51] of knowledge of God to be convicted and rendered inexcusable before God. We may make believe what we will, but God pronounces that we are darkness. And how so? Let us not attribute that to God, but to our vice. Now God must enlighten us by His brightness. Otherwise there would be nothing but darkness in us, and we would surely trip if we wished to walk a pace forward without His leading. And yet it is true (as I have already said) God has not left us so destitute that we are entirely abandoned by Him so that none of His gifts remain in us. And that it may be so, there is some semblance of religion in men. They still have relics of their original creation. So we see even in the most wicked and depraved there is some impression of the image of God. That makes us all the more inexcusable. Inasmuch as they will not have made use of it, their condemnation will be all the heavier. It will be doubly heavy. That, then, is how, although our nature has been so corrupted, yet we still retain some spark of the grace which God had put in our father Adam. So this sentence is true, "The light shines in darkness."

However, the Gospel-writer says, *"The darkness comprehended it not."* By which he shows the ingratitude of men. God makes His light to shine in us. His Word shines there. However, we obscure that light by our wickedness. To be sure, the Gospel itself is to us a declaration and a manifestation of this light. But still the wickedness and ingratitude which are in us would entirely extinguish the light in us, unless God remedied it by an infinite power and goodness. That is what Saint John wishes to show in this place. However, he begins to prepare us for what he will say later: that is, the purpose for which this Word (Who is Jesus Christ) was sent to us by God His Father. It is that He might be manifest to us in the flesh for our salvation. He wishes, then, to show the mystery of our redemption and how we needed it when he says, *"We have not comprehended the light*[52] which was in

51 Fr., *clarté,* which I have usually translated "brightness." *La lumière* is the word for "the light." *clarté* here may also be rendered by "clarity" or "clearness," one of Calvin's virtues as an expositor.

52 Again, *la clarté,* as distinguished from *la lumière,* which is Christ.

us." As if he said, "It would not have been profitable to have the light which shines in us,[53] unless we had been so wonderfully redeemed and this Word had fulfilled the love of God toward us to restore His image which had been blotted out by our sin and entirely disfigured in the first man."

That is how (say I) Saint John wishes to prepare us to know the effect of our redemption. Then he also wished to show how the Word of God declares Himself in His creatures, since all things are preserved by His power. However, he exhorts us to know the graces God has given us, by which we excel other creatures, so that we magnify Him. Besides, to know that, since He has imprinted on us His living image from the beginning and He makes us to experience His power, it is only reasonable that we should learn to cling to this Word and to know in general, the benefits God has given to mankind, in order that the light[54] He has poured upon us by His grace may not be extinguished by our wickedness, but that Jesus Christ may so dwell in the midst of us that, being led by the Holy Spirit, we may be able to have such access to the Father that He may introduce us into His heavenly glory.

Now I have treated things as briefly as was possible for me, always hoping to attain the object which was before the Gospel-writer. However, if I have omitted something because I could not remember everything, let each one of you say what God has revealed to him about it. And if there is any doubt let him suggest the things, so that declaring them they may be explained, and so that the Church of God may be fully edified by it when things do not remain in doubt, but they are understood according to their true sense, after they shall have been appropriately discussed and according to God.

---

53 Fr., *la clarté qui luit en nous.*
54 *la clarté.*

SERMON 2

The Nativity of Jesus Christ * [1]

Now it happened in those days that an edict was made by Ceasar Augustus that all the world should be registered. (This first registration was done when Cyrenius was governor of Syria.) They all went to be registered, each one to his own city. Joseph also went up from Galilee, from the city of Nazareth, into Judea, to the city of David, which is called Bethlehem, because he was of the house and lineage of David, to be registered with Mary, who had been given to him as a wife, who was with child. Now it happened while they were there that the days were accomplished for her to give birth. And she gave birth to her first-born son, and wrapped him in swaddling bands, and laid him in a manger, because there was no place for them in the inn.

Now in the same country there were Shepherds abiding in the fields, keeping watch over their flock by night. And, behold, the Angel of the Lord stood near them, and the brightness of the Lord shone around them and they feared with great fear. Then the angel said to them, "Fear not. For, behold, I announce to you great joy, which will be to all the people. Today is born to you the Savior, who is Christ the Lord, in the city of David. And you will have this sign. You will find the baby wrapped in swaddling bands, and laid in a manger." And suddenly with the Angel was a multitude of heavenly knighthood, praising God and saying, "Glory be to God in the highest places, and on earth peace to men. Good will."—Luke 2:1-14

WE KNOW that it is our good, our joy and rest to be united with the Son of God. As He is our Head, we are His body, so also from Him we hold our life and our salvation and all good. In fact, we see how miserable our condition would be unless we had our refuge in Him, to be maintained under His

---

* From: *Corpus Reformatorum, Calvini Opera,* vol. 46, pp. 955-968.
1 Title given by the editors of the *Corpus.*

keeping. However, we could not reach so high (seeing that scarcely can we crawl upon the earth), unless from His side He approached us, and already He had approached in His birth, when He clothed Himself in our flesh and He made Himself our brother. We could not now have our refuge in our Lord Jesus Christ's being seated at the right hand of God His Father in heavenly glory, unless He were abased as far as being made mortal man and having a condition common with us. That is also why, when He is called "Mediator between God and men," this title "man" is especially attributed to Him. As also for the same reason He is called "Emmanuel," that is, "God with us."

Yet when we seek our Lord Jesus Christ to find in Him alleviation of all our miseries and a sure and infallible protection we must begin at His birth. Not only is it recited to us that He was made man like us, but that He so emptied Himself that scarcely was He reputed to be of the rank of men. He was, as it were, banished from every house[2] and fellowship. There was nothing except a stable and a manger to receive Him.

Since it is so, then, we know here how God displayed the infinite treasures of His goodness when He willed that His Son might be thus humbled for our sakes. Let us recognize also how our Lord Jesus Christ from His birth so suffered for us that when we seek Him we need not make long circuits to find Him nor to be truly united to Him. For this cause He willed to be subject to every shame, in such a way that He was, as it were, rejected by the rest of men. But let us also learn to be little to be received by Him. For it is reasonable at least that there be conformity between the Head and the members. Men need not empty themselves to be of no value. For by nature already they will find such poverty in themselves that they will have good reason to be thoroughly dejected. But let us know of what sort we are, that we may offer ourselves to our Lord Jesus Christ in true humility and that He may recognize us and acknowledge us as His own.

---

2 Fr., *logis,* more inclusive than *la maison.*

However, we also have to note that, in the history which St. Luke here recites, on the one hand we learn how the Son of God emptied Himself of everything for our salvation, nevertheless, on the other hand He did not fail to leave certain and infallible testimony that He was the Redeemer of the world promised from all time. Even though He took our condition, He was able to maintain His heavenly majesty. Both sides are here shown to us. For our Lord Jesus Christ is here in a manger and He is, as it were, rejected by the world. He is in extreme poverty without any honor, without any reputation, as it were, subject to servitude. Yet He is magnified by Angels from Paradise, who do Him homage.

In the first place, an angel bears the message of His birth. Then the same one is accompanied by a great multitude, even by an army, who are all present and appear as witnesses sent by God to show that our Lord Jesus Christ, being thus abased for the salvation of men, never ceases to be King of all the world and to have everything under His dominion.

Then the place, Bethlehem, gives proof that it was He who had been promised from all time. For the prophet Micah had spoken thus: "And thou Bethlehem, though thou be in great contempt, as a village which is not much to look at, and which is not densely populated, yet from thee shall come forth to Me He Who is to govern My people, and His goings forth will be from all eternity."[3] We see, then, here on the one hand how our Lord Jesus Christ did not spare Himself, so that we might have easy access to Him and that we might not doubt that we are received even as His body, since He willed to be not only a mortal man clothed in our nature, but, as it were, a poor earthworm stripped of all good. May we never doubt, then, however miserable we may be, that He will keep us as His members.

On the other hand, we see Him here marked, as it were, by the hand of God, so that He may be received without any difficulty, as Him from Whom we must expect salvation, and by Whom we are received into the Kingdom of God, from which

3 Calvin here gives the gist of what he understands by the prophecy, possibly since the Hebrew, the Septuagint, and the Gospel according to Matthew do not entirely agree upon the exact text of the prophecy.

we were previously banished. For we see that He has in Himself a Divine majesty, since the Angels recognize Him as their superior and their sovereign King. We ought not to doubt, when we shall be under His keeping, that He has all that is needed to maintain us. Let us know, however much He was abased, it in no wise takes away from His Divine power nor hinders us from being securely under His guidance.

Now we see the summary of this history. That is, in the first place, we know that the Son of God, even our Mediator, has united Himself to us in such a way that we must never doubt that we are sharers both of His life and of all His riches. Let us know also that He brought with Himself to us everything that was required for our salvation. For (as I have already said) He was not thus emptied without always retaining His Divine majesty. Although before men He was made of no reputation, yet He always remained not only heir of this world (since He is the Head of the Church), but also always true God.

Besides, let us learn from those who are here ordained as teachers and leaders how we must come to our Lord Jesus Christ. To be sure, the wise men of this world are so inflated with pride and presumption that scarcely will they condescend to be scholars of unlearned men and poor shepherds[4] from the fields. But it is all our wisdom, nevertheless, that we learn from these shepherds (of whom it is here spoken) to come to our Lord Jesus Christ. For although we may have all the sciences of the world stuffed into our heads, of what use will it be when life fails us? How will it help us to know "Him in whom the treasures of all wisdom are hidden," as St. Paul says? Now we see where we must begin. It does us no harm to follow those who have shown us the way to come to our Lord Jesus Christ.

God gave this honor neither to the great ones of this world, nor to the wise, nor to the rich, nor to the nobles, but He chose shepherds.[4] Since it is so, let us follow that order. It is true

4 Fr., *bergers.* The nice word for "shepherds" is *pasteurs; bergers* is here used in a somewhat derogatory sense.

that Wise Men came from the East to pay homage to our Lord Jesus Christ. But the shepherds[4] had to come first, in order that all presumption might be abolished, and that he who would be reputed Christian must be as a fool in this world. So, let us not bring a foolish presumption to judge by our imaginations the admirable secrets of God, but let us adore them in all simplicity.

Further, let us look at the faith which was in these shepherds. Then it will no longer be difficult to follow them. They come to adore the Redeemer of the world. And in what condition do they find Him? There He is laid in a manger and wrapped in a few little cloths, and it is the sign which had been given to them by the Angel. Now it surely seemed that this was to astonish them and even to make them turn their backs in such a manner that they might no longer recognize Jesus Christ as their Savior.

For the Scribes and Teachers of the Jews surely thought that the Redeemer who had been promised must come in great pomp, and that He must subject all the world, in such a way that He would have only prosperity, that they would get wealth in abundance to glut themselves, and they would amass all the riches of the world. Here, then, was a scandal which could make these poor people lose courage, so that they would never have come to our Lord Jesus Christ, but rather that they would have been entirely alienated from Him, when it is said to them that they will find Him in a stable and wrapped with rags. The sign given to them of the Redeemer is that He will be laid in a manger as if He were cut off from the rank of men. Yet even that does not turn them away. They come, then, to know Him as Lord, confessing how God has had pity on them and that finally He willed to fulfil His promise which He had given from all time, and they are assured by such a spectacle.

Since, then, the faith of these shepherds was so great that it fought against everything that could turn them from coming to our Lord Jesus Christ, we shall be doubly guilty and stripped of every excuse, unless we learn in their school, and unless the birth of our Lord Jesus Christ (although He appeared without dignity or pomp or nobility of this world) be not a scandal to hinder us, or to make us turn away from the good way,[5] and unless we come to yield to Him as to our sovereign King, and to Him to Whom all dominion is given both in heaven and on earth. In fact, we need such an admonition. For, as I have already mentioned, the doctrine of the Gospel brings only scandal to those who are preoccuppied with pride and folly and who repute themselves wise men.

We see also how many fanatics reject everything which is contrary to their brains. There are, on the other hand, many mockers who have never been touched by any feeling of their sins. Because they are profane people who think they will never be brought to an accounting and they do not know whether there is a better life than the one they see here below, they reckon that it is only foolishness so to follow the Son of God and to acquaint oneself with Him. Let us see, then, how much more ought we to be strengthened by this admonition: namely, that the Son of God loses nothing of His majesty and of His glory, and that it is not decreased in His humiliation for our salvation; but rather we ought to be enraptured by it, knowing His inestimable goodness and the love He has borne toward us.

This, then, is how we must practice this doctrine, that we do not fail to come to our Lord Jesus Christ, although at first sight we do not find in Him what our flesh, that is, our natural senses, desire. But although He was wrapped in rags at His birth, and although He had been laid there in the manger, may we know and be resolved that He did not, however, cease to be Mediator to draw us to God His Father, to give us an entrance into the Kingdom of heaven from which we were entirely shut out. Still more today, although He does not rule in pomp, and although His Church is despised, and although there is a simplicity in His Word which the great men of this world reject, as for us, may we never cease on that account to cling to Him and to subject ourselves to His dominion in a true obedience of faith. For example, when one preaches, according to our custom it is not anything to draw us much. We

---

5 Fr., *le chemin.* Gr., HO HODOS.

hear a man speaking. And who is he? He is not of great dignity and reputation. Then, in summary, there is only the word. On the other hand, in what is preached by the Gospel there are many things which seem to us to be against all reason, when we wish to judge them according to our taste. So let us know we cannot draw near to what God shows and declares to us, unless we have first bowed down.

As a confirmation which He adds for our sakes to His Word we have the Sacraments. And would a drop of water suffice to assure us of the remission of our sin, and that God adopted us as His children, and, though we are feeble and frail,[6] yet we shall be clothed with His heavenly glory which will never fail us? Could we find a guarantee and assurance[7] of things so great and so excellent in a little water? In the Holy Supper would a piece of bread and a drop of wine suffice to assure us that God accepts us as His children, that we live in Jesus Christ, and that He has shared everything with us? For it seems that such ceremonies which have no great pomp can have no value. So then, we see still better how what is here mentioned about the Shepherds[8] pertains to us and how we should profit by it today. That is, let us not cease to draw near to our Lord Jesus Christ and to be assured that it is He in Whom we shall find all good, all rejoicing, and all glory, although it seems that He is still, as it were, in the stable and in the manger, wrapped with swaddling clothes. That is to say, there might be many things which could debauch us and dazzle the eyes of a few that they might not perceive the heavenly glory which was given to Him by God His Father, I say, even in the human nature He took from us. For since He is God, He has everything from Himself (as it is said in the 17th chapter of St. John), but with respect to His humanity He received as a free gift everything that He brought to us, that we might draw from His fullness, and that we might find in

6 Fr., *caduques et fragiles.* These words are nearly parallel and approximately interchangeable. Both are Latin derivatives. *Caduque* is more colloquial.

7 Fr., *un gage et seureté.* Parallel words again, *gage* being more colloquial.

8 Here *Pasteurs,* the nicer word for "shepherds."

Him everything that is desirable, and that we might have all our rest and contentment in Him alone.

Besides, let us note well that the Holy Spirit also wished to assure us that in following the shepherds[9] who are here ordained as teachers[10] and guides, we should have no fear of making a mistake. For if the shepherds[9] had had no other sign than the stable and the manger, we could say, "Look at the poor idiots who make themselves believe foolishly and without reason that He was the Redeemer of the world." That would be altogether too easy for us. We could, then, be in doubt. But the Shepherds[11] were confirmed by other means to be certain that He was the Son of God, He Who was thus laid in the manger. That is, when the Angel appeared to them, then they heard this song which St. Luke adds, where all the Kingdom of heaven renders testimony to our Lord Jesus Christ, that He has all power over creatures, in heaven as well as on earth.

Let us learn, then, to receive (to be assured in the faith of Jesus Christ) everything here proposed to us. For it is certain that God willed to convict of ingratitude all those who today do not condescend to do homage to His Only Son,[12] when He sent such a multitude of Angels to declare that He was the Redeemer Who had been promised. It is vain, then, for us to be satisfied in our unbelief, as we see many stupid people who do not take account of everything that is contained in the Gospel. There are even mockers of God, who are so careless[13] that it makes no difference what is preached to them.[14] They pay no more attention than they would to fables.

There is also something to convict of an obstinate and devilish rebellion all those who do not subject themselves to our Lord Jesus Christ to do Him homage. For since there are unbelievers, they will have an infinite multitude of Angels from Paradise who will testify against them. For these[15] are the

---

9 *pasteurs.*
10 *maistres.*
11 *bergers.*
12 *son Fils unique.*
13 *qui s'anonchalissent tellement*
14 *que ce leur est tout un de ce qu'on leur preschera.*
15 these angels.

ministers of the truth of God. So then, though all the wicked and all those who are steeped[16] in their vices and corruptions, take pleasure in it and are hardened as much as they wish in their unbelief, they have more-than-sufficient witnesses to testify their condemnation. For the Angels of Paradise appeared so that there might no longer be any excuse for us not to receive Jesus Christ as our sovereign King, humbly bowing ourselves before His majesty.

However, let us note on the other hand that God procured our salvation when He sent such a multitude of Angels, so that we might be able to come to our Lord Jesus Christ with a ready courage and that we might no longer be held back by dispute or scruple, but that we might be fully resolved that we shall find in Him all that is lacking in us and that He will have something to supply all our wants and miseries. Briefly, it is He by Whom God willed to communicate Himself to us. Do we wish to seek our life except in God?

There is all fulness of the Godhead[17] in Jesus Christ. When, then, we have such a testimony, it is just as if God extended His two arms to make us feel His inestimable goodness: and to show that only when we have faith in Jesus Christ (I say a faith without hypocrisy) leaning only upon Him, knowing that it is from Him that we must receive everything, then we shall be sharers of all the benefits which are lacking in us and for which we starve. Besides, although today we do not see the Angels who appeared only for an instant,[18] yet this testimony is registered so as to be authentic. For the Holy Spirit spoke by the mouth of St. Luke. Let us be satisfied, then, to have such a witness from God, Who[19] declares to us that the Angels rendered testimony of the birth of our Lord Jesus Christ, so that, knowing how He was made man, that is, that He emptied Himself for our sakes, we may be so delighted as to aspire to the Kingdom of heaven, so as to adhere to Him in true union of faith.

---

16 I think this is a pun on *confier* (to confide) and *confire* (to can or preserve).
17 *toute plénitude de Divinité.*
18 *pour un coup seulement.*
19 God through St. Luke.

Next we consider the place of His birth, Bethlehem. This is no slight or unimportant confirmation when we see how the Son of God was born as such, a long time before the Prophet had made mention of it. If Joseph and Mary had had their dwelling-place in Bethlehem and had made their residence there, it might not have been strange that she delivered there and Jesus Christ was born there. But this which ought today to help us has been much obscured. For one might at least know that not without cause the Prophet had said, "Thou, Bethlehem, although thou art today despised as a little village, yet thou wilt produce Him Who is to be Head of My people." But when Joseph and Mary are living in Nazareth and they come into the city of Bethlehem just when she must be delivered and Jesus Christ is born there, who will not see that God guided the whole thing by His hand? Men, then, must knowingly and with sure knowledge be blind when they are not willing to recognize here the Word of God, Who marked His only Son, so He could be received without any doubt as Him Who had been promised.

Surely there was sufficient occasion to cause Joseph to come to Bethlehem in the edict published by the Roman Emperor. But to bring there a woman with child and about to be delivered, it is certain that was not governed by man and God was at work there. We see how even God uses strange means to accomplish His will. For the edict of Ceasar, though it was carried out without tyrranical subjection, made it necessary that the Jewish people were then tagged, they had a check upon each person, and it was to show them that they need no longer expect any liberty. Jesus Christ was promised to deliver the Jews and all believers from the subjection of Satan and from all tyranny. It seemed that this edict was to close the door, that God might never accomplish what He had promised to His people. However, it is the means of accomplishing it. For when Joseph and Mary come as poor people subject to a tyrant, a pagan and an unbeliever, and so Jesus Christ is born in Bethlehem, it shows the Prophecy to be true. God (as I have said) here gives full certainty to His own so that they must not doubt the birth of our Lord Jesus Christ. That, then, is how we must apply to our use and instruction the things here discussed. For it is not the intention of St. Luke, or rather of the Holy Spirit Who spoke by his mouth, simply to write us a history of what had happened. But He[20] expressed here on the one hand how the Son of God did not spare Himself for our sakes, and then on the other hand how He bore infallible testimony that He was the Redeemer in order that He might be received as such.

Let us bethink ourselves to profit from this history, so that we may be able to be in tune with the song of the Angels in glorifying God, and to so receive what He here gives us for the rejoicing of our souls.[21] In the first place the Angel says (that is the one who bears the message of the shepherds[22]), *"Fear not. I announce to you a great joy."* Then there is this testimony in common from all the army that God sends, *"Peace on earth to men."* This, then, is what we have to remember first of all: that we seek our joy in Jesus Christ. For, in fact, even though we had all kinds of delights and luxuries, it would only be a matter of drowning ourselves in our pleasures. Yet even if we are too sleepy, even entirely stupid, our conscience will never have rest. We shall be tormented without end and without ceasing. This worm (of which the Scripture speaks) will eat us away, we shall be condemned[23] by our sins, and we shall feel that with perfect right God is opposed to us and is our enemy. So, there will be a curse upon all the enjoyments of the world, since they will be changed into gnashing of teeth,[24] until men are right[25] with God.

Cursed then are all enjoyments, all honors, all things desirable, until we feel that God received us in mercy. Being thus reconciled with Him we can enjoy ourselves, not merely with an earthly joy, but especially with that joy which is promised to us in the Holy Spirit, in order that we may seek it in Him.

---

20 The Holy Spirit through St. Luke.
21 Fr., *ames.* Lat., *anima.* Soul, spirit, mind, feeling, conscience.
22 *bergers.*
23 Lat., *redarguo.*
24 Fr., *grincement de dents* is more onomatopoetic than the English.
25 Fr., *appointez* in the sense of Lat. *a punctum.* In tack with God, right with God, having God's approval, agreeing with God even to the smallest point in space and time.

For peace and joy are inseparable things. For how, seeing we are surrounded by so many miseries, can we enjoy ourselves? Then, seeing we are cursed in Adam, we are children of wrath, God being our Judge is armed with vengeance to cast us into the pit, what joy can we conceive of, being in such a state? Certainly when we think of it, not only must we be overcome with unrest[26] but in a horrible gehenna which surmounts all the anguishes of this world, unless the devil has bewitched us. As we see many who do not cease to make merry,[27] although they make war on God. But if we have a single particle of feeling in us, it is certain that we shall always be in torment until God is declared favorable toward us.

This peace, then, must precede, that we know that God owns us as His children, even since He does not impute to us our sins. Are we thus at peace with God? Then we really have something over which to rejoice, even with God, following what I have already mentioned. For unbelievers have indeed some peace (that is to say they are so thick[28] that they are not concerned about the judgment of God; they even defy it), but it is not with God. For they never have peace nor rest, except when they forget both God and themselves and they are altogether insensible. But St. Paul exhorts us to have peace with God, that is, to look to Him, and seek as we are able to be peaceable. That is, that when we draw near to Him we be certain and assured of His love. How will that be? By the remission of our sins, by the free unmerited love which He bears toward us in our Lord Jesus Christ.

Let us note well, then, that the peace which the Angels of Paradise preach here carried with it this joy, which the first Angel had mentioned, saying, "I announce to you a great joy," that is, the salvation you will have in Jesus Christ. He is called our Peace, and this title declares that we would be entirely alienated from God unless He received us by means of His only Son. Consequently we also have something to boast of when God accepts us as His children, when He gives us liberty

---

26 *accablez d'inquiétude.*
27 *qui ne laissent pas de s'esgayer.*
28 *eslourdis,* heavy, dull-witted.

to claim Him openly[29] as our Father, to come freely to Him, and to have our refuge in Him.

However, let us deduce from this that God has so ordained that the Gospel be preached by the mouth of men. Yet the Angels have preached it beforehand. Today it is true that the Church must be taught by means of mortal creatures. Though that may be, we bear nothing new. We only recite the preaching[30] which was done by the Angels of Paradise, and not in a small number, but an infinite multitude and a great army. Besides, it cannot be that we are as inflamed to magnify our God as when we shall be made fully certain of His goodness. That is why these two things are joined: that the Angels exhort all the world to glorify God, since He has given such a peace on earth. We rejoice, then, over the good that God has freed us by means of our Lord Jesus Christ His only Son. He has taken possession of this peace, in order that praises ascend on high and that they pierce the clouds, and that all the world may re-echo this song, that is, that God may be blessed[31] and magnified everywhere.

We have to deduce from this that we shall always be dumb and that we shall never be able to praise God until He has made us to experience His goodness. For example, how shall poor sinners, while they have troubles and remorse in themselves, who do not know whether God loves them or hates them, be able to bless His Name? But on the contrary the anguish, as it were, will keep them restrained so that they will not be able in any wise to open their mouths. It must be, then, in the first place that God knowingly testified to us the love He bears toward us in such a way that we may be resolved that He will always be Father to us. Then surely we shall have something for which to bless His Name.

But as we cannot praise God until He has declared to us His goodness, let us also learn not to have a faith dead or idle, but may we be incited to bless the Name of God, when we see that

---

29 *à pleine bouche.*

30 *la prédication,* the more formal Latin word. Usually Calvin perfers the more colloquial *presche.*

31 Fr., *benit.* Lat., *benedictus.*

He has so displayed the great treasures of His lovingkindness[32] toward us. May our mouth, on the one hand, perform its function, and then may all our life correspond to it. For this is the true song, that each one dedicates himself to the service of God, knowing that, since He has bought us at such a price, it is reasonable enough that all our thoughts and our works be applied to this use, that His Name be blessed.

When we shall know that we really are His own, may we know that it is inasmuch as it has pleased Him to accept us to Himself, and that everything proceeds from His free unmerited bounty. So not without cause is added the word that peace is given to men—not for any merit, not that they had acquired it, but by the good pleasure of God. For the word which St. Luke uses means that we must not seek any other reason why our Lord Jesus Christ appeared to us than that God has had pity and compassion on our miseries. As also it is said in John 3:16[33] that God so loved the world that He spared not His own Son, but delivered Him to death for our sakes.

Let us learn, then, to come to our Lord Jesus Christ in this way: that is, that the message which is here published by the Angels be to us as a burning lamp to show us the way, that faith lead us, and that we know that it is now God in us, as much as it is God with us. Our God with us is declared when He willed to dwell in our human nature as in His temple. But now it is God in us, that is, we feel Him joined to us in greater power[34] than when He showed and declared Himself mortal man. He is even both God and man in us. For first by the power of His Holy Spirit He makes us alive. Then He is man in us, since He makes us sharers of the sacrifice which He offered for our salvation, and declares to us that not without cause He pronounced that His flesh was truly meat and His blood was truly drink.

---

32 *miséricorde*, mercy.

33 This is the first place I have found chapter and verse reference in the text of one of Calvin's sermons. The practice of using verse numbers began about 1551. I think this sermon was preached in 1559.

34 *vertu*.

This is also why the holy table is made ready for us, so that we may know that our Lord Jesus, having descended here below and having emptied Himself of everything, was not, however, separated from us when He ascended into His glory in heaven. But rather it is on this condition that we are sharers of His body and His blood. And why so? For we know that His righteousness and His obedience is the satisfaction for our sins and that He appeased the wrath of God by the sacrifice of His body and of His blood which He offered in this humanity which He took from us.

Since this is so, may we not doubt when Jesus Christ invites us to this table, although we perceive only bread and wine, that He really dwells in us, and that we are so joined to Him there is nothing of Himself that He is not willing to communicate to us. May we recognize, I say, that in order that we know how to profit from this Sacrament which has been established for us from Him. However and whenever we receive it, may we know assuredly that God might have delivered us from the depth of condemnation in which we were by another means if He had so willed. But He willed to give us more assurance of the love which He bears toward us when we have Jesus Christ for a Guarantee, so that we seek all our good in Him. May we know that we cannot fully appreciate what this is, until He be given, as it were, in the midst of us and He be so approached by us that by means of Him we are led into the Kingdom of heaven, from which we were banished and deprived because of our sins.

That is how our Lord Jesus Christ must be applied to our salvation, if we wish to approach God, if we desire to have a real spiritual joy, contentment, and rest, also if we desire to be armed against the temptations which the devil can stir up. But to be sharers of this holy table, let us examine ourselves, and let us in the first place recognize our miseries, that we be displeased by them and entirely confounded by them. Besides, let us know that God willed to sweeten all our sadness and anguish when He so shed Himself abroad in His only Son, and that He willed that we should enjoy Him fully.

Although we are subject to much poverty in this world and besieged by enemies who are like ravenous wolves, though the devil on the one hand ceases not to seek to prey upon us and unbelievers bark like mastiff dogs, although, I say, we are agitated by many troubles and menaced from all sides, although we must endure many annoyances, let us hold it as a certainty that we shall never cease to have peace toward our God. Let us pray to Him that He will make us experience it by His Holy Spirit, since that is one thing that surpasses all human understanding[35] (as already we have noticed from St. Paul) and let us so learn to be content with our Lord Jesus Christ and the spiritual benefits of which He makes us sharers, that we may be able to bear patiently all the miseries and afflictions of this world.

May it not prove to be evil to us to be molested from all sides, in brief, to be exposed to all shame and disgrace, provided that Jesus Christ is with us, and He blesses all our miseries and afflictions, and we gain such fruit from it that we realize in the midst of all our poverties we ask nothing except to glorify our God. And when worldlings gain their triumphs to their confounding, since they cannot enjoy themselves without fighting against God, may our true joy be to serve Him in all fear and humility, and to give ourselves entirely to His obedience. That is how we have to profit from this doctrine.

Now we shall bow in humble reverence before the majesty of our God.

---

35 *qui surmonte tout sens humain.*

SERMON 3

First Sermon on the Passion of Our Lord Jesus Christ*

Then Jesus went with them to a place called Gethsemane, and said to his disciples, "Sit here while I go yonder and pray." Then he took Peter and the two sons of Zebedee and began to be sad and sorrowful. Therefore he said to them, "My soul is sad even to death. Stay here and watch with me." And going a little further he threw himself to the ground on his face, praying and saying, "Father, if it be possible, let this cup pass from me. Nevertheless not as I will, but as Thou wilt." — MATTHEW 26:36-39

WHEN Scripture speaks to us of our salvation it proposes to us three aims. One is that we recognize the inestimable love God has shown toward us, so that He may be glorified by us as He deserves. Another, that we hold our sin in such detestation as is proper, and that we be sufficiently ashamed to humble ourselves before the majesty of our God. The third, that we value our salvation in such a manner that it makes us forsake the world and all that pertains to this frail life, and that we be overjoyed with that inheritance which has been acquired for us at such a price. This is what we ought to fix our attention upon and apply our minds to when it is mentioned to us how the Son of God has redeemed us from eternal death and has acquired for us the heavenly life. We ought, then, in the first place to learn to give God the praise He deserves. In fact, He was well able to rescue us from the unfathomable depths of death in another fashion, but He willed to display the treasures of His infinite goodness when He spared not His only Son. And our Lord Jesus in this matter willed to give us a sure pledge of the care which He had for us when He offered Himself voluntarily to death. For we never shall be keenly

* From: *Corpus Reformatorum, Calvini Opera*, vol. 46, pp. 833-846.

touched nor set on fire to praise our God, unless on the other hand we examine our condition, and see that we are as sunk in hell, and know what it is to have provoked the wrath of God and to have Him for a mortal enemy and a judge so terrible and appalling that it would be much better if heaven and earth and all creatures would conspire against us then to approach His majesty while it is unfavorable toward us. So it is very necessary that sinners should be broken-hearted with a feeling and an understanding of their faults, and that they should know themselves to be worse than wretched, so that they may have a horror at their condition, in order that in this way they may know how much they are indebted and obligated to God, that He has pitied them, that He sees them in despair, and that He has been kind enough to help them; not because He sees in them any dignity, but only because He looks upon their wretchedness. Now the fact is also (as we have said), forasmuch as we are surrounded by too much here below and that when God has called us to Himself we are held back by our affection and covetousness, that it is necessary to prize the heavenly life as it deserves, that we may know at how great an expense it was bought for us.

And that is why it is here narrated to us that not only our Lord Jesus Christ has been willing to suffer death and has offered Himself as a sacrifice to pacify the wrath of God His Father, but in order that He might be truly and wholly our pledge, He did not refuse to bear the agonies which are prepared for all those whose consciences rebuke them and who feel themselves guilty of eternal death and damnation before God. Let us note well, then, that the Son of God was not content merely to offer His flesh and blood and to subject them to death, but He willed in full measure to appear before the judgment seat of God His Father in the name and in the person of all sinners, being then ready to be condemned, inasmuch as He bore our burden. And we need no longer be ashamed, since the Son of God exposed Himself to such humiliation. It is not without cause that St. Paul exhorts us by his example not to be ashamed of the preaching of the Cross; however foolish it may be to some and a stumbling-block to many. For the more our Lord Jesus abased Himself the more we see that the offenses on account of which we are indebted to God could not be abolished unless He were abased to the last degree. And, in fact, we know that He has been made weak in order that we might be made strong by His virtue, and that He has been willing to bear all our sufferings, sin excepted, so that He may be ready today to help us. For if He had not felt in His person the fears, the doubts, and the torments which we endure, He would not be so inclined to be pitiful toward us as He is. It is said that a man who knows what neither hunger nor thirst is will not be moved with compassion or humanity toward those who endure them, because he has always been at his ease and has lived in his pleasures. Now it is true that God, although in His nature He endures none of our passions, does not cease to be humane toward us, because He is the fountain of all goodness and mercy. However, in order that we may be assured that our Lord Jesus knows our weaknesses in order to relieve us of them, and that we may come so much more boldly to Him and we may speak to Him more familiarly, the Apostle says that for this cause He was willing to be tempted like us.

So, then, we have to notice in the text we have read that when our Lord Jesus came into this village of Gethsemane, and even on the mountain of olives, that it was to offer Himself as a voluntary sacrifice. And in that He willed to fulfil the office and the charge which was committed to Him. For why did He assume our flesh and nature, unless to make reparation for all our rebellion by His obedience, to acquire for us full and perfect righteousness before God his Father? And still He came to present Himself for death, because we can not be reconciled nor can we pacify the wrath of God which had been provoked by sin, except by His obedience.

This, then, is why the Son of God came boldly to the place where He knew that Judas would find Him. And thus we know that it was necessary, since our father Adam by his rebellion had ruined us all, that the Son of God, who has sovereign control over all creatures, should subject Himself and assume the condition of a servant, as also He is called both a Servant of God and of all His own. And that is also why

St. Paul, showing that we must have some support to call upon Him in full confidence that we shall be heard as His children, says that by the obedience of our Lord Jesus Christ we are recognized to be righteous. For it is as a mantle to cover all our sins and offenses, so that the thing which could prevent us from obtaining grace is not taken into account before God. But on the other hand we see that the price of our redemption has been very dear, when our Lord Jesus Christ is in such agony that He undergoes the terrors of death, indeed, until sweat as drops of blood by which He is, as it were, beside Himself praying if it be possible that He might escape such a distress. When we see that, it is enough to bring us to a knowledge of our sins. There is no possibility of lulling us to sleep here by flattery when we see that the Son of God is plunged into such an extremity that it seems that He is at the depth of the abyss. If that had happened only to a righteous man, we might be touched, of course, because it was necessary that a poor innocent endured for our ransom that which happened to the Son of God. But here is He Who is the fountain of life Who subjects Himself to death. Here is He Who sustains all the world by His power Who is made weak to this degree. Here is He Who rescues the creatures from all fear Who has to undergo such a horror. When, then, that is declared to us, we would be more than stupid, if each one of us would not meditate on that, and, being disgusted by his faults and iniquities, would not be ashamed before God, gasping and groaning, and if even by this means we were not led to God with a true repentance.

Now it is impossible that men become rightly converted to God unless they are condemned in themselves and they have conceded both the terror and the agony of the malediction which is prepared for them unless they are restored to grace with God. But again, to better understand the whole it is said that our Lord Jesus took only three of His disciples and left the company at quite a distance, and again those three He did not take all the way with Him, but He prayed to God His Father in secret. When we see that, we must notice that our Lord Jesus had no companion when He offered Himself as a sacrifice for us, but He alone completed and accomplished that which was required for our salvation. And even that is again better indicated to us, when the disciples sleep, and cannot even be awakened, although they had already been warned so many times that the hour was approaching in which our Lord Jesus would have to suffer for the redemption of mankind, and that He had exhorted them for three or four hours, never ceasing to declare to them that His death was approaching. However true all that may be, they do not cease to sleep. In this it is shown to us as in a vivid picture that it was most necessary that the Son of God bear all our burdens, for He could not expect anything else. And that is in order that our attention may be fixed so as not to wander in thought, as we see the poor unbelievers who cannot fix their attention upon our Lord Jesus Christ but who imagine that they must have patrons and advocates as if there were many redeemers. And we see even the blasphemies which are the rule in this wicked papacy, that the merits of the saints are to help the death and passion of our Lord Jesus Christ, in order that by this means we may be freed and acquitted before God. Even if there had been, say they, general remission as far as the guilt of original sin as well as of actual sins is concerned; still there must be an admixture and the blood of Jesus Christ is not enough unless it is supplemented by the blood of the martyrs, and we must have our refuge in them in order to have God's favor. When the devil has thus broken loose we ought all the more to be watched that we hold fast to our Lord Jesus Christ, knowing that in Him alone we must find the full perfection of salvation. And that is why it is said notably by the Prophet Isaiah that God marveled, seeing that there was no help anywhere else.

Now it is true that God well knew that He alone had to perfect our salvation, but it is in order that we may be ashamed and that we may not be hypocrites as if we have brought anything to help in the remission of our sins and to make God receive us in His grace and love, so that we do not run from one side to the other to find mediators. So that any such idea may be banished, it is said that God has used His own arm, and that He has completed all by His righteousness, and He has found no one to help Him. Now that is declared to us with extreme clearness when it is said that three of the disciples, those who were the flower of all, were sleeping there as poor beasts and that there was nothing else than brutal stupidity in them, that which is a monstrosity against nature to see that they slept at such a fatal moment. Then in order that our confidence be turned away from all creatures and that it be entirely shut up to our Lord Jesus Christ, therefore it is said that He advanced to the combat. Besides in addressing God His Father He well shows us the remedy for our relief from all our agonies, to soften our sorrows, and even to raise us above them, even though we were, as it were, sunk under them. For if we are troubled and in agony we know that God is not called in vain the Father of Consolation. If, then, we are separated from Him, where shall we find strength unless in Him? We see, however, that He has not willed to spare Himself when we needed Him. So it is the Son of God Who leads us by His example to the true refuge when we are in sorrow and agony.

But let us notice also the form of prayer which He uses: "Father, if it be possible let this chalice be removed from me," or this drink, for it is a figure of speech whether He speaks of a goblet or of a glass or of a cup, all the more so because Scripture calls afflictions bitter drinks in order that we may know that nothing happens by chance, but that God as a father of a family distributes to each one of his children his portion, or as a master to his servants, thus God shows that it is from Him and from His hand that they are beaten and afflicted, and also when we receive good things that they proceed from His unmerited loving-kindness and He gives us as much as He wants to give us. Now according to this way of proceeding our Lord Jesus says that death is for Him such a bitter drink that He would prefer that it were taken away from Him, that is, "if it were possible." It is true that one could raise here many questions, for it would seem that for an instant Jesus Christ forgot our salvation or, still worse, that fleeing from the struggle He willed to leave us in a lost estate on account of the terror which He felt.

Now that would not agree with what we have said. And even the love which He has shown us would be much obscured. But we do not have to enter upon any dispute so subtle, because we know that suffering sometimes so ravishes the spirit of a man that he does not think of anything; but he is so weighed down by present suffering that he lets it get him down and has no regard for the means of restoring himself. When, then, we are thus temporarily out of ourselves that does not mean that everything else is entirely blotted out from our hearts and that we have no affection. As for example, he who will think on some affliction of the Church, especially a particular affliction, will pray to God as if the rest of the world were to him as nothing. Now is that to say that he has grown inhuman and that he is not concerned for his brothers who also have need that he should pray for them? Not at all, but it is that this feeling drives him with such a vehemence that everything else is cut off from him for a time. Moses prays to be removed from the book of life. If we would want to split hairs about it we would say that Moses blasphemed against God in speaking as if He were variable. For those whom God has elected to eternal life can never perish. So it seems that Moses fights here against God and that he wants to make Him like us whose counsel and talk often changes. And then what honor does he to God when he knows that he is of the number of His elect, and he knows that God had marked him from his infancy to be committed to a charge so excellent as being a leader of his people and yet he asks to be, as it were, rejected and exterminated by God? And what would that lead to? One could, then, do much arguing. But the solution is easy in that Moses, having such an ardent zeal for the salvation of the people, seeing also the horrible threat that God had pronounced with His mouth, forgets himself for a little time and for a minute, and only asks that he may help his people. To this state of mind our Lord Jesus had been brought. For if it had been necessary for Him to suffer a hundred deaths, even a million, it is certain that He would have been prepared previously. But so He has willed not so much for Himself as for us to bear the agonies which plunge Him even to that point, as we see. So much for point one.

Now for the second. If anyone asks how Jesus Christ, Who is entirely righteous, Who has been the Lamb without blemish, and Who has been even the rule and the mirror of all righteousness, holiness, and perfection, has a will contradictory to that of God; the answer to that is that God has in Himself all perfection of uprightness, while the angels, however much they conform to the will of God and are entirely obedient to Him, nevertheless have a separate will. For inasmuch as they are creatures, they can have affections which do not belong by rights to God. As for us who are surrounded by this mass of sin, we are so burdened that we are far removed from the will of God, for in all our appetites there is some excess, there is even rebellion manifest oftentimes. But if we consider man in his integrity, that is to say without this corruption of sin, again it is certain that he will have his affections far removed from God, and yet they will not on that account be vicious. As when Adam was not yet perverted and he persisted in the estate and condition in which he had been created, it happened that he was both hot and cold and that he had to endure both anxieties and fears and like things.

That is how it was with our Lord Jesus Christ. We know that in all His feelings He had neither spot nor blemish, that in everything He was ruled by obedience to God, but still He was not prevented (because He had taken our nature) from being exposed both to fear, and to that horror of which it is now spoken, and to anxieties, and to like things. We are not able to perceive that in ourselves, as in troubled water one can distinguish nothing. So, the human affections make us drift from one side to the other to give us such emotions that we need to be restrained by God. But such as men have, being descended from Adam, are as a mire where there is a more and more mixed up infection of the kind that we cannot contemplate what this passion of our Lord Jesus Christ must have been, if we judge it by our own persons. For even if we have a good aim and an affection is upright in itself and approved by God, still we always lack something. Is it not a good and holy thing when a father loves his children? And right there we sin again. For there is never rule or moderation such as is required. For whatever virtues there are in us God shows us vices in them in order that all pride be more abased and that we have all the more occasion to bow our heads, even to be confounded with shame, seeing that even the good is corrupted by the sin which dwells in us and of which we are filled to excess.

Besides, as far as our Lord Jesus Christ is concerned (as I have already said) we ought not to be surprised if He had (insofar as He was man) a will different from that of God His Father, but on that account we must not judge that here was any vice or transgression in Him. And even (as we have already noted) in that let us see the inestimable love He bore toward us when death was to Him so dreadful and, nevertheless, He submitted to it of His own good pleasure. And even if He had not had any repugnance toward it, and even if without reluctance He tasted that cup, without feeling any bitterness in it, what kind of a redemption would that have been? It would seem as if it had only been a play, but when it happened that our Lord Jesus Christ endured such agonies it is a sign that He loved us to such a degree that He forgot even Himself and suffered that all the storm fell on His head in order that we might be delivered from the wrath of God.

Now it still remains to note that when the Son of God agonized in such a way it was not because He had to leave the world. For if it had only been the separation of body and soul, with the torments which He had to endure in His body, that would not have borne Him down to such a degree. But we must observe the quality of His death and even trace its origin. For death is not only to dissolve man, but to make him feel the curse of God. Beyond the fact that God takes us out of this world and that we are as annihilated with respect to this life, death is to us an entrance, as it were, into the abyss of hell. We would be alienated from God and devoid of all hope of salvation when death is spoken of to us unless we have this remedy—that our Lord Jesus Christ endured it for our sakes in order that now the wound which was there shall not be fatal. For without Him we would be so frightened by death that there would no longer be hope of salvation for us, but now its sting is broken. Even the poison is so cleansed that death in humiliating us serves us today like medicine and is no longer fatal now that Jesus Christ swallowed all the poison that was in it.

This, then, is what we must bear in mind, that the Son of God in crying out "Father, if it be possible, let this drink be removed from me" considers not only what He had to suffer in His body, nor the disgrace of men, nor leaving the earth (for that was easy enough for Him), but He considers that He is before God and before His judicial throne to answer for all our sins, to see there all the curses of God which are ready to fall upon us. For even if there be only a single sinner, what would the wrath of God be? When it is said that God is against us, that He wants to display His power to destroy us, alas! where are we then? Now it was necessary for Jesus Christ to fight not only against such a terror but against all the cruelties one could inflict. When, then, we see that God summons all those who have deserved eternal damnation and who are guilty of sin and that He is there to pronounce sentence such as they have deserved, who would not conceive in full measure all the deaths, doubts and terrors which could be in each one? And what a depth will there be in that! Now it was necessary that our Lord Jesus Christ by Himself without aid sustained such a burden. So then, let us judge the sorrow of the Son of God by its true cause. Let us now return to what we have already discussed—that in one respect we may realize how costly our salvation was to Him and how precious our souls were to Him when He was willing to go to such an extremity for our sakes, and knowing what we deserved let us look at what would have been our condition—if we had not been rescued by Him. And yet let us rejoice that death has no more power over us that could hurt us.

It is true that always we naturally fear death and we run away from it, but that is in order to make us think of this inestimable benefit which has been acquired for us by the death of the Son of God. This is in order to make us always consider what death is in itself, how it involves the wrath of God, and it is, as it were, the pit of hell. Besides, when we have to fight against such fear may we know that our Lord Jesus Christ has so provided for all those fears that in the midst of death we can come before God with uplifted heads. It is true that we have to humble ourselves before all things, as we have already said, that it is very necessary in order that we should hate our sins and be displeased with ourselves that we be touched by the judgment of God to be frightened by it. But still we must raise our heads when God calls us to Himself. And this is also the courage which is given to all believers! So we see that St. Paul says, Jesus Christ has prepared a crown for all those who wait for His coming. If, then, we no longer have hope of life in coming before the heavenly Judge, it is certain that we shall be rejected by Him and that He will not know us, even that He will disown us, however much profession of Christianity we may make.

Now we cannot really wait for our Lord Jesus Christ unless we have understood and are persuaded that He has so fought against the terrors of death that nevertheless we are freed from them and that the victory has been gained for us. And even if we have to fight to make us feel our infirmity, to make us seek refuge in God, always to bring us to a true confession of our sins, so that God Himself alone be righteous, it is nevertheless true that we are assured that Jesus Christ has so fought that He has won the victory not for Himself but for us and we must not doubt that by means of Him we can now surmount all anxieties, all fears, all dismays, and that we can invoke God, being assured that always He has His arms extended to receive us to Himself.

This, then, is what we must consider: that we may know that it is not a speculative teaching that our Lord Jesus endured the horrible terrors of death, forasmuch as He felt that He was there before our Judge and He was our Pledge, so that today we can by virtue of His fight win over all our infirmity and persist constantly in calling upon the Name of God, not doubting a single moment that He hears us, and that His goodness is always ready to receive us to Himself and that by this means we shall go through both life and death, through water and fire, and we shall feel that it is not in vain that our Lord Jesus fought to win such a victory for all those who have come to Him by faith. This is, then, in a word, what we have to keep in mind.

Now, however, we see how we must fight against our affections, and unless we do it is impossible for us to move a finger by which we do not in full measure provoke the wrath of God. For behold our Lord Jesus Christ Who is pure and entire, as we have already declared. If one asks what His will was, it is true it was weak as the will of a man, but it was not vicious as the will of those who are corrupted in Adam, for there was not a single spot of sin in Him. Behold, then, a man Who is exempt from every vice. But, however that may be, it is still necessary that He efface Himself and that He exert Himself to the limit and that He finally renounce Himself, and that He put all that underfoot, to yield obedience to God His Father. Let us look now at what shall become of us. What are our affections? What of our thoughts? All those are enemies that battle against God, as says St. Paul. Here God pronounces that we are altogether perverse and that all that man can imagine is but falsehood and vanity. Even from our infancy we show that we are steeped in the complete infection of sin. Little children coming into the world, though the malice does not appear, do not always fail to be little serpents full of poison, malice and disdain. In this we truly realize what is in our nature even from the beginning. And when we have become of age, what of us then? We are (as I have said) so evil that we do not know how to conceive a single thought which is not at the same time rebellion against God, so that we do not know whether to apply ourselves to this or to that, since we are always led astray from the true norm, even if we do not come to a clash with God in a provocative way. What a fight, then, is necessary to draw us back to the good! When we see that our Lord Jesus, in Whom there was nothing but integrity and uprightness, had to be subject to God His Father, even to renouncing Himself, is it not important that we should give ourselves entirely to it?

So then, let us learn to fight more valiantly. But seeing that we are not able and that rather all our powers and faculties tend to evil and that we have not a single particle of good in our nature and that there is such a weakness that we would be conquered a hundred times each minute, we come to Him Who was made weak that we might be filled with His power, as St. Paul says. Next, so it is, then, that our Lord Jesus Christ has thus renounced Himself, that we might learn, if we wish to be His disciples, to do likewise. Seeing that we are not able of ourselves to succeed in it but that we always tend to go the wrong way, let us pray to Him that by virtue of His Holy Spirit He may rule in us to make us strong. As it is said, He suffered in the weakness of His flesh, but by virtue of His Spirit He was raised from the dead in order that we may be made partakers of the fight which He sustained and that we may realize the effect and the excellence of His power in us. This, then, in summary, is what we have to remember when it is said that Christ resigned all His will in order to submit fully to God His Father.

Now, however, we have always to remember that the Son of God does not here propose Himself to be only an example and a mirror, but He wishes to show us how dearly our salvation has cost Him. For the devil, wishing to obscure the infinite grace of God which was shown us in our redemption, has said that Jesus Christ was only, as it were, model of every virtue. Behold how the whining pretenders in all the Papal See prattle. Not only do they not know how to deduce what obedience is, nor what self-renunciation is, but they say, what the Gospel-writer recites of Jesus Christ is in order that we may follow Him and that we may be conformed to Him. Now that is, to be sure, something, but it is not all nor even the principal thing. For an angel could well have been sent that we might have followed him, but when Jesus Christ was the Redeemer of the world He submitted and was subject of His own free will to that condition so miserable, as we see here. We must always recognize that we find nothing in us which can give hope of salvation. And therefore we must seek in Him what we lack. For we never can obtain the grace of God nor approach Him unless we come to Jesus Christ as poor beggars, which thing cannot be done until we have recognized our poverty and our indigence, in brief, that we lack everything.

This, then, is what we have to bear in mind in order that, after having heard that all the perfection of our life is to render us obedient to God and then to renounce our affections and thoughts and our whole nature to conform to Him, also after having heard that we must ask God for what we do not possess, we may know that our Lord Jesus Christ is given to us not only as an example, but He has fully declared to us that if we are separated from Him our life will necessarily be cursed and when in death we see the depth of misery that we shall see the pit of the wrath of God ready to swallow us up and that we be not seized with a single terror, but with a million, and that all creatures shall cry out vengeance against us. So we must feel all that, then, in order to recognize our sins and to groan and to be confounded in ourselves, and to have a desire and to have the courage to come to God with a true humility and repentance and that we should appreciate the goodness and mercy of our God according as it is seen here and that we should have mouths opened to give Him a sacrifice of praise, and that we should be turned away from the wiles of Satan, who has his nets spread out to retain us in the world, and that we leave also our conveniences and our comforts in order to aspire to this inheritance which was bought for us at such a price.

And since next Lord's Day we are to receive the Holy Supper and because God, after having opened to us the Kingdom of heaven, presents there to us a spiritual banquet that we may be even more touched by this teaching: In fact when we eat and drink daily for our restrengthening God declares sufficiently to us that He is our Father and that He cares for these earthly and frail bodies, so that we cannot eat a piece of bread without having the testimony that God cares for us, but in the Lord's Supper there is a special reason. For God does not fill our stomachs there, but He transports us to the Kingdom of heaven. He sets before us our Lord Jesus His Son for meat and drink. Jesus Christ is not satisfied only to receive us at

His table, but He wishes to be in every respect our Food. He makes us feel by the effect that His body is truly meat to us and His blood drink. When, then, we see that our Lord Jesus so gently invites us to Him, must we not be the worst of villains if we are not drawn away from that which turns us away from Him? And even though we were coming with dragging foot, let us not fail to be grieved for our vices in order to draw near to Him and compel ourselves as far as it shall be possible for us to be detached from this world and to aspire to the Kingdom of heaven.

So then, let each one observe what benefit the Holy Supper ought to confer on us. For we see that our Lord Jesus calls us to it to be partakers of His death and passion that we should enjoy the benefit He acquired for us and by this means we should be fully assured that God declares that we are His children and that we can claim Him openly as our Father. Let us bring a true faith knowing why our Lord Jesus was sent to us by God His Father, what His office is, and how He is still today our Mediator as He always was. Beyond that, let us try to be so united to Him, that it may be not only for each one of us that such a thing may be said, but for all in general. Let us have mutual concord and brotherhood together, since He has sustained and borne the condemnation which was pronounced by God His Father upon us all. So let us aim at that, and let each one come here not only for himself (as I have said), but let him try to draw his companions to it, and let us so urge one another on to walk stedfastly, noticing always that our life is as a road which must be followed to the end, and that we must not grow weary in the middle of the journey, but let us profit so much day by day, and let us take trouble to approach those who are out of the road; let this be all our joy, our life, our glory and contentment, and let us so help one another until God has fully gathered us to Himself.

Now let us bow in humble reverence before the majesty of our God.

SERMON 4

Second Sermon on the Passion of Our Lord Jesus Christ *

Then Jesus comes to His disciples and finds them sleeping, and says to Peter, "Can you not watch one hour with Me? Watch and pray that you enter not into temptation, for the spirit is ready but the flesh is weak." Again He went away for the second time and prayed, saying, "Father, if it is possible that this cup pass from Me without My drinking it, Thy will be done." Then He comes again and finds them sleeping, for their eyes were heavy. And having left them, again He went away and prayed for the third time, saying the same words. Then He comes to His disciples and says to them, "Sleep now and rest. Behold! the hour draws near when the Son of Man will be delivered into the hands of wicked men. Rise, let us go. Behold! he who betrays Me draws near." And while He was still speaking, behold! Judas, one of the twelve, comes and with him a great crowd having swords and clubs, from the chief priests and elders of the people. Now he who betrayed Him had given them a sign, saying, "He whom I shall kiss is the one; seize him." And forthwith addressing himself to Jesus, he said, "Hail, Master," and kissed Him. Jesus said to him, "Friend, why hast thou come?" Then they drew near and laid their hands upon Jesus and seized Him.

— MATTHEW 26:40-50

WE HAVE seen this morning how the Son of God, having to sustain so difficult a fight as to appear before the judgment-seat of God His Father to receive sentence of condemnation as our security, was made strong by prayer. For it was necessary that human weakness appear in Him, and it takes nothing away from His divine majesty when He has so bowed down to the dust to bring about our salvation. Now we have to note that

* From: *Corpus Reformatorum, Calvini Opera,* vol. 46, pp. 846-859.

it was not only once that He prayed. By which we see that by His example He has exhorted us not to faint if we are not heard as soon as we would wish. So, those who lose courage when our God does not respond to their first wish show that they do not know what it is to pray. For the certain rule for finding our refuge in God involves perseverance. Thus it is that the principal exercise of our faith is prayer. Now faith cannot exist without waiting. It is not possible for God to humor us as soon as we have opened our mouths and formed our request. But it is needful that He delay and that He let us languish oftentimes so that we may know what it is to call upon Him sincerely and without pretense, so that we may declare that our faith is so founded upon the Word of God that it checks us as a bridle so that we may be patient to endure until the opportune time to help us shall have come. Let us note well, then, that our Lord Jesus Christ did not pray to God His Father only once, but that He returned to it a second time.

Besides, we have to consider what we have already touched upon: that is, to know that our Lord Jesus has not formed here any trivial prayer, but He has, as it were, been willing to lay aside all selfish considerations. He Who is the power of God His Father, by Whom all the world is supported, nevertheless, forasmuch as He had to show Himself a weak man, taking our place, being there in our stead; He has declared when He thus reiterated His prayer that it was not as a spectacle that He did it (thus several profane people imagine that when Jesus Christ appeared He suffered nothing), but it was so that we might be taught that we cannot escape the hand of God and His curse except by this means. Now it is here declared to us (as it was this morning) that our Lord Jesus was crushed to the limit, even so far as that the burden He had received was unsupportable unless the invincible power of the Spirit of God had operated in Him. We must not think that it was superfluous language when He repeated these same words. For what is said in the other passage, that in praying to God we must not use a long babble, as those who believe that in dabbling in words they get much more, does not imply that we should not continue in our prayers, but it is to tax the hypocrisy and superstition of those who believe in breaking God's ear drums (after a manner of speaking) to persuade Him of what they want. As we see, how this folly has prevailed in the world! Again, how many there are among us who use this sorcery, how many who say no more than their Ave Maria, to whom it seems as if they have gained a great deal every time they say their Lord's Prayer, and that God will count all their words in which they dabble when they pray! Now I call that real sorcery. For they wretchedly profane the prayer which has been given us by our Lord Jesus Christ, in which He has comprehended in a brief summary all that we can ask of God and what is lawful for us to desire or ask for.

However, that does not imply that if a man is crushed in agony he should not return often to God, and that when he shall have heaved some sighs he should not begin again immediately afterwards. Supposing we come to it without ambition and without display and then that we have no idea of having gained anything by our babble, but that a deep feeling urges us on, then we have the true perseverance, similar to that of our Lord Jesus Christ. Now there is this article to note, as we have said, that the principal thing in all our prayers is that God should control us to such a degree that there is an agreement on our part to conform to His good will. That, surely, is necessary for us. Behold our Lord Jesus Christ, though all His affections were upright, holy, and conformed to righteousness, that, however, insofar as He was natural man, yet He had to fight against the agony and sorrow which might have crushed Him and He had to hold Himself captive under obedience to God His Father. How will it be with us who have nothing but malice and rebellion and who are so corrupted that we did not know how to apply our senses to anything whatever? Would not God be utterly offended? Since that is so, let us learn in praying to God so to hold ourselves in check that no one may give himself such license as he is accustomed to in following his own appetites. But let us know that we shall have profited much, being able to hold ourselves captives, in order that God may be complete master over us.

It is also a noteworthy sentence when our Lord Jesus says to His disciples, *"Watch and pray in order not to enter into temptation; for if the Spirit is ready, the flesh is weak."* He showed here, then, that the principal spur which ought to goad us to call upon God is that we have to fight, that our enemies are near, and that they are strong, and that we shall not be able to resist them without being helped and aided from on high, and that God fight for us. Now we know that when man is assured, he asks only to be given all his comforts and to sleep. For we do not voluntarily accept anxiety or melancholy unless necessity forces it upon us. To be sure, it is a sovereign good to have rest, or else we would be tired out. Nevertheless it is very necessary that necessity press us to be vigilant. Our Lord Jesus, then, not without cause declares that we have to sustain many alarms. For what is said only once to His disciples pertains to all of us in general, since in our lives we must always be ready to meet many temptations. For the devil is our perpetual enemy, if we are members of our Lord Jesus Christ. There will be, then, open war without ending and without ceasing.

Then let us notice what kind of enemy we have to deal with. It is not only one, but the number is infinite. Moreover the devil has a vast number of means to cast us down; now he strikes openly, now he plots underground, and by craftiness he will have surprised us a hundred thousand times before we have thought of it. When it is only as St. Paul says that our enemies are powers who dwell in the air over our heads and that we are here as poor earthworms who only crawl below, that certainly ought to cause us to be concerned.[1] As also St. Peter alleges this reason, that our enemy is like a lion who roars and seeks prey and who never rests. That, then, is what we have to observe in the saying of our Lord Jesus that we must be on our guard in order not to enter into temptation. Besides, although we are vigilant, though we keep good watch, yet we cannot be exempt from the devil's raising himself against us or our being assailed by him in many and diverse ways. We cannot, then, repulse the blows from afar. But

1 Lat., *sollicito.*

before entering into combat, we must be on our guard lest we be plunged into temptation.

Let us learn, then, although the believers and children of God desire to have rest, nevertheless, they must not desire to be here at their ease. But let it be sufficient for them that God perfects His power in their weakness, as also St. Paul says that he had to pass through that. It is, I say, the condition of all the children of God to battle in this world, because they cannot serve God without opposition. But although they are weak, although they can be impeded, even often beaten down, may they be content to be helped and aided by the hand of God, and may they always lean upon this promise, that our faith will be victorious over all the world. Yet also the remedy proposed to us is that we fight. To be sure Satan is always making new beginnings to assail us, but Jesus Christ also commands us to watch. Besides, He shows that those who presume upon their own strength will be conquered by Satan a hundred thousand times before they obtain a single victory. What is needed, then? That, confessing with all humility that we can do nothing, we come to our God.

Here, then, are our real arms. It is He Who takes from us all fear and terror. It is He Who can give us assurance and resolution, that even to the end we shall remain safe and sound, that is, when we call upon God. As Solomon says,[2] "His Name is a strong tower and the righteous man will have in Him his good and assured retreat." Also says the Prophet Joel, "Although the world be turned upside down, whoever calls upon the Name of the Lord will be saved." That is especially applied to the reign of our Lord Jesus Christ, in order that we may be entirely persuaded that, although our salvation may be, as it were, in suspense, and though we may see, as it were, a thousand hazards, yet God will always keep us in His protection, and we shall feel that His power is always near us, and ready to help us, provided we seek it by prayer of mouth and heart.[3] That, then, in summary is what we have to remember. In order that we may be better confirmed in this

2 Proverbs 18:10.

3 Fr. *oraisons et prières*. Nearly synonymous, but showing two aspects of prayer, the inner urge to request and the outward speech.

doctrine, let us note that our Lord Jesus in praying not only called upon God for Himself and for His own use, but He has dedicated all our requests and prayers so that they are holy and God approves them and finds them acceptable. As it says in the seventeenth chapter of Saint John, He sanctifies Himself in order that we all may be sanctified in Him. Surely we must also conclude that He prayed in order that His prayer may avail today, and that it might have its full strength, and that by this means we might all be heard.

This consideration is very valuable when he adds, "*The Spirit* is ready, but the flesh is weak." For it is to show that all have need of the advice which He here urged upon His disciples. For many think that they have gained all if they have some good desire. That makes them indifferent. Soon afterwards they are seized with such laziness and coldness that they recoil from God and despise His help. That is also the cause why God often withdraws Himself and hides His power. For it is a good thing that men who confide too much in themselves find themselves frustrated and God mocks their arrogance and foolish imagination. In order, then, that both great and small may know that they cannot dispense with the help of God, and whatever graces they have received, God must still maintain in them what He has put there and even augment it that they may be strengthened, it is here said, "*The Spirit is ready, but the flesh is weak.*" That is, since we feel in us some good will, and God has already set us on the way, and has extended to us His hand, may we experience that He really governs us by His Holy Spirit. Although, then, we may have all of that, yet we must not be slow to pray. And why not? Let us consider whether there is in us only the Spirit. Surely we shall find many infirmities remaining. Although God may have already worked in such a way that we may have whereof to offer thanks to Him and to magnify His goodness; yet there is reason to bow our heads and to see that if He left us we would very soon be, I do not say weakened, but altogether fainting.

In a word, our Lord Jesus here wished to show that those who are the most perfect, the most advanced, and upon whom God has poured the graces and powers of His Holy Spirit, still must be humble, and they must walk in fear and carefulness, must call upon God every hour, knowing that it is not enough that He has begun if He does not finish.[4] Surely every good must come from Him. When He has given the goodwill He must continue to carry it out more fully, since perseverance is the most singular and the most rare gift there is. That is why our Lord Jesus wished to exhort us. Now if those who can be called spiritual, that is, who have an ardent zeal to serve God, who are fully accustomed to have recourse to Him, who are exercised in prayer of mouth and heart to God,[5] are still so weak that in a single moment they can be ruined unless they are calling upon God; what will happen to those who are still so earthly and so pitiably weighed down that they cannot drag their legs and they hardly have a good impulse or a single good thought? How they must have to struggle for the prize! So then, may each one of us examine himself, and we shall find that we are so lax[6] and so dull[7] in the matter of praying to God that there is sometimes more ceremony than feeling. Seeing that, may we learn to be displeased with ourselves for such a vice and such laxity.[8] May we even detest such a corruption, may we take pains to call upon God, and to raise our spirits on high and to seek the remedy which is here proposed for us. That, then, in a word, is what we have to remember.

Now when it is said that the disciples went to sleep for the third time, even though they had been spurred so sharply (beyond what we discussed this morning, that is, that we see how Jesus Christ to perfect our salvation sought no other companion) let us also contemplate how slow we are.[9] For it is certain that we have no more ability than these three who are here mentioned, and yet they were the most excellent of the company, and those whom Jesus Christ had marked as the flower of the twelve, who were to publish the Gospel to all the world. Although, then, there was already such a good beginning, yet we see how they weakened. Now it is in order that

4 *parfait,* perfected, completed.
5 *en prières et oraison.*
6 *lasches,* sloth, loose, lazy, cowardly.
7 *hebetez,* besotted, blockheaded.
8 *laschcté.*
9 *quelle est nostre tardivité.*

we may have recourse only to the Son of God and that we may seek in Him all that is lacking in us, and that we may not lose courage when we feel such a weakness in us. It is true that the example of the Apostles gives us no occasion at all to flatter ourselves (as many will say that they have as much right to sleep as Peter and John and James) but rather to make us displeased with our vices, that we may always know that our Lord Jesus is ready to receive us, provided we come to Him. Furthermore, there is always this special reason that we declared this morning, that it was necessary that everything that is man should give way in order that we may know that the accomplishment of our salvation is in Him who was appointed by God as our Mediator. We must also note when we are near our Lord Jesus Christ that it is then that we must be more vigilant. For the worldlings and those whom God has cut off entirely as rotten members[10] whom He abandons, have no great fight. For the devil already has dominion over them. And that is why they can sleep at their ease. But according as our Lord Jesus exercises toward us the grace to call us to Himself, and to draw near to us familiarly, the battles are also instigated by Satan, because he wishes to draw us back from the obedience of the Son of God. When (I say) he sees that we are on the right track, then we have all the more rude assaults. Thus may each one prepare himself, knowing for what he was called by God, and what is his charge. This, then, is, in summary, what we have to remember.

Besides, when it is said *"Sleep and rest, the hour has come"* that is, as it were, a declaration that they would soon be surprised unless God watched over them. However, He rebukes them[11] by saying, "How now? Look where you are. For the devil is making every effort for the perdition of mankind, and in My Person the Kingdom of God must be recovered, or all creatures will perish. Yet here you are sleeping." Now this admonition hardly served for that time. But as time passed the disciples knew they must attribute all praise for their salvation to God, in view of their ingratitude, which was dis-

10 *membres pourris.*
11 Lat., *redarguo.*

played in such brutish cowardice.[12] So now we are admonished (as I have already mentioned) that the Son of God had to be shown to be our Redeemer by Himself alone and without aid. Besides, let us also learn that it is absolutely necessary that God watch over us even while we sleep. For how many times will it happen that the devil would have oppressed us a hundred thousand times? Yet what means have we to resist him, unless God have pity on us, although He sees us, as it were, reduced to insensibility. So that must not give us occasion to go astray and to quit addressing God in prayer.[13] But still we must always remember this sentence from the Psalm, "He who watches over Israel never sleeps; what is more He slumbers not."[14] So for our part let us be vigilant, even as we are urged by this exhortation. But let us recognize that however vigilant we ourselves may be, God must still keep a careful watch. Otherwise our enemies would soon win against us.

It follows that Jesus Christ says to His disciples, *"Let us go; he who betrays Me draws near."* He does not wish them to keep Him company (as we have already declared) except that they see how He does not spare Himself for their sakes, nor for the sake of the human race. For He presented Himself to receive all the blows and to exempt them from them, as it was necessary that this word might be fulfilled. *"He let nothing* perish of that which the heavenly Father had given Him and committed to His charge and protection." But by that he declares that He went voluntarily to death, following what we have treated this morning, that the sacrifice of obedience had to answer to wipe out all our rebellions. If Jesus Christ of His free will[15] had not been offered to appease the wrath of God His Father, His death and passion would not have been of any use to us. But He holds Himself to it and declares that as He has put on our nature in order to accomplish our redemption, now in the supreme act, He did not wish to fail in His office.

According to the narrative, *"Judas had given a sign of Him Whom he betrayed, that it was Jesus, and that He was seized,*

---

12 Fr., *lascheté*.
13 *oraisons et prières*.
14 Psalm 121:4.
15 *de son bon gré*.

and having arrived he kisses Him and says to Him, 'Hail, Master!' " Now let us note that this was a manner of greeting. As in some nations they embrace, in other nations they shake hands. The Jews were entirely accustomed to this kiss, as one sees by Holy Scripture. Besides, one would find it strange that Judas, being part of the company of Jesus Christ a little while before, that is, even that same night, returns and kisses Him as if he came from a distant journey. But he uses this ceremony, because he comes there as a frightened man. And that is why the other Gospel-writer says, "Rabbi, Rabbi, Hail!" He makes believe, then, that he is very sorry that his master is thus assailed. When he sees such a company who come to surprise Him, he draws near and kisses Jesus Christ, as if to say, "O my Master, they are looking for You, here are Your enemies who surround You, they seek to exterminate You, You will be cut off from the midst of men, once they put their hands upon You." That, then, is a sign of pity and compassion which Judas gives.

Further, it is said that Jesus Christ reproaches him, "Friend, why art thou come?" which is as if He said, "You villain, you who have been with Me at My table, you have been, as it were, of My blood, when we were united as children of God (for I being your Head, so I have recognized you as My members) and yet you come to betray Me, even by a kiss." Upon which let us note that the Son of God had to be marked, in order that Scripture might be so much better proved, and that it might be known that it was He Whom God had elected as our Redeemer. For all this had been typified[16] in the person of David, who was, as it were, a mirror and image of the Son of God. Now it says that it is not strangers nor those who have openly declared themselves His enemies who molested and tormented Him, but "He (says He) who ate bread at My table has kicked up his heel for betrayal, he has surrounded Me, he has betrayed Me falsely." Indeed, even he (as He says in the other passage) who accompanied Me to go together into the house of the Lord." As if God said there was not only a

16 *figuré.*

private and human friendship, as it would be between those living in common, but that there was holy brotherhood dedicated to the name of God. This, then, is what the Holy Spirit wished to show us, that nothing happened to the Son of God which had not been testified previously and which had not been typified,[16] in order that we may be all the better assured that it is He Who from all time had been established by God, since He bears such infallible marks.

Besides, in the person of Judas we see that the Church of God will always be subject to many betrayals. To be sure, it is something to have Satan with all his paraphernalia for an enemy, and everything we have already declared, and to have also those who fight openly against God and seek only the confusion of His Church. It is something (I say) that we have to fight against such enemies, but God still wills to prove our patience in this respect, that in our midst there may always be domestic enemies, who are full of betrayal and disloyalty. Although this plague is detestable, yet the Church never will be purged of it. Surely we must guard against it, and each one must try, as much as it is in his power, to scrape such an odor and infection. But when we shall have done all, still God will always permit that there be Judases. For since it was typified in David, and since it was fulfilled in our Lord Jesus Christ, we must be conformed to Him (as Saint Paul says), for He carries, as it were, the coat of arms of the house of God, being the first-born[17] among all believers. We must, then, have this condition in common with Him. But we can see here that it is from a frightened conscience, when God put there the spirit of disturbance, frenzy or stupidity, as He often spoke of it by His prophets. Judas, then, shows us the penalty of those who knowingly fight against God, that they must be so lost that they no longer have either sense of reason. However, they try to hide everything by hypocrisy even to saying that God forces them and that He leads them even to their final condemnation. At first glance it surely seems that these two things are opposed: (1) that a man comes to throw himself

---

17 *avant la primogéniture.*

like a savage bull against God, that he has forgotten that it won't do him any good to spit at the sun, that often he wishes to spite nature, and (2) yet tries to hide himself by subterfuges, and he thinks to gain something by his hypocrisy. One will say that those two things are incompatible. But they are seen in Judas. For he had experienced the heavenly power of our Lord Jesus Christ, he had seen so many miracles, and on his part he had done them, even in the Name of our Lord Jesus Christ. Having known, then, that the Son of God has all power both over life and over death, he betrays Him, and says he did justly. For otherwise he would have immediately escaped. Judas, then, is entirely depraved of sense and reason, and is, as it were, frantic. So it is only by a kiss and by these sweet words, saying "Alas my Master," he does not yet allow himself to have subterfuges, thinking he will be acquitted by this means. But that is how Satan dazzles his lackeys.

Let us learn, then, in the first place, to humble ourselves that no one throw himself against this rock which is too hard. That is, may we not wage war against our Lord Jesus Christ. Let us watch carefully, then, lest we stand in this devilish rage, lest we fight against the truth, and lest we contend against our conscience, so that we knowingly provoke the wrath of God, as if we wished to defy Him. Let us guard against that. Let us not so flatter ourselves in our hypocrisy and in our fictions that we are finally cheated and deceived by them. For we see what happened to Judas (as it is mentioned in the account), that it was not necessary that a judge condemn him, that it was not necessary to compel him to recant. But he confessed that he had sold and betrayed righteous blood. However, he did not ask pardon for his misdeed, but he went away in despair to hang himself and he burst asunder. Let us be well advised, then, not to give such access to Satan that he tears our eyes when we are asleep in our sins, and not to expect[18] by this means to escape the hand of God. But let us remove all this make-believe.

---

18 *et que nous cuidons.*

Besides, let us recognize that it is certainly commanded to us to kiss the Son of God in Psalm 2:12,[19] but that is to do Him homage as our King and as Him Who has sovereign Dominion over all creatures. For the word "Kiss" implies only reverence and a solemn protestation[20] that we are His own. As He said, "You call me Master, and you do well." But in coming to Him let us be advised not to call Him Master from the tip of the tongue while we are yet enemies to Him, not to practice toward Him a false reverence in order to kick against Him and to give Him the boot.[21] That is, may we not be stubborn and peevish by our disloyalty, but may we show that we have sought to maintain ourselves in His Church only in order to serve our God. Let us, then, be admonished of all that. Besides, although the word of our Lord Jesus Christ did not immediately take effect upon Judas, finally by virtue of this word he had to hang himself without waiting for other condemnation.

In fact, Saint John tells us how our Lord Jesus struck like lightning, although He used only a single word against all those who came to seek Him, saying, *"I am He."*[22] There is a band sent by Pilate. There is a force of men gathered by the Priests. They come there furnished with clubs, swords, and other blades. Jesus Christ is alone. He is as a lamb led to the slaughter-house, as Isaiah says. And what word does He use? *"I am He."* And all are thrown down. All fall immediately. And how comes this fall? By it we see that our Lord Jesus, although He is humbled for a time, even emptied of everything, never ceased to retain, when it seemed good to Him, His heavenly power in order to cast down all His enemies, if He had wished. Let us compare our times with what was done then. Jesus Christ had to be bound and fastened (as we shall see later). He had to let His enemies rule. For Satan had unleashed the bridle to urge them on to every rage and cruelty.

---

19 Note that chapter and verse are given in the text. I think this sermon was preached in January, 1564, a few months before Calvin's death.

20 Calvin usually uses Fr. *protester* in the original Latin sense of *protestari,* to bring forth a witness. It refers to making a solemn affirmation.

21 *pour luy donner du talon.*

22 In the Greek it is simply "I am," the "He" being understood. John 18:5.

This is what is said by St. Luke, "This is the reign of darkness." Be that as it may, when He said "I am He" His enemies had to be confounded. What will it be, then, when He comes in His majesty with all His Angels? When He comes to make all those who have resisted Him His footstool? When He comes with a dreadful face and an incomprehensible wrath? As Saint Paul says in 2 Thessalonians 1:8. Then how can wicked despisers of the majesty of God and of the word of our Lord Jesus Christ exist before His face? When He had thus thrown down His enemies, then He was ready to suffer and He did not use any defense. I say, even that of God His Father. As He said, He could ask that a million Angels might be sent to Him. But He abstained. Yet He surely wished to show that by His voice alone He could cast down everyone who was against Him, if He had wished.

By that we are taught to fear the word of our Lord Jesus. Although He does not converse here in a visible manner in our midst, yet since the Gospel is preached by His authority and He says, "He who hears you, hears Me;" let us learn to receive what is preached to us in His name with all reverence and to subject ourselves to it. We shall find that this word, which so caused to fall the guards and those who came against Him, will be our only foundation and prop. For how can we rejoice, except when the Son of God appear to us, and we see that He is near us, and He show us Who He is, and why He has been sent to us by God His Father? So then, it is in this word *"I am He"* that we may know, when it will please our Lord Jesus to manifest Himself as He does to all His believers, that in this word He declares to us why He calls us to Himself, why He has descended to us, and why He dwells in us by the power of His Holy Spirit, and that is wherein consists all our good and all our rest. But if we wish to be peevish and scorn the Word of God like many profane people, let us be assured that it will be a thunderbolt to cast us down into the depth of hell. So let us fear, and yet may our Lord Jesus open to us the door, and may He say to us in another fashion "Here am I," as He has not done to those who were already His declared enemies. Let us learn to come to Him.

Besides, let us also learn so to bear in patience the betrayals which we see today in the Church no matter how outrageous they may be to us, so that we shall show that we really cling to the Son of God, for He is our Head. Then may we have His truth. May we so converse with one another that we may be united in true concord and brotherhood together. That is what we have to remember.

But whatever else may be, may we accept the principal article of instruction which we must remember from this passage: namely, that the Son of God made Himself obedient in everything and by everything in order to make reparation for our rebellions. It is true (as I have said) that all the members of His body ought to be ruled by His example. There is good reason, since He Who has entire mastery and superiority is so humbled, that we be ready to obey our God unto life and unto death. Yet let us recognize that the obedience of our Lord Jesus Christ in this place is special, that is, because of the fruit and the effect which proceeded from it. The Apostles have well chosen the death of Jesus Christ for an example. For they were strengthened for their needs when they had to fight for the witness of the Gospel. They were not then asleep. We see the vigilance which was in them and that they were ready to follow their calling. They even had fear neither of torments nor of the death which was presented to them when God called them for the glory of His Name, and the confession of our Lord Jesus Christ. Yet they insisted principally on showing that by the pouring out of the blood of our Redeemer we are washed and cleansed of all our spots, that He made payment to God His Father for all our debts by which we were obliged, that He acquired for us perfect righteousness.

Let us recognize, then, the difference between the Head and the members. Let us learn that though by nature we are entirely given to evil, and although God may have regenerated us in part, still our flesh does not cease to chafe[23] against God. However, by virtue of the obedience which we see in our Lord Jesus Christ, we do not cease to be acceptable to our God. If we do not yet do the good that we will, but the evil oftentimes

23 *de se rebéquer.*

pushes us, and there may be many failures, or perhaps we may be too slow to do good, let us look at what the Son of God suffered in order to make reparation for all our faults. Let us notice how He fought in such a way that there was no contradiction in Him when our crimes and sins were imputed to Him, as was explained more at length this morning. Let us see, then, how our Lord Jesus has made satisfaction in everything and for everything, but we today, although having taken the trouble to obey God, are not able to succeed, but we always droop our wings, must constantly repeat this: that we know that we shall not cease to be acceptable to God and that our imperfections will always be abolished by the obedience of our Lord Jesus Christ, so that they will not come into account before God. Besides, may each one according to the measure of his faith and of the grace which he has received exert himself to fight until we come to the heavenly rest. Seeing our weaknesses are still so great, being convinced that we shall not even know how to have a single good thought, and that having stumbled we shall not be able to raise ourselves, unless God extended to us His hand and strengthened us each minute,[24] may we be advised to pray that He may augment in us the graces of His Holy Spirit; as He has promised it to us, and offers to us Jesus Christ for our Head and Captain, in order that after we are able to arrive at the victory which He acquired for us, of which we already experience the fruit, we shall experience it in perfection.

Now we shall bow in humble reverence before the majesty of our God.

---

24 I think this paragraph reflects Calvin's ill health and sense of approaching death.

SERMON 5

Third Sermon on the Passion of Our Lord Jesus Christ *

And behold, one of those who were with Jesus, putting forward his hand drew his sword, and struck the servant of the high Priest, and cut off his ear. Then Jesus said to him, "Put your sword back into its place. For all those who handle the sword will perish by the sword. Do you think that I cannot now pray to my Father, and he will give me more than twelve legions of Angels? How then would the Scriptures be fulfilled? For thus it must be done!" At that hour Jesus said to the crowds, "You have come out having swords and clubs, as after a robber to take me. Everyday I was seated with you, teaching in the temple and you did not capture me. But all this was done in order that the Scriptures of the Prophets might be fulfilled." Then all the disciples left him and fled. Then others, having captured Jesus, led him away to Caiaphas the high Priest, where the Scribes and Elders had assembled. And Peter followed him from afar as far as the courtyard of the high Priest, and having gone inside, he sat with the servants, in order that he might see the end. Now the chief Priests and the Elders and all the counsel were seeking false witness against Jesus, in order that they might put Him to death. And they found none. Although many false witnesses had come, they found none of the same. But finally two false witnesses came and said, "He said, 'I can destroy the temple of God, and in three days rebuild it.'" Then the high Priest arose and said to him, "You answer nothing? Why do these men testify against you?" And Jesus kept silence. Then the high Priest answering said to him, "I adjure you by the living God that you tell us if you are the Christ, the Son of God." Jesus said to him, "You said it. Yet I tell you, hereafter you will see the Son of man seated at the right hand of the power of God, and coming upon clouds of heaven. Then

* From: *Corpus Reformatorum, Calvini Opera,* vol. 46, pp. 859-873.

the high Priest tore his vestments, saying, "He has blasphemed. Have we further concern about witnesses? Behold, you have heard now his blasphemy. How does it seem to you?" They answering said to him, "He is guilty of death."

— Matthew 25:51-66

If we wished to judge superficially according to our natural senses the capture of our Lord Jesus Christ, we would be troubled by the fact that He offered no resistence. It would not seem consistent with His majesty that He suffered such shame and disgrace without hindering it. On the other hand, we would prize the zeal of Peter, since he exposed himself to death. For he saw the great multitude of enemies. He was alone, and a man who was not skilled at arms. Yet he draws out his sword on account of the love which he bears toward his Master, and prefers to die on the field rather than allow such an injury to be done to Him. But by that we see that we must come with all humility and modesty to know where all that the Son of God did and suffered was leading, and that what seems good to us is worth nothing, but we must pray to God that He lead us and guide us by His Word and that we judge not except according to what He will have shown us. For that is how the Gospel is a scandal to many people. Others make fun of it, and all to their perdition. It is that they are inflated with presumption and are rash judges. But in order not to be deceived, we must always in the first place come back to what our Lord Jesus declares. It is the will of God His Father. That is one item. Then we have to consider the end of that which may seem strange to us. When, then, we shall have these two considerations, then there will be occasion to adore God and to know that what seems to be folly according to men is an admirable wisdom even to the Angels.

But to arrive at that, let us consider what is here told about Peter. It is said, *"Having drawn out his sword, he cut off the ear of Malchus, who was servant of Caiaphas."* Here we see how men are too bold, when they follow their foolish opinion. Then they are so blind that they do not spare themselves under any conditions. But when they ought to obey God they are so cowardly that it is a pity. They even forget themselves in such a manner that it takes nothing to make them turn aside. That is how we shall always have hundred times more courage to follow our foolish imaginations than to do what God commands us and to do what our calling implies. We see too much of that in the example of Peter. For after he has shown that he has made confession and witness to our Lord Jesus, he blasphemes to his perdition. Yet he is content to die, even when it is not commanded to him. What moves him to draw out his sword? He does it as if in spite. For he received no such instruction from his Master. And when he renounces Jesus Christ, did he not already know the saying, "Whoever denies me before men, him I shall deny before God My Father Who is in heaven"? But (as I have said) he is hot-headed.[1] This foolish desire to support our Lord Jesus in his own way and according to his fancy carries him on. Now by his example let us learn to exert ourselves to walk where God calls us. May nothing that He commands us be too difficult for us. But may we attempt nothing, not even to move our little finger, unless God approves it and we have testimony that it is He Who guides us. That is one item.

In fact, in the first place, our Lord Jesus shows him that he has offended grievously, because he was not ignorant of the law, where it is said, "Whoever spills human blood, his blood will be spilled." St. Peter, then, should well remember this lesson, that God does not will that either force or violence be used. And (what is more) in what school had he been nurtured during more than three years? Had not our Lord Jesus held back as far as it was possible for Him in humaneness and gentleness?[2] Where, then, does he expect to get approval for his boldness? We must observe further what we have already said. That is, if our zeal is prized by men and we are applauded, to that extent we shall not cease to be

---

1 *il a le cerveau bouillant.*

2 *en humanité et mansuétude.* It would be profitable for someone to make a careful study of what Calvin means by *humanité*. He seems to have put an extremely high value upon the possibilities of simple human kindness as a means of witnessing for God. Despite the fact that he was attacked most of his life, he seems to have been a kindly soul. Lat., *mansuétude* has been dropped from modern French.

condemned before God if we transgress His Word ever so slightly. There is then no praise except in walking as God shows us by His Word. For as soon as a man goes beyond this line, all his virtues only stink. That is how it is with all our devotions. As soon as we have worked to do what we have imagined in our brain, God will condemn everything, unless we have heard His Word. For apart from that there is no truth which He approves and which is legitimate before Him.

But as for the account we are treating now, the second reason which our Lord Jesus alleges is more noteworthy. What we have already touched upon is general. But there is here a sentence which is peculiar to the death and passion of our Lord Jesus Christ, when he says, "*Do you not think that I can now pray to my Father, and he will send me more than twelve legions of angels?*" Now one legion in that time customarily made four or five thousand men. "There is, then, a heavenly army which I can have," says He, "and yet I do without it. And why, then, do you come here to usurp more than God either wills or permits?" Now it is surely permissible to call upon God and to pray to Him that He may be willing to sustain our life; and as He holds it precious, that He may keep it in His protection. Our Lord Jesus declares that He does not wish it now and that He ought not to do it. How, then, will Peter use violence, seeing it is outside the order which God has permitted and established by His Word? If a means which is permissible in itself ought not to come into use, how distinguish what God has defended and what He has declared worthy of punishment? Here (as I have already mentioned) we see how the Son of God subjected Himself to such shames and that He preferred to let Himself be bound and tied like an evil-doer and a criminal rather than to be a deceiver by miracle and that God employed His arm to protect[3] Him. By that we have to recognize how He prized our salvation. Here is a point which I have already noted: namely, that He refers us to the will and to the decree of God His Father. For apart from that one

3 *garantir.*

would find it strange that He did not wish to implore His aid, as He might surely know that He could have it. It seems that He tempts God when He does not pray to Him at all. We have the promise that Angels will surround those who fear God, even that they will follow them to prevent them from hurting themselves, and that they may not have to meet any evil in their paths.[4] Now when God has promised us something, He wills that it may be to invite us to prayer. Yet when we are in need we ought to run back to Him in order that He may use His Angels to guide us, for which cause He has given them this office. We see also that this was practiced by the holy Patriarchs[5] and the Fathers. "The Angel of the Lord who has never failed me will be in thy way with thee and he will make thee prosper," said Abraham.[6] Thus, then, have the holy Fathers used it. Why, then, did Jesus Christ not wish to have the Angels? For already He had been comforted (as St. Luke mentions) and Angels[7] had waited upon Him in order to sweeten the anguish in which He was.

It seems, then, that He despises a necessary help from God. But He takes it into account when he adds *"How will the Scriptures be fulfilled?"* As if He said, "If we doubt something, we can, then, and ought to pray to God that He may look upon us in pity and that by all means He may make us to feel His power. But when we are convinced that He must pass by some need, and that the will of God is known to us, then it is no longer a matter of making of Him another request, unless that He may strengthen us in power and in invincible constancy, and that we may make no complaint, or that we may not be carried away by our affections; but that we may go with a ready courage through everything to which He calls us." For example, if we are persecuted by our enemies, and we do not know what God has in store for us, or what ought to be the outcome, we have to pray to Him as if our life were precious to Him and since He holds in His

4 Psalm 91:10-12, a very free paraphrase.
5 The first time I have found *Patriarchs*. Usually Calvin used a paraphrase.
6 I think a vague reference to Gen. 24:40, although it is somewhat garbled.
7 In Luke 22:43 it is only one angel who appears.

guard that He demonstrates this by the result and that He delivers us. But when we are persuaded that God wills to call us to Himself and that there is no longer any remedy, then we must cut off every dispute and fully resign ourselves that nothing any longer remains but to obey the decree of God which is immutable.[8]

That, then, is the intention of our Lord Jesus. For He surely prayed throughout His whole life, and even previously in this great combat which He had sustained, He prays to God that if it were possible this drink might be turned away from Him. But now He has taken up His conclusion, because He was so ordained by God His Father and He saw that He must acquit Himself of the charge which was committed to Him, that is, to offer the perpetual sacrifice to blot out the sins of the world. Since, then, He saw Himself called to that place, and the matter was finished, that is why He abstains from praying to God to do the contrary. He wishes, then, to be helped neither by Angels nor by men. He does not wish that God make Him to feel His power to withdraw Him from death. But it was sufficient for Him to have this spirit of constancy, that He might be able to go by His free will to perform His office. That is what satisfies Him.

Now we see in the first place that the will of God ought to stop us and hold us in check so that, when things seem to us savage and against all reason, we may value more what God has ordained than what our brain can comprehend. Our imaginations, then, ought to be put under foot when we feel that God has proved otherwise. It is part of the obedience of our faith when we consider God to be wise, so that He may have authority to do everything that pleases Him. If we have reasons to do the opposite, may we know that it is only smoke and vanity and that God knows all and that nothing is hidden from Him, and even that His will is the norm of all wisdom and of all uprightness. Besides, what our spirit[9] argues to the opposite, that comes from our rude-

8 Probably Calvin is here reflecting upon his own life and death, as well as upon the death of Jesus Christ.

9 *esprit*, spirit, mind.

ness. For we know that the wisdom of God is infinite, and scarcely have we three drops of sense. We need not, then, be astonished if men are scared when God does not govern Himself according to their appetite. And why not? For we are poor fools. In fact, there is only brutality in us however much our sense and reason rule. But since we do not understand the profound depth of the judgments of God, let us learn to adore what is hidden — to adore it (I say) in humility and reverence, confessing that everything God does is just and upright, though as yet we may not perceive how. That is one item.

Following that, since it is so that God willed that His Son might be thus exposed to death, may we not be ashamed of what He endured. May we not think that wicked men were in control and that the Son of God did not have the means to defend Himself. For everything proceeded from the will of God, and from the immutable decree which He had made. That is also why our Lord Jesus says in St. Luke, "Indeed, it is your reign now, and the power of darkness."[10] As if He said, "Take no glory in what you are doing; for the devil is your master." However, He shows that it is by means of the permission which God gave them. Although the devil possessed them, nevertheless, neither they nor he could attempt anything unless God had unleashed for them the bridle. That, then, in summary, is how we must have our eyes and all our senses fixed upon the will of God, and upon His eternal plan, when the death and passion of our Lord Jesus Christ is spoken of to us.[11] Now He declares that such is the will of God, because it is written. For if Jesus Christ had not had testimony of what was ordered by God His Father, He might still have been in doubt. But He knew His office. God did not send Him here below that He might not have given Him fully to His express charge. It is true, inasmuch as our Lord Jesus is eternal God, He did not need to be taught by any Scripture; but inasmuch as He is our Redeemer and that

---

10 A free paraphrase of Luke 22:53b.

11 This paragraph seems to me supralapsarian. Cf. chart on p. 31 and article on "Calvinism" on p. 87 in Benjamin B. Warfield, *The Plan of Salvation.* Cf. pp. 118-125 in Louis Berkhof, *Systematic Theology.*

He clothed Himself in our nature to have a true brotherhood with us, He had to be taught by Holy Scripture, as we see, above all, that He did not refuse such instruction.

So then, since God has shown Him to what He was called, that is upon what He relies. That is why He is taken as a captive, in order not to draw back when He knew that He had to achieve[12] the charge which was committed to Him, that is, to offer Himself in sacrifice for the redemption of us all.[13] So, then, we must learn that, inasmuch as the will of God is secret to Himself and incomprehensible, we must have recourse to Holy Scripture. It is true that God does not cease to have His counsel ordered by things that we imagine[14] to be by chance. But that is not declared to us. We shall not always have special revelation to say that God has determined this or that. Then, we must withhold judgment. That is why we pray to God that He may heal us of an illness or that He may deliver us from some other affliction when we have fallen into it. And why? We do not know what He wills to do. To be sure, we ought not to impose a law upon Him. This condition ought always to be added: that His will may be done. But all our prayers ought to lead here: to ask Him that He may know us to be necessary and useful, and that we may meanwhile refer everything to Him in His secret counsel in order that He may do as seems good to Him. But when we have testimony through Holy Scripture that God wills a thing, then it is not proper to offer any reply, as I have already said.

Here we are still better assured as to the person of our Lord Jesus Christ, that He was afflicted cruelly and treated with such shame and haughty, scornful abuse, not only according to the desire of wicked and lawless men, but since God had so decreed it. And how do we know? By Holy Scripture. For had not the sacrifices been ordained in the Law two thousand years before Jesus Christ was born? And

---

12 *exploiter*, sometimes "to farm" or "to cultivate."
13 Not unlimited atonement, but sacrifice for the redemption of all of us who are to be redeemed.
14 *nous cuidons*.

before the Law was given or written, had not God already inspired and taught the Ancient Fathers to sacrifice? And could the blood of brute beasts acquire remission of sins? Could it render men acceptable to God? Not at all,[15] but it was to show that God would be reconciled by the blood of the Redeemer Whom He had established. Then He gives explicit testimony and declaration through the Scriptures. We see, indeed, that the Prophets have spoken of Him, and He also refers especially to them. When Isaiah said that He Who was to be the Redeemer, would be disfigured, that He would be held in disdain, that He would have no form or no more beauty than an adder, that he would be beaten and struck by the hand of God, that He would be a terrible thing to see, in summary, that they would take away His life, by what power did he prophesy that? Is it that God cannot resist Satan or all the wicked men? No but He pronounced by the mouth of Isaiah what He had previously ordained. In Daniel there is a still greater expression. Since it is so, then, that God had declared that His only Son had to be sacrificed for our redemption and salvation, now we are better assured of what I have said, that is, that we must always contemplate the hand of God Who governs when we see that our Lord Jesus is subjected to such shameful things at the hands of men. That is also why St. Peter says in Acts 4:27 that Judas and all the Jews and the police and Pilate did not act except as the counsel and the hand of God had determined, as will be declared still more at length.[16] Here, then is where we must look, if we wish not to be troubled by our foolish imaginations. It is that God sent here below His only Son in order to accept the obedience when He would offer to Him in His death and passion to abolish all our faults and iniquities.

Now the second point which I have mentioned is the benefit[17] which comes back to us from what our Lord Jesus suf-

15 *Nenni.*
16 Since Calvin preached from memory there are sometimes slight inaccuracies on secondary points, as here the list of personalities involved. This habit of quoting roughly from memory nowhere, as far as I have discovered, affects his main points.
17 *le fruit.*

fered. For if we did not know why, that would be to take away the taste of what is here narrated to us. But when it is said that He has been bound and tied for our deliverance, then, indeed, we see our condition by nature, that is, that Satan holds us under the tyranny of sin and death, that we are slaves, so that instead of our being created in the image of God there is in us only entire corruption, that we are cursed, and that we are dragged like poor beasts in this cursed captivity. When, then, we know that and we see, on the other hand, that the Son of God did not refuse to be shamefully bound in order that the spiritual bonds of sin and death, which hold us under the servitude of Satan, might be broken, then we have to glorify God, we have to triumph with full voice in the death and passion of our Lord Jesus Christ and in the capture which is here mentioned. So that is what we must remember from this passage.

Thereupon the Gospel-writer says that our Lord Jesus healed the servant who had been wounded by Peter. Not that he was worthy of it, but in order that the offense might be removed. For it would have been to defame the doctrine of the Gospel and the redemption of our Lord Jesus Christ if this wound had remained (I call "redemption of our Lord Jesus Christ" what he acquired for us) so that it could be said that He had resisted the governor of the country and all the priests and that He committed, as it were, robbery in this lonely place. That, then, might have obscured all the glory of the Son of God and it would be to put the Gospel in perpetual shame. Also let us see that this action of Peter was by zeal of Satan. For the devil schemed to make Jesus Christ be rendered infamous with all His doctrine. That is also the tendency of all our beautiful devotions when we wish to serve God according to our desire and each one is given leave to do what he imagines to be good. Jesus Christ, then, wished to abolish such a scandal in order that His doctrine might not be defamed at all.

However, we see here a detestable ingratitude in those who were not moved by such a miracle. There are the police who come to bind our Lord Jesus Christ. They see that the power of the Spirit of God is at work in Him in so many ways. He made them fall back a little before a single word. Now He heals a man who has his ear cut off. All that is nothing to them. We see, then, when the devil has once bewitched men and he has dazzled their eyes, that neither the graces of God nor all His powers can touch them that they do not follow and walk always in their deeds, and they have, as it were, the snout of a pig which pokes itself everywhere. Whatever God does, whatever He says, they remain always in their obstinacy, which is a horrible thing. Yet we surely have to pray to God that He may give us prudence to profit from all His graces in order to be drawn by His love and also to touch us when He raises His hand to show us that He is our Judge in such a way that we are then frightened into returning to Him in true repentance. This, then, in summary, is what we have to remember.

Whatever it may mean, the mouths of the wicked men were closed when Jesus Christ healed the servant of Caiaphas. Thereupon it is said *"Jesus is led into the house of Caiaphas, where He is questioned,"* etc. For to abbreviate we omit what St. John tells of Annas, who was the father-in-law of Caiaphas, and perhaps Jesus Christ is led there out of respect, or maybe it was along the road while they were waiting for everyone to be assembled. Jesus, then, is led as far as the house of Caiaphas and is there questioned. Especially is it said, *"The priests sought everywhere for false witnesses, and found none. Finally two false witnesses stood up and said, 'He said he would rebuild the temple in three days.'"* Here we see how Jesus Christ was charged. Not that the priests were moved by some holy zeal. Often those who persecute innocents imagine they are performing a service acceptable to God, as in fact we see that Saint Paul was possessed by such a rage, that, being, as it were, a brigand (so he is called) he spoiled and destroyed more. Even then he imagined himself to be a good zealot. But this was not so of Caiaphas and all his band. For what did they seek, except that Jesus Christ be unjustly oppressed? So we see that their ambition led them to fight openly against God, which is a horrible thing. For as for Caiaphas and all his band, they are sons of Levi, the holy line which God had chosen. It was not by men that they had been elected, but God had so ordained by His law. It is true that there was a villanous and enormous corruption, inasmuch as the office of the priest was sold in that time, and instead of being obligated for life (so God had ordained it) each one brought his companion and he who brought the most money carried away that dignity. It was, then, a villainous and detestable corruption that intrigues and underhanded practices were used in so holy and honorable an estate. However, the Priest always remained in this line of Levi which God had dedicated to His service. Nevertheless, look at them! all enemies of God, look at them! all intoxicated by Satan, indeed enraged against the Redeemer of the world, Who was the final purpose of the Law.

So let us note that those who are in high estate and dignity will not always acquit themselves so faithfully that it is not necessary to keep watch over them, as over those who can be enemies of God. By that one can see the altogether too dull-witted foolishness of the Papists, when they adopt the title and estate of Priest. Suppose that God had commanded that there be a Pope (which He never did). Suppose that He ought to have His throne at Rome (still less). Though all that might be true, yet in the person of Caiaphas and of his kind it is seen that all those who have been raised to honor can abuse their power. So then may we not be so foolish as to amuse ourselves with masks. And when there is some honorable title, may God not lose His authority over it, as we see the Papists renounce the whole Holy Scripture and do homage to their idols. Let us learn, then, that under shadow of some human dignity God must not be decreased, but He must retain His sovereign Dominion. That is one item. As for the scandal which we could here conceive according to our fancy, let us note what is said in Psalm 118 (as also our Lord Jesus had previously alleged) that He is the rock which had to be refused[18] by the builders. And who were the build-

18 *reprouvée*, disallowed, disapproved of.

ers of the house of God and of His Church? The Priests. At least they ought to acquit themselves of that office. Yet they refused the stone which God had established as the corner-stone.[19] And this stone, although it might have been rejected, has nevertheless been seated at the principal place of the building, that is, that God did not cease to fulfil what He had ordained by His counsel, when he raised from the dead His only Son, and raised Him higher than He was before He was emptied. For every knee must bow before Him.

When it is here said that the Priests sought false testimony, this was not simply to contrive a crime, but to have some pretext and disguise[20] to burden and oppress the Lord Jesus. In truth He had pronounced these words, "Destroy this temple, and I shall raise it up in three days." Those, then, are the words of our Lord Jesus, just as they came out of His mouth. The witnesses who are produced recite them. One could say that they are good and faithful witnesses. Yet the Holy Spirit calls them false, since they have wickedly perverted this remark. For our Lord Jesus spoke of His body, which is the true temple of the divine majesty. The material temple which was built in Jerusalem was nothing but a figure. It was only a shadow, as we know. But in our Lord Jesus all fulness of the Godhead[21] made His residence, as says St. Paul, indeed, bodily and in true substance. So then, let us note that we must look not simply at the words of a witness but at the intention of him who speaks. This is a good and useful instruction for us, because we see men are so given to their evil deeds and lies that when they have some cover it is enough for them and it seems to them that they are absolved before God when they have by this means falsely charged a man. May we not, then, be stopped simply at the words or at the formality or ceremony, but may we look at the true nature of the cause. For those who could always maintain that they gave no evidence except what

19 *le principal fondement,* a more accurate term than the English "cornerstone." The modern "cornerstone" is not essential to the structure of the building.

20 *couleur et fard,* make-up and rouge.

21 *toute plénitude de Divinité.*

was there, will not cease to be reputed before God false witnesses, as we see.

Whereupon it is said that Caiaphas says to Jesus Christ, *"How now? You answer nothing? Do you not see those who testify against you?"* Yet Jesus still remains entirely quiet and receives all those slanderous words in silence. One might find it strange that Jesus Christ, Who had a just enough occasion to repulse such a falsehood does not contradict. But (as already we have mentioned, as we shall see still more fully) Jesus Christ was not there to maintain His doctrine as previously. We must, then, distinguish prudently among all circumstances. For Jesus Christ, after having fasted in the desert, was sent by God His Father to publish the doctrine of the Gospel. During all that time we see with what magnanimity He always defended the doctrine of which He was minister. We see how He was opposed to all contradictions. That, then, is how He acquitted Himself of His office, since He was sent as minister of the Word. But here there is a special regard. It is that He must be Redeemer of the world. He must be condemned, indeed, not for having preached the Gospel, but for us He must be oppressed, as it were, to the lowest depths and sustain our cause, since He was there, as it were, in the person of all cursed ones and of all transgressors, and of those who had deserved eternal death. Since, then, Jesus Christ has this office, and He bears the burdens of all those who had offended God mortally, that is why He keeps silence. So, let us well note that when there was need that Jesus Christ maintained the doctrine of the Gospel, and that His office and His calling demanded it, He faithfully acquitted Himself of it. But when by keeping silence He performed the office of Redeemer, as if He accepted voluntary condemnation, it was not out of regard for Himself that He kept His mouth closed, for He was there (as I have already said) in our name. It is true that He speaks (as we shall see presently) but it is not for His defense; it is not without inflaming the anger and fury of the wicked men all the more against Him. That, then, is because He did not wish to escape death, but allowed Himself voluntarily to be oppressed, in order that He might show that

He forgot Himself in order to acquit us before God His Father. So, He had no regard for Himself, neither for His life itself nor even for His honor. It was all one to suffer the shames and disgraces of the world, provided that our sins be abolished and we be absolved from our condemnation.

Whereupon it is said, *"The high Priest adjures Him by the living God that He tell them if He is the Christ, if He is the blessed*[22] *Son. He answers that so He is, but they will see His majesty when it is too late,"* that is, for them, since it will be to their confounding.[23] Here our Lord Jesus speaks, but it is not to bow as a human being to the great Priest and all his band. Rather He uses threats to sting him still more. If previously he was full of malice and cruelty, this is to light still more fire. But we have already declared that Jesus Christ had no regard for Himself and that rather He acquits Himself of the duty of which He has taken the charge, that is, to be our Redeemer.

Besides, here we have in the first place, as it were, despisers of God, those who are entirely possessed by Satan, who yet will abuse some kind of cover of religion, for one might say that this great Priest still performs well his office, when he adjures Jesus Christ by the Name of the living God. But that is where men are plunged once Satan has bound their eyes. He flings them into such impudence that they have no reverence for God, no more than they are ashamed before men. In this answer of our Lord Jesus we have to note that He wishes to declare both to Caiaphas and to all the rest that if He is thus, as it were, crushed for a little time, that ought not to lessen His majesty, that always He may be held and reputed Only Son of God. But He has here a still higher consideration. It is that we may be assured that, having thus abased Himself for our salvation, nothing has been lost of His heavenly majesty, but that before men He was willing to be so oppressed, in order that we may be made fully certain that we shall be found honorable before God, because all the shames which we might have deserved will be abolished. Since, then, our Lord Jesus kept silence and He did not

22 *beni,* a higher type of blessedness than *bonheur.*
23 *confusion.*

defend Himself in His good cause, now we have our mouths open to call upon God as if we were righteous. He is even our Advocate, Who puts in a word for us. When, then, our Lord Jesus stood by, it was in order that now in full liberty He intercedes for us before God His Father, although we are nothing except poor vermin. There is in us only all misery. Yet we have access to God to call upon Him privately and to claim Him openly as our Father.

This is what He wishes to show when He said, "*You will see afterwards* the Son of Man seated at the right hand of the power of God. We must, then, be turned away from every regard which could bring us scandal, when we see that our Lord Jesus was thus humiliated. So let us look at what was the end of it. He willed, then, to be condemned without any resistance in order that we might be able to appear before the judgment-seat of God, and that we come there freely without any fear. Let us learn, then, in summary, every time the history of the Passion is recited to us so to groan and sigh seeing that the Son of God had to suffer so for us, that we tremble at His Majesty until it may appear to us. May we be so resolved that when He comes, it will be to make us experience in effect the fruit which He acquired for us by His death and passion. Besides, may we fear to be numbered with those whom He threatens so, saying, "*You* will see henceforth." For it must be that the wicked and reproved will feel how terrible is the judgment-seat of God and how great is His power to cast them down when He will rise against them. When St. Paul also wishes to speak of the condemnation which the wicked and those who are cursed by God will endure, he says that they will be before His infinite majesty trembling and frightened at His look.

Since it is so, let us learn to humble ourselves before the Lord Jesus. Let us not wait to see with the eye the majesty which He will show at His second coming, but by faith let us contemplate Him today as our King, and the Head of the Angels and of all creatures, and let us receive Him as our sovereign Prince. Let us attribute to Him the honor which belongs to Him, knowing that since He is given to us for wisdom, for redemption, for righteousness and holiness by

God His Father, we must attribute to Him every praise, and that it is from His fulness that we must draw to be satisfied. Let us be advised, then, to do this honor to our Lord Jesus Christ, although today we do not yet see His judgment-seat prepared. But let us contemplate Him by the eyes of faith and let us pray to God that He may enlighten us by His Holy Spirit, that He may strengthen us to call upon Him in time of trouble, and that this may carry us above the world, above all of our senses and all our apprehensions, in such a way that our Lord Jesus may be magnified today by us as He deserves. That, then, in summary, is what we have to remember.

Touching the saying that Caiaphas and the Priests have condemned Him to death, may we learn not to be astonished by the obstinacy of the wicked and of the enemies of the truth. Today this doctrine is very necessary for us. For we see the great ones of this world blaspheme openly against the Gospel. We see even in our midst that those who make profession of the Gospel and wish to be considered reformed people and in whom it seems there is only the Gospel, yet condemn like devils incarnate, or even like furious beasts possessed by Satan, the doctrine of the Gospel. One need not go far to see all these things. So, may we be assured against such scandals, and may we learn to always glorify our God. Though Caiaphas and all his kind cough up their blasphemies as much as they wish, and though they say that Jesus Christ is deserving of death, it is necessary to keep silence on such an article, though it is bad. Though, then, they so infect the air by their villainous and execrable blasphemies, yet let us cling to this voice of our Lord Jesus Christ. If today His truth is so condemned by men falsely, and it is doubted, it is falsified, it is depraved, and people deliberately turn their backs on it, it is strong and powerful enough to maintain itself. Let us wait in patience until He appears for our redemption. Yet may all of us learn to humble ourselves, and to give Him all the glory, since He was so willing to stoop, indeed, to empty Himself of everything for our salvation.

Now let us bow in humble reverence before the majesty of our God.

SERMON 6

Fourth Sermon on the Passion of Our Lord Jesus Christ *

Then they spat in his face and slapped him, and others struck him with their fists, saying, "Christ, prophecy to us, 'Who hit you?'" Now Peter was sitting outside in the courtyard, and a chambermaid came forward to him, saying, "You also were with Jesus the Galilean." And he denied it before them all, saying, "I do not know what you are saying." And as he went out the door another chambermaid saw him and said to those who were there, "This man also was with Jesus the Nazarene." And again he denied it with an oath, saying, "I have not known the man." And after a little while those who were present came and said to Peter, "Surely you also belong to them, for your language gives you away." Then he began to curse and swear, saying, "I do not know the man." And immediately the cock crowed. And Peter remembered the word of Jesus, who had said to him, "Before the cock crows, you will deny me three times. So he went out and wept bitterly. But when morning had come, all the chief Priests and the Elders of the people took counsel against Jesus in order to put him to death. And they led him away bound and delivered him to Pontius Pilate the governor. Then Judas who had betrayed him, seeing that he was condemned, repenting, brought back the thirty pieces of silver to the chief Priests and elders,[1] *saying, "I have sinned in delivering innocent blood." But they said, "What does that matter to us? You worry about it." So, after having thrown down the pieces of silver in the Temple, he departed and went away and hanged himself. Now the chief Priests, having taken the pieces of silver, said, "It is not lawful to put them in the treasury, for it is the price of blood." And after they had taken counsel, they bought the potter's field for the burial of strangers. Therefore this*

* From: *Corpus Reformatorum, Calvini Opera,* vol. 46, pp. 873-887.

1 *prestres,* not the usual word for elders, which is *les Anciens.* Fr. *prestres* and Eng. "priests" are derived from Gr. PRESBUTEROS, meaning "elders."

field has been called "the field of blood" until today. Then was fulfilled what was spoken by Jeremiah the Prophet, saying, "And they took thirty pieces of silver, the price of him who was appraised, who was bought at a price set by some of the children of Israel; and they gave them for a potter's field, as the Lord had directed me."

— MATTHEW 26:67-27:10

AS SAINT PAUL says that the preaching of the Gospel is odor of life to those whom God calls to salvation and odor of death to all reprobates who perish,[2] also we have two noteworthy examples who are here proposed to us to show that the death and passion of the Son of God was to the salvation of one and pushed another into condemnation. For in the fall of Peter is seen the need which he had of being drawn out of the pit in which he was trapped. For while he was there he was banished from the Kingdom of heaven, he was alienated from all hope of salvation and cut off from the Church, as a rotten member. Nevertheless the death of our Lord Jesus did not fail to benefit him, although he may not have been worthy of it. As for Judas, it is said that, seeing that Jesus Christ is condemned, he is seized with despair. Now in this condemnation of our Lord Jesus (as we have said) one must take courage to hope in God. For we are absolved by virtue of the fact that our Lord Jesus was condemned. But it was necessary that we had here these two mirrors in order that we might be able so much the better to know that unless we are by special grace called to be sharers of the fruit of the death and passion of the Son of God, it will be useless to us. It is not enough, then, that our Lord Jesus Christ has suffered, but the good which He acquired for us must be communicated, and we must be put in possession of it. That is done when we are drawn to Him by faith.

But to better understand all this let us follow the thread of the history which is here narrated to us. It is said that our Lord Jesus was treated with every shame in the house of Caiaphas, that they spit in His face, that He was insulted and made fun of by calling Him "Prophet," indeed in dis-

2 A summary statement of 1 Corinthians 1:18 and 2 Corinthians 2:15, 16.

grace. Now that was in order that we might know that what He suffered in His person was to deliver us before God and before His Angels. For no one needs to spit in our face in order for us to bear many spots and blemishes before God. All of us are not only disfigured by our sins, but full of infection, and abominable. Besides, here is the Son of God, Who is His living image, where His glory and majesty shine, Who suffered such shames, in order that in His name now we can appear before God to obtain grace and that He may know us and own us as His children, and that all our stains and spots may be wiped away. That (I say) is what we have to consider in the first place.

Now we come to the fall of Peter. It is said, *"A chamber-maid, seeing him, accused him of being a disciple of Jesus. He denies it."* Another chamber-maid returns. He denies it again. Then, more press him and make quite an issue of it. Then he begins to swear, and even to curse, and to use the form of execration. As if he said, "May I be damned, may I perish, may the earth swallow me up if I know Him." There, then, is the fall of Saint Peter, and not one, but three which are so heavy and so enormous that we surely ought to be frightened reading this history. Now we know the zeal which was in him. Moreover, he had been praised by our Lord Jesus Christ, and the name of Peter had been given to him to note the firmness and constancy of his faith; he had been taught in such a good school. He had heard this doctrine: "Whoever will renounce Me before men, him will I also renounce before God My Father to disavow him from Me." Yet we see how he stumbles. Each one, then, ought surely here to have occasion to tremble. For unless we are sustained from on high, the weakness of Peter was no greater than ours. So, in the first place, we see how frail men are as soon as God has let go with His hand. For this is not spoken of some mocker, of some profane man, of someone who had never heard a particle of the Gospel, who had no fear of God, and who had borne no reverence to our Lord Jesus Christ. It is entirely the contrary. For there were already some excellent gifts in Peter. It had been said to him from the mouth of the Son of God, "Flesh and blood have not revealed to you these things, but My Father." It is, then, the Spirit of God which dwells in Peter. Yet how little he resists renouncing our Lord Jesus! A chamber-maid! If a man had assailed him, or if it had been some honorable person who had assailed him, there might have been some excuse. But we see that it required only a chamber-maid to make him give up hope of life and of salvation.

Let us contemplate, then, in the person of Peter, that it is very necessary that God strengthen us each minute of time. For it is impossible to persevere otherwise. Although we may have tried to draw near to God, and though we may have done many deeds of virtue, all the same at the least little turning of the hand we shall be entirely changed unless God continues to give us invincible constancy. Let us learn, then, to practice the admonition of Saint Paul, "Let him who stands take heed lest he fall."[3] It is true that we cannot maintain ourselves. But let us have recourse to Him Who has the means. However, let us walk in all humility. As Saint Paul says in the other passage. "Since it is God Who gives the will and the deed and He does it by His good pleasure, be advised (says he) to work out your salvation in fear and trembling."[4] As if he said that all presumption surely ought to be beaten down, and indeed all indifference. When we see what necessity we have to be helped by God, and in so many ways, is it not right that we be on our guard, indeed that we do not presume at all on our own strength, but that we be solicitous to call upon God evening and morning, and to put ourselves in His keeping and leading?

That, then, is what we have to observe in the first place. It is even very necessary for us to assume that the temptations, although they may not be large, will have soon overwhelmed us, unless God by His grace works on it and He remedies it. And those who imagine themselves to be the most hardy, when they are far from blows, find themselves, as it were, lost if there is only a little wind that blows. It is true that if God assists us, we shall persevere, however great storms arise. For we know the figure of speech that our Lord Jesus Christ

3 1 Corinthians 10:12, not quite literal.
4 Philippians 2:13, 12b.

drew: that a building with a good foundation and built of good material, although there comes a great torrent, always remains whole; but what is built upon sand will soon go away in decay. So then, when we shall be founded upon our God and He will extend to us His strong hand, we shall surely be able to sustain great and very rough alarms. But although there may not be any enemy who fights us, yet we shall be conquered immediately when God withdraws from us or lets go of our hand, as we see in Peter.

But it is still worse that it is not only once that he denies the Lord Jesus. But he repeats it as many times as he is questioned. We see that it did not matter at all to him that he was going from bad to worse, even until he adds execration, as it were, asking that God may curse him and swallow him up. When we see that, let us know that he who has fallen, instead of wanting to be raised soon, will plunge himself ever more deeply into ruin, until he completely perishes in it, unless God remedies it. This is the condition of men. From the beginning they make themselves believe that they are marvels in their own power. Yet our Lord shows by experience that it is nothing, and that only a little wind blows, and they are beaten down. Still they are persuaded that they can stand up again. But on the contrary they only augment their evil, adding fault upon fault, overflowing still more with preposterous deeds. If Saint Peter had been tempted a hundred times in a day, he would have renounced Jesus Christ a hundred times, and a thousand besides. That is where he would have been unless God had had pity on him. But He spared him, and did not wish to prove him further. Yet the three falls mentioned here are enough to show a dreadful example, and it ought to make our hair stand up on end when we see that for the third time Peter so forgot himself and that he was as senseless as a brute to renounce his salvation. Besides, we must always observe that if still other temptations had come upon him, he would have resisted them no better and he would have been put into the most profound depths unless God had spared him that much.

That, then, is how we have to profit from this doctrine. Now we do not hear these things in order to judge Peter and to condemn his cowardice. To be sure, we cannot do it justly, but if it is necessary in the first place to receive instruction, may we know our weakness, may we even know that we can do nothing at all, may we not be inflated with pride, attributing to ourselves by foolish opinion some virtue. However, may we also know, since the devil has so many means to plot our ruin, he would soon put an end to us, since St. Peter fell without his making any appearance. Then finally, let us know that our Lord Jesus has pity on us when He does not permit us to be tempted without limit. For it is certain that always so much more evil would be uncovered, and that there would be no end, unless we were held back by His goodness. These are all the things we have here to observe.

However, it is said, *"Peter, after having heard the cock crow* (as St. Luke tells) *after Jesus Christ looked at him, went outside and wept bitterly."* By this conclusion it is shown us (as I have already mentioned) that the death and passion of our Lord Jesus has already produced its effect and its power in that Peter has been raised from such a horrible fall. For is it not a miracle that God had pity on him and that he still obtained mercy after having committed such a detestable fault? We have declared that he could not have the excuse of ignorance, as if his fault of having renounced Jesus Christ were small. For it had been said and pronounced to him that if he did not make confession of his faith and give testimony before men he would deserve to be entirely cut off before the Angels of God and that his name be erased from the book of life. However it does not matter to him that he sells this miserable and frail life by so villainous and so strange a renunciation. Indeed, he is not yet even led before the judges. He is not questioned to the limit. There is only a chamber-maid who speaks to him. When they might already have been rude to him, and well so, he had fought only as a poor ill-starred creature. Nevertheless, he did not forget all fear of God. When, then, we see that, let us think how much more necessary it was for us that God displayed the infinite treasures of His goodness, when He still made Peter sharer of the fruit of the death and passion of His Son.

It is, then, a miracle which ought to enrapture us, that Peter obtained remission for such a great offense, indeed, as it appears, by his repentance. For it is certain that if a man is touched to the quick, after having failed, and he moans and wails before God to obtain pardon, it is a sign that God has already received him, and that He has reconciled him to Himself. For also repentance is a peculiar gift proceeding from the Holy Spirit, Who shows us that God has pity on us and that He does not will that we perish. But He draws us to Himself. Now we see that in Peter. It follows, then, that already the death and passion of our Lord Jesus Christ was profitable to him, indeed, in a marvelous way, as I have already said. But in the first place let us note that St. Peter always remained sleepy and stupid until he received the sign of which our Lord Jesus Christ has warned him, that is, that the cock would not crow until he renounced Him three times, or better, that the cock would not crow for the second time unless Peter had already made his renunciations. Since it is so, then, that if he had not been warned by our Lord Jesus Christ he would have remained there in his sin[5] and he would be forever plunged into perdition, let us know that we need to be solicitous after we have committed some fault. For if we were deprived of the grace of God and He did not exhort us to return to Him, it is certain that we would be preoccupied by Satan and all our senses would be brutalized so that we would have neither any scruple nor good movement to return to the way of salvation.

That, then, is what we must contemplate further in the person of Peter. But when Saint Luke tells that Jesus Christ looked at him, through that we are so much better taught that it is not sufficient to be stung and that someone tug on our ears to make us return to God, but Jesus Christ must cast His glance and His look upon us. Now it is true that it is here spoken of only the look of the eyes. However our Lord Jesus does not converse with us in a visible manner. Yet it is certain that until He has cast His glance upon us we shall always be blockheaded dullards in our faults and we shall never

5 *cropissant en son péché.*

think to moan and wail, although we may have provoked the wrath of God. Although He may have His bow bent and His sword unsheathed, we shall always remain in our indifference until our Lord Jesus has made us feel that He has not forgotten us and that He is not willing that we perish, but wishes to draw us back to Himself. And that it may be so, we hear daily sermons, by which we are exhorted to repentance. And how are we touched by them? There are as many admonitions as there could be. Does not all creation incite us to come to God? If our senses are well ruled so as to have some particle of prudence, when the sun rises in the morning, does it not call us to adore our God? After that, if we notice how the earth and all elements perform their offices, the beasts and the trees, that shows us that we must draw up to our God, in order that He may be glorified in us, and that we may not think of doing otherwise. The cock, then, has well crowed, and not only the cock, but God makes all his creatures above and below to crow[6] to exhort us to come to him. What is more, He surely deigns to open His sacred mouth through the Law, through His Prophets, and through the Gospel, to say, "Return to me." However, it is seen, as it were, that we are dullwitted.[7] Such a stupidity is seen in us that we are, as it were, monsters. It is very necessary, then, that our Lord Jesus regard us in pity, as He did Peter, in order to draw from us true wailings to give testimony of our penitence. For when it is said that Peter wept bitterly, it is to note the sorrow of which Saint Paul speaks in 2 Corinthians, when he says that it works toward salvation[8] and that we ought not to flee it but that we even ought to seek it. Although naturally we wish to enjoy ourselves and not to experience any nuisance, yet we must have some melancholy. As when God touches us with anguish, we must be tormented in our hearts after having offended Him. For such unrest is to lead us to real rest and such sorrow is to make us rejoice both before God and before Angels.

---

6 This is awkward in English. Fr. *chanter* means both "to crow" and "to sing." The pun is lost in English.

7 *eslourdis*, made heavy.

8 2 Corinthians 7:9, 10.

Soon we shall well see that Judas repented, but it is in another and diverse fashion. But as for Peter, he wept to show that he was greatly displeasing in his sin and he has fully returned to Jesus Christ. Let us note also that *"he went out to weep."* It is true that it still proceeded from his weakness, that he feared to show his repentance before the crowd. But though that may be, when he weeps alone, he well shows that he is touched by his fault and offense. For he does not seek men to witness his repenting, but being alone, he weeps before God. That is also how we must do it. For if we weep only before men, by that we show our hypocrisy. But when each one has collected his thoughts, and he examines his faults and sins, if he is then touched with anguish, it is a sign that there is no make-believe in him, and that he knew his Judge, and that he is there to ask pardon, and he well knew that it is the office of God to draw back from the depths those who are already, as it were, damned and lost. That, then, in summary, is what we have to remember from the account here given of the fall of Peter, and concerning these three renunciations, by which he had deserved to be cut off from the Kingdom of God, unless Jesus Christ had already displayed the power of His death and passion in order to draw him to repentance, as we see that it came to pass.

Next it is said, "The priests and governors took counsel to condemn Jesus." But because that was not in their power, they led Him bound and tied to the governor who had jurisdiction over the country, that is, Pontius Pilate. After that the Gospel tells that Judas repented, seeing that Jesus Christ was condemned, and threw down the money which he had received as the price and payment for his betrayal and completely confessed his fault. However the Priests are not willing to receive the money, but it buys a potter's field, where there had been some tile-making so that the field was useless and could be neither cultivated nor seeded. They buy, then, this field to bury passers-by. Indeed, they do it under cover of some devotion. For they said that it was not lawful that this money be put with the offerings of the Temple. Whereupon the Gospel-writer says what was said by the Prophet was fulfilled, that the thirty denarii, by which God had been appraised by the people of Israel, could be used for the pottery. We have here to consider what was already begun, that is, that the death and passion of our Lord Jesus does not bear fruit in all men, because it is a special grace that God gives to His elect when He touches them by His Holy Spirit. Although they have fallen, He raises them. Although they have gone astray like wandering sheep, He corrects them and extends to them His hand to bring them back to His fold. For there is Judas who is entirely cut off from the number of the children of God. It is even necessary that his condemnation appear before men and that it be entirely obvious.

So let us learn (following what I have already mentioned) to know in everything and by everything the inestimable goodness of our God. For as He declared His love toward mankind when He spared not His Only Son but delivered Him to death for sinners, also He declares a love which He bears especially toward us when by His Holy Spirit He touches us by the knowledge of our sins and He makes us wail and draws us to Himself with repentance. The entrance, then, that we have to come to our Lord Jesus Christ does not proceed from us, but it is inasmuch as God governs us and it pleased Him to show His election. And these circumstances are good to note. Behold Judas who had been a disciple of our Lord Jesus Christ. He had done miracles in His Name. Yet what is the issue of it? May we, then, learn to fear and to walk in solicitude, casting ourselves entirely upon our God; and may we pray that He may not permit us to fall into such confusion as this miserable wretch. And even when we have fallen, that He may raise us again by His power, and that we may return to Him; not with such a repentance as that of Judas, but with a true and right confession. For the wicked mock God as much as they can. They are pleased in their sins. They even take glory in them, and in the end they become as shameless as prostitutes,[9] as it is said by the Prophets Jeremiah and Ezekiel. Besides, in the end God makes them feel their sins, and they are in such fright that they fret and

9 I think the explicit reference is to Jeremiah 6:15 and 8:12, which are nearly identical. In Ezekiel are many general references to "bearing shame."

cry "alas!" But it is not in order to conceive some hope and to present themselves to God. Rather it is a fury which drives them. They flee as far as possible and they would like to pull down God from His throne. It is only a matter of fretting and of gnashing their teeth in complete rebellion against Him.

Now we surely must come to another kind of repentance; that is, not that we be frightened, seeing that we cannot escape the judgment and the hand of God; but that we confess our sin, and detest it; and next that we do not cease to draw near to God, indeed, being summoned before Him without being drawn to Him by force; but that of our own good pleasure we come to do Him homage, and to confess that we deserve to perish; nevertheless, being assured that although we deserve a hundred thousand deaths, He will not, however, cease to have pity on us. That was the repentance of Peter. But that of Judas ought to show us that it is not sufficient to have some feeling of our faults and some scruple, but we must be fully converted[10] to God. This is very noteworthy, because we see how many, and nearly all, flatter themselves. When they have made confession in a word of their faults, however grievous they are, it seems to them that they are free and clear, as if all they had to do was to wipe their mouths. And even if some instance is mentioned to them, they imagine that they are done a great wrong. "Why?" they say, "Have I not recognized my fault? Have I not done penitence?" That is all the payment they make, as if God were a little child Who was appeased by some laughter, even a false laughter which is full of hypocrisy and lying. But since it is common among men that they wish to appease God I do not know how all, so it is said that Judas repented. Let us fear, then, when God admonishes us and He makes us feel our faults, but let us not stop everything there. For that is not properly repentance. But here is the test by which we can know whether we are truly repentant or not. It is when of our free will we seek complete accord[11] with God and we do not flee

10 *reduits,* perhaps "brought under."

11 *appointement,* not in the modern sense of the word, but in the sense of the Lat. idiom *a punctum.* See note 25, p. 45 above.

being judged by Him, indeed, provided that He receives us in mercy. This is what He will do after we plead guilty. For he who will judge himself in order to plead guilty before God, before Angels, and before men will be justified and absolved, since he asks only that God may be favorable toward him. That then, in summary, is what we have to observe.

Now this confession of Judas had to be made in order to render the Priests all the more inexcusable. Also the Gospel-writer gives this account so that we may contemplate so much the better the blindness that Satan had put into all these reprobates, and that each one may think of himself. When God proposes to us such examples of His wrath and of His vengeance and He shows that men are, as it were, mad, that they are depraved of sense and of reason, that they are (briefly) brutish to fling themselves with an infernal fury; it is in order that each one of us may bow his head and that each one of us may know that we could often come to that, unless we were preserved by the goodness and grace of our God. However, let us be advised not to fight against our own consciences as the Priests did. For all those who so harden themselves against God in the end will fall into such a reprobate condition that they will no longer have any reason in them. Even after being thus undone before God, they will also cease to be at all ashamed before men. For it is a good thing that their baseness[12] is shown to all and that they be put in such disgrace that everyone may be horrified by their villainy.

That, then, is why the Gospel-writer has here related to us that when Judas came to pay back the money, the Priests were not at all moved by it. It is true that they do say that it is not lawful to put it into the coffer of the treasury, but that it is the price of blood. That is how hyprocrites always guard well I do not know what appearances to make a shadow and a covering for their iniquities. But this in only mocking God. For they never come in integrity and openness to Him. For what is there to say? "Oh, we shall not put this money with

12 *turpitude.*

the sacred oblations, because it is the price of blood." Then this money, had it been stolen? It is known that the Priests lived on the oblations of the Temple. As today in the Papacy those who are called Prelates and people of the Church gobble up the oblations and do not care for what purpose they apply them. Although the Priests had drawn from the oblations of the Temple the money which they had given to Judas, it does not matter to them; they have no regard. Now they make an issue of putting this money back into the coffer of the oblations. By which means they repulse Judas, as it were, by mockery, and as if they said, "Perhaps this wicked man has betrayed his master. We have only to determine whether he has done good or evil. Yet in order that we may not be sharers in his offense on our part, and in order to keep our hands clean (since they had used this money for such a purpose) we shall buy with it a field for the burial of strangers." Indeed, to say that they have surely satisfied God and that He might not know how to ask more, though there was some fault in what they did.

That is how hyprocrites will always have their satisfactions, thinking to buy their way out, but this is only child's play. Yet let us know that this is recited to us in order that we may learn when we have fallen to recognize our faults in truth and not to make circuits from one side or from another, but in everything and by everything to frankly bear condemnation. That, then, is what is shown to us. Meanwhile, let us pray to God that He remove from us the blindfold Satan is trying to put on in order that we may not croak[18] on our flatteries, wishing to excuse evil, but that more and more we may take the trouble to examine well all our vices to condemn them and to make an upright confession of them. Besides, we see also how God overthrows the opinion of hypocrites, that in the end they remain frustrated by what they had pretended. For the Priests had surely wished to erase their fault and that no one might ever mention it. That is why they pretend when they buy a field for the burial of strangers.

---

13 *cropissions.* I think it is a colloquial onomatopoetic word.

But God turns that entirely to the contrary of their intention. For this field must be called "field of blood" or "field of murder." That memorial must be perpetual and it remains forever on the mouths of men, women and little children, so that this detestable crime which had been thus committed by the Priests is daily known and manifest, and they say, "Behold, the field of blood, that is, the field that was bought with the price of betrayal. And who did it? The Priests and the chiefs of all the people." So then, we see when hypocrites try to hide themselves in their crimes and to disguise themselves, that God uncovers their villainy all the more and causes their shame to be known by all men and that everyone hold them in detestation. That is why I have said it is all the more necessary that we be advised to come to God and there to uncover all our offenses, in order that it may please Him to bury them before Him, before His Angels, and before all the world, when we have thus recognized them on our part.

Finally the Gospel-writer cites a passage from the Prophet to show that this is not recited only on account of the sin of Judas, or on account of the devilish obstinacy of the Priests, but on account of the condemnation of all people in general. He says, then, "*What was written by the prophet has been fulfilled, that God was appraised at thirty denarii and that was applied on a potter's field.*" Now Zechariah,[14] from whom this passage is drawn, compares our Lord Jesus Christ to a Shepherd,[15] and says that wishing to govern the Jewish people, He had taken His staff, or His shepherd's crook, which was called "Beauty," in order to say that He had a condition so well ordered that it was possible among those people, indeed, that He might be allowed to be led by the hand of God. For is there anything more desirable? And that it may be so, where is our sovereign joy and bliss, unless God cares for our salvation and He performs the of-

---

14 Zechariah 11:12, 13. Matthew 27:9, where this passage is ascribed to Jeremiah, is plainly in error. Calvin frankly recognized the error in his *Commentary*, but makes no mention of it in a sermon.

15 Calvin is relating Ezekiel 34:11-16, 23 to Zechariah 11:4-17.

fice of shepherd among us? That, then, was a government of God in those people, when it is spoken of this rod, not of a staff which is to strike and break everything, but to lead and govern peaceably the sheep which become docile. Now it is said that again He took a second rod. As in fact, when the people have been returned from the captivity of Babylon, God has then gone back to His position as shepherd. After such a horrible dissipation as had existed previously, He gathers in the people to govern them peaceably under His hand. But in the end there was such villainous ingratitude that God had to quit everything. So He says, "Oh, I see what it is; I need not lose My time or My trouble with you." He speaks here in the common fashion of men. "Let us get on the march at once. Pay me, that I may go away." Whereupon they brought Him thirty denarii. "What?" says He, "is this the reward and the payment I get from you?" For when He speaks of thirty denarii, He considers the oblations which they made in the Temple. They were (since they used them in hypocrisy without faith and without repentance) only vain ceremonies which, nevertheless, the Priests and the Jews prized highly. As today the Papists, when they have done many "holies"[16] and all their beautiful devotions, it seems to them that God is almost indebted to them. Now God says all that is only rubbish. "How," says He, "have I gained from your having gone through it? Perhaps that is the payment for a shepherd, I am much obliged to you. Oh, oh, no! I have nothing to do with it. Go, throw that in the pottery, and may you decorate the mouths and handles of your pots with it![17] Go! I am leaving you. Use that in your tile." As if He said, "If it rains in your Temple, fix it yourselves. As for Me, I no longer have any part or portion with you. I wish you would go away. And do not think to appease Me here by bringing Me, as it were, the payment of a scoundrel. I do not approve at all of any

---

16 *agios*. I think the use af the word here is a transliteration of the Greek, rather than the word in its modern sense.

17 *refaciez vos trous et vos pertuis*. It was impossible for me to identify these more closely.

of it." That, then, is what the Prophet, in summary, has intended.

Now we know that what was predicted of our God then, was fulfilled in the person of our Lord Jesus Christ, Who is our true God manifest in the flesh. So it was necessary that in a visible manner this passage be verified, and that Jesus Christ was appraised at only thirty denarii, that is, that the people showed such villainous ingratitude toward Him, Who was the Eternal Shepherd, Whom God had established over His people. It is certain that since the people had left being governed by God, also our Lord Jesus always performed the office of Mediator, indeed, although He had not yet appeared in human flesh. We must remember this well, in order that we may learn on our part, if God has exercised the grace to receive us, as it were, under His hand, and we are His flock, and He gives us our Lord Jesus Christ for a Shepherd, not to sting Him so that His Spirit is saddened and wearied by our acts of rebellion and ingratitude. Also may we not throw Him any bouquets of flowers[18] (as they say in common proverb), but since He gives Himself to us, may we cling to Him as our God and King, may we dedicate our whole lives to Him, and may we not bring Him a payment that He rejects; but may we present to Him both our souls and our bodies. For it is also very right that He should have all pre-eminence over us and that He possess us entirely, when we see that He seeks only our salvation.[19]

Now to end it and come to the conclusion, it is said, *"Our Lord Jesus having been led before Pilate answered nothing. Pilate asked him, saying, 'Do you not speak at all? Do you not see the witnesses they have brought here against you?' And he held his peace, so that the judge marvelled greatly."* In the first place we have to keep in memory, when our Lord

18 *que nous ne le payons point de nèfles,* not directly translatable. I have given what I think is the nearest current American expression.

19 According to Calvin's outline the sermon ended here. The rest is strictly impromptu.

Jesus Christ is judged before an earthly judge, that it was in order that we might be exempt and absolved from the condemnation which we deserved before the heavenly Judge. We know that we cannot escape what is written by the Prophet Isaiah, that every knee must bow before God.[20] Since God is the Judge of the world, how can we subsist[21] before His face and before His majesty? There is not one of us who is not constrained to condemn himself a hundred thousand times. When we have lived only a year in the world, there are already a hundred thousand faults, by which we deserve to be condemned. There is no one who has not this testimony engraved upon his heart, and who is not convinced of it. Now God, Who sees much more clearly than we, how will He not condemn us when each one is constrained to condemn himself, indeed, in so many ways? But here our Lord Jesus is subjected to this extremity of being accused before an earthly judge, even before a profane man, before a man who was pushed only by his greed and his ambition. When, then, the Son of God is humiliated to that extent, let us know that it is in order that we may be able to come with heads raised before God, and that He may receive us, and that fear may no longer cause us to draw back from His judgment-seat, but that we may dare to approach it boldly, knowing that we shall be received there in mercy. We even know that Jesus Christ acquired authority and power and sovereign dominion to be Judge of the world. And when He is thus condemned by Pilate, it is in order that today we may come boldly to Him, indeed, knowing that power is given to Him to judge us. Since He stood there, may we know that He wished to bear our condemnation and that He did not intend a trial to justify Himself, also knowing well that He had to be condemned, indeed, in our person. For although He was without spot or blemish, He bore all our sins upon Himself. We need not be astonished, then, that He stood there

20 Isaiah 45:23.

21 *subsister*. In Calvin there is a subtle distinction between *subsister* and *exister*. I have not yet found the key, except to note that *subsister* includes more than *exister*, *subsister* being almost equivalent to *vivre*. Calvin does not like to think of mere existence, apart from real living.

as if He had been convicted. For otherwise He could not have performed the office of Mediator except by accepting sentence and confessing that in our persons He had deserved to be condemned. That, then, is what the silence of our Lord Jesus Christ implies, in order that today we can call upon God with full voice, and that we can ask Him for pardon for all vices and offenses.

Now let us bow in humble reverence before the majesty of our God.

SERMON 7

Fifth Sermon on the Passion of Our Lord Jesus Christ *

Now Jesus was before the Governor, and the Governor asked him, saying, "Are you the King of the Jews?" Jesus said to him, "You said it." And when he was accused by the chief Priests and Elders, he answered nothing. Then Pilate said to him, "Do you not hear how many things they witness against you?" And he answered him not even a word, so that the Governor marveled greatly. Now at the feast he was accustomed to release to the people a prisoner, whomever they wished. And at that time he had a notorious prisoner, who was Barabbas. When, then, they had assembled, Pilate said to them, "Whom do you wish that I release to you? Barabbas or Jesus who is called Christ?" For he well knew that they had delivered him through envy. Also when he had sat upon the judgment-seat, his wife sent a messenger to him, saying, "Have nothing to do with that righteous man. For today in a dream I suffered much on account of him. But the high Priests and the Elders persuaded the people to ask for Barabbas and to cause Jesus to die. And the governor answering said to them, "Which of the two do you wish that I release to you?" They said, "Barabbas." Pilate said to them, "What shall I do, then, to Jesus who is called Christ?" They all said, "Let him be crucified." The governor said to them, "But what evil has he done?" And they cried still more loudly, saying, "Let him be crucified." Pilate, seeing that he was not improving matters at all, but that the tumult was rising still higher, took water and washed his hands before the people, saying, "I am innocent of the blood of this righteous man. You attend to it." And all the people answering said, "His blood be upon us and upon our children." Then he delivered to them Barabbas. And after he had whipped Jesus, he gave him to them in order that he might be crucified. — MATTHEW 27:11-26

* From: *Corpus Reformatorum, Calvini Opera*, vol. 46, pp. 887-901.

We have already seen by the preceding verses that our Lord Jesus so offered Himself of His own will as a sacrifice to make reparation for all our iniquities by His obedience and He was willing to be condemned to wipe them out. That is why it is said that He did not answer at all the accusations that were raised against Him. He had enough wherewith to answer, but He was silent, as is also mentioned by the Prophet Isaiah. That was not only to show his patience, but in order to acquire for us liberty to be able today to glory in being righteous and innocent before God (indeed, notwithstanding that our conscience accuses us and condemns us), knowing that God has received us in mercy, and that all our faults are abolished by the perfection which was found in our Lord Jesus Christ. That, then, is how the Son of God acquired for us the liberty to be able to glory boldly that we are the children of God and reputed righteous before Him, that is, when He willed to offer no reply to show His integrity. Besides, one might at first find it strange that He is thus captured and nevertheless responds that He is King of the Jews. For these things seem contradictory; but Saint John proceeds still further, and says that He declared that His Kingdom was not of this world, and then He declared also that He was Son of God, indeed, He protested[1] that He had come into the world to maintain the truth. But all this agrees easily. For our Lord Jesus surely had to declare Himself to be King of the Jews, unless He wished to reject the Phophecies. Also He had to be declared Son of God. But that did not lead to His absolution. It was rather that there might not be a long drawn-out trial, but that He might be condemned. Let us note well, then, when the silence of Jesus Christ is spoken of, that it was inasmuch as He did not wish to offer any excuse. As for His person, He kept His mouth closed. However, He did not cease to make such confession as He had to make. That is also why Saint Paul says that He made a good confession before Pontius Pilate.[2] For if it had been a matter of Jesus Christ's entering into His own self-defense, already the judge was persuaded

1 Note again the usage of *protesté*.
2 1 Timothy 6:13.

of His integrity. He could, then, easily have won His case by speaking. That is what amazes Pilate. Yet our Lord Jesus Christ did not cease to render such testimony as God had committed to Him — not tending to instruct (for this was not the place) but to confirm and ratify the doctrine to which He had previously borne witness.

However, we have to note on the one hand that the crime which troubled the Jews most was that He had stirred up trouble and prevented them from paying tributes to the Emperor of Rome. That also was to irritate the Governor, a pagan man who was sent there by the Emperor. Now it is very certain that our Lord Jesus had declared Himself to be King, but not an earthly king. As, in fact, we see that when the Jews wish to crown Him, He withdraws Himself and hides on the mountain. Still further He dulls the edge of that calumny, because it would have been a slander against the Gospel, if He had perverted the order and law-enforcement of the world. For He Who has come to call us all to the heavenly Kingdom and to make us sharers in it did not wish to abolish earthly kingdoms, since even they are sustained by Him and in His power. The Gospel, then, need not be blamed, saying that Jesus Christ had come to usurp any power or worldly authority. That is why He said to Pilate especially that His kingdom is not of this place.

In fact, what would happen if the Kingdom of our Lord Jesus Christ were earthly? What would we gain by hoping in Him, since our condition is so miserable in the world? Unbelievers have a much better lot than we, concerning the afflictions which we must endure. True it is that the chastisements of God have effect everywhere and that those who wish it as much as they possibly can do not cease to be subject to many miseries and afflictions. But all the same let us always be ready for more rigid discipline. For God must begin His chastisements in His house and in His Church. If, then, our Lord Jesus were an earthly King, it would seem that we might be entirely alienated from Him. Further, suppose we had everything easy in this world and that by means of the Son of God we had here, as it were, a paradise, yet our life is only a shadow. Our happiness, then, would be very brief and frail. So we must surely know and be entirely persuaded that the Kingdom of our Lord Jesus is heavenly, in order that we may reach the life everlasting[3] to which we are called. That, then, is how the Kingdom of Jesus Christ is perpetual, because it does not consist in anything which is of this world, here where everything is corruptible.

Let us learn, then, to bear patiently our adversities, knowing that they neither diminish nor impair at all the grace which was acquired for us by our Lord Jesus Christ. For indeed, these are aids to our salvation, as St. Paul shows in Romans 8:28. When we are despised and mocked by the world, that we have to suffer many reproaches, that we are hungry and thirsty, that our wings are clipped, that we are harassed from all sides; we must consider "So it is that God accepts us." That is as if He said to us, "Look on high. Do not set your minds on what is in this world." That, in summary, is what we have to observe. In fact, it is not without cause that our Lord Jesus wished to add as a confirmation that He was born and came into the world to speak the truth. Whoever has clearly heard it stops at the sound of His voice. By this we see that it is a doctrine of importance to know that the Kingdom of our Lord Jesus Christ is not from this world. For if it had been a trivial sentence, He might have passed it quickly. But when He pronounced that He had come into the world to speak the truth, it is as if He wished to render us attentive, and that each one should meditate in his heart, and apply well his study to this doctrine. That is, that we be withdrawn from the world and from all creatures, in order to come to this heavenly King, and to seek in Him the spiritual benefits which are here communicated to us, in order that we might enjoy them according to the measure which He knows to be useful to us for our salvation. Indeed in all that we see to be of the summary of the Gospel, let us note particularly this word: that Jesus Christ came into the world to speak the truth, in order that we may come to the

---

3 *la vie permanente.*

conviction from it, when we are attentive to His doctrine that we shall not be at all disappointed, since it is an entirely sure and certain thing that what He has promised He will bring to pass. When David wishes to be assured against all temptations, he says that the Word of God is as silver purified seven times and which has been well tried by fire.[4] So as often as we shall enter into doubt about the promises of our Lord Jesus Christ, and as we shall be troubled and molested (as the devil also uses such craftiness in order to dishearten us and to make us lose courage), let us return to this testimony, that in any case our Lord Jesus appeared in the world in order to be to us a faithful witness. Let us wait today for Him to show in effect that it is not in vain that He gave us all these promises, because they are infallible. That, then, in summary, is what we have to remember.

Besides, when Pilate says, *"What is truth?"* let us note that it was not, as it were, through a desire to learn that he asked such a question, but it was, as it were, through spite and in mockery, as today this vice is seen in many. When we speak of the truth of God, we mean the doctrine of the Gospel. Saint Paul (in the first chapter of the Epistle to the Ephesians)[5] attributes to it this title in order that we may be able to distinguish it from all other knowledge.[6] To be sure, if someone gives us an account of something which has happened, it is truth; but when God calls us to Himself, and He wishes to withdraw us from this world in order that we may arrive at the heavenly life, that is a truth which ought to be put in sovereign position and by comparison all the rest should be nothing. Now let us notice how the world bears reverence toward the doctrine of the Gospel. The wisest men in the world (who are considered to be such) are so blinded by presumption that when it is spoken of to them, "How now?" they say, "Have we lived such a long time in the world, and we should know the Gospel only and nothing else that exists?" All of them, then, will be scandalized when

4 Psalm 12:6. Note that Calvin substitutes "the word of God" for "the words of the Lord."
5 "the word of truth, the gospel of your salvation." Ephesians 1:13.
6 *la discerner d'avec toute autre science.*

it is said to them that the truth of God has been buried and that it is now necessary to guard it more closely. We hear how they scoff at that idea. So it was with Pilate. For inasmuch as he was sent by the Emperor to be his lieutenant in the country of Judea, it seemed to him that a great wrong was done to him when a truth was spoken of which was unknown to him. "And how so? Must we, then, act like idiots? Is there nothing but lies in us? Can we not discern between good and evil? And I who am appointed to office, who take the place of the Emperor, representing his person, must you reproach me just because I have not known what truth is?" This, then, is the intention of Pilate. He is inflated with pride like a frog and he does not wish to have the reputation of not knowing the difference between good and evil. In fact, we do not see that he waits for the answer of our Lord Jesus, but he throws in this word as if in spite, and leaves the place. Since it is so, then, let us be advised. If today there are many Pilates who refuse to be taught in the school of God and become teachable, as if they were already wise enough, may we not be hindered from placing ourselves under the obedience of faith, in order to accept what our Lord shows and proposes to us; that is, knowing that the truth does not grow in our minds, inasmuch as there is only vanity and falsehood there and we are plunged in darkness until our Lord draws us out of it. Let us recognize, then, that the truth surpasses all our senses and faculties and God must surely be our Master to keep us in it; also that we are little to receive what He shows us. May we hold this truth so precious that, when we shall have circled the heaven and the earth, and it seems that we have learned everything, we may know that it is only smoke and that it will prove ephemeral until we are founded upon this Word, Who is certain and immutable. That, then, in summary, is what we have to remember.

Now it is said, *"As Pilate was seated* upon his throne his wife commanded him not to condemn Jesus Christ, because she had been tormented by many dreams." There is no doubt that God wished to testify to the innocence of Jesus Christ in many ways; as even by the mouth of Pilate (as already we have mentioned and as we shall see still more fully), not that God had not already concluded what ought to be done by His Only Son. So, since He willed that He be the Sacrifice to wipe out the sins of the world, Scripture had to be fulfilled. Yet our Lord Jesus also had to be proved righteous and innocent, in order that we might know all the better that He suffered the condemnation which was due to us and which we deserved, and that we might always look at our faults and sins in everything that is here told us of the death and passion of our Lord Jesus Christ.

Whereupon it is said, "*Pilate desires to be able to acquit our Lord Jesus.*" For although he had sovereign authority beyond appeal, still he was in a foreign country and with a mutinous people, though he had a garrison in the city, the sedition troubled him. That is why he wished to proceed by subtle and amiable means, in order that the people might be appeased. It is then said that he presents what was his custom, "*At the feast of the Passover he released a prisoner whom the people willed.*" He allows them to choose either Jesus Christ or Barabbas, who was (as says Saint John) a robber. The other Gospel-writers say that he was a well-known malefactor, who had even been a murderer, and had stirred up sedition and trouble in the city. He is a pest who should be detestable to everyone. Yet, nevertheless, the people cry, "Let us have Barabbas, and let him be pardoned, and let Jesus Christ be crucified."

As for this custom of releasing a prisoner at the Passover, we see where men are led by their foolish devotions. For it surely seemed that the feast was so much better kept by delivering a prisoner, and that it was a service of God. Nevertheless, all that was only an abomination. For it is said that he who justifies the malefactor is just as blameworthy before God as he who punishes the innocent. There must, then, be a sense of equity in those whom God sent and established upon the throne of justice. For in arming them with His sword, He has not said to them, "Do what seems good to you." He surely wishes that they have a fatherly care over the people and that they guard well against rising in cruelty to do wrong to others by abusing their credit and authority, but rather that they be humane and pitiful. However, evil-doers must be chastized, and so God commands it. But what do men do? They imagine they are keeping the feast of the Passover, when they are offending God and they are transgressing openly His Word. By that we ought to be admonished not to follow our fancies when it is a matter of honoring God, but to please His will in everything and by everything. So then, let us not conjure up[7] any devotion according to what seems good to us, but let us be satisfied to do what God orders us to do and what He approves. We even see what this custom is, which men make law today, that everything that is received as a common statute seems to be lawful. Though that may be, God does not fail to condemn it. We see the abuse that took place, that this corruption brought about—that Barabbas was preferred to the Son of God.

Also at first, one might find it strange that our Lord Jesus is thus cried down and that a robber and murderer is more privileged than He, that he finds more favor among men, and that Jesus Christ has received such shame and disgrace. For was it not enough that the Son of God be crucified and that He endured a kind of death full of opprobrium and that furthermore there were great torments? For death by the cross was, as it were, the punishment of robbers. It was not only like the gallows[8] would be today, but like the wheel.[9] Would it not have been enough, then, that Jesus Christ, after having been whipped and spat upon in the face, should be plunged into the depths, with its being necessary by comparison to show Him to be execrable to all the world? For if we judge by our senses and we do not look beyond what appears, surely we shall be confounded, but we must raise our eyes higher by faith and come to what we have previously mentioned: namely, that God governs all this by His counsel. Let us not stop then with what the people did with Pilate, but let us contemplate this immutable decree of God: that to better humble us He willed that His Son be plunged into complete confusion and that He be put even below all the malefactors of the world, as He was crucified be-

---

7 *se forger.*

8 *le gibet.*

9 *la roue,* in Calvin's time an instrument of torture upon which bones were gradually pulverized by a crowbar dragged over the body of the victim.

tween two robbers, as we shall see later. That, then, is what we have to observe when it is here said that Barabbas had to be set free and Jesus Christ put there, as it were, the most detestable man in the world.

Pilate, even after all that, tries to make our Lord Jesus escape, but by a devilish means: namely, he whips Him (what was then called "chastise") and wished to release Him after having thus chastised Him, as one who had committed some fault. For by that he pretended to quiet the people. Now if our Lord Jesus had thus escaped, what would have become of the Gospel, what would have become of the salvation of the world? For this "correction" as Pilate called it, might forever have been a mark of shame, as if the Gospel had been a wicked doctrine, since the judge of the country condemned it, and our Lord Jesus in His person would have been entirely rejected. Meanwhile we would have perished, since there was no other means to reconcile us to God, except by the death of His only Son. This, then, is the overture of life—the death of our Lord Jesus. So we see that the devil exerted himself very greatly that our Lord Jesus might not die at all. Yet who drove the Priests and their kind to pursue Jesus Christ to death, unless the devil? It is true, for he works, as it were, like a madman. According as we see that God sends a spirit of disturbance and of frenzy upon all wicked men so that they contradict themselves and are like waves of the sea which beat upon one another, so the devil was carried away when he tried to abolish the memory of our Lord Jesus on the one hand and then, however, wished to prevent the redemption of mankind. But God so worked that He willed that the innocence of His Son might have witness through the very mouth of the judge; however, He also willed nevertheless that He should die in order to make the sacrifice for our salvation and redemption. God has only a single and simple will, but it is admirable to us, and He has such strange ways of proceeding that we must bow our heads in awe and yet recognize that our Lord Jesus suffered, not at all according to the desire of men, but because we had to have such a gage[10] of the infinite love of our God, and Jesus Christ had to declare it to us to show how precious our souls are to

10 security, pledge, etc.

Him and how dear[11] is the salvation of them to Him. Let us, then, consider all these things.

Besides, it is said at the end by St. John, although Jesus Christ had been whipped, the people strive still more by crying that He be put to death. Then Pilate questions Him again; indeed, because he heard that Jesus made Himself the Son of God, and this word touches him, and he is more frightened by it than before. That is why he asks Him, "Where are You from?" When Jesus Christ does not answer at all, "Do You not know says he) that I have power to release You or power to condemn You?" Now here we see why the Jews bring such an accusation against our Lord Jesus Christ. It is true that the crime which could better move the Governor of the country was having attributed to Himself kingdom and dominion; but when they see that their malice is discovered, and that Pilate well understands that they are only trumped-up lies, thereupon they say, "*We* have the law by which He ought to die." For that privilege had been reserved for them, in order that they might not have any religious disputes. For the Romans, who were profane people and who served their idols only through ceremony, wished to maintain their empire by means of letting each one do according to his religion.

Whereupon they say, "*He made Himself* the Son of God and thereby He blasphemed." It is true that, if our Lord Jesus had not been the Redeemer of the world, it would have rendered Him subject to the death penalty to make Himself the only Son of God. For we are all children of God when He has adopted us through His grace. That is the common manner of speaking of it in Holy Scripture. Those who have received some special grace are called "Sons of God" in still another manner, as Princes and Magistrates. With greater reason, then, Jesus Christ, Who was supremely anointed with graces and powers by the Holy Spirit, might well be called "Son of God." But if He had not been Redeemer of the world at all and called Himself "Only Son of God" *par excellence,* that would truly have been a mortal crime. But how is it that the Jews accuse Him of that? It is first of all by ignorance of the Scripture, inasmuch as they do not know

11 costly.

that He Who should be the Redeemer should be the living God manifest. Since, then, they did not have the real understanding of Scripture, and they were not trained in it, but they were made brutish by their indifference, that is why they are so bold to condemn Jesus Christ. Now we see a like temerity in all ignorant people. Today when they cry "Heretic" it is not that the proofs are on hand, but the most blockheaded people are driven by such a rage that they wish to be zealots to honor God, and they know neither why nor how. Further, it was necessary to investigate whether Jesus was Christ the Messiah or not. But the Jews rejected Him without making any inquiry.[12] Let us learn by that, if we wish to have a zeal which God approves, we must be ruled by true knowledge[13] and be taught by His Word. For we may be able to skim the surface, but it will be only by wild arguments of Satan, if we do not speak as scholars of God's truth; because He is the only competent Judge, and He reserves to Himself the office of showing us what is His will. Since it is so, then, let us follow the Word of God with simplicity, and also let us be peaceable. Then may our zeal be ruled by that. That is what we must observe in the first place.

But when it is said that *Pilate* feared more than ever to hear the Son of God spoken of, here we see in the person of a poor Pagan some semblance of religion which moves him, and stings him, and speaks to his conscience, so that he does not know which way to turn. There stands Jesus Christ entirely disfigured and with the marks of the whipping still upon Him. He had previously suffered so much reproach and ignominy,[14] so many drops of spit, so many blows on the head[15] which had been given to Him in the house of Caiaphas. Briefly, here is a man who is despised and rejected by everyone. Yet, nevertheless, the name of God moves Pontius Pilate and arouses in him fright and astonishment. What of us, then, when we behave like savage beasts? And when one wishes to speak to us of God, if we are not

12 *inquisition.*

13 *reglez en droite science.*

14 *tant d' opprobres et ignominies.*

15 *soufflets.* Strictly, I think, a cuff on the ear.

held in check at all, must not the example of Pilate condemn us even to the last day? We see today mockers, people full of the devil. If one proposes to them, "Look what God shows us," if one declares to them His Word, if one wishes to prove what they reject; one thing is as good as another to them. They stop up their ears, they bind up their eyes, they are entirely preoccupied in their natural senses, and they are so proud that they would not even consider giving any audience. For they are satisfied as they are. "We have ordained it," they say, "and so it must be done." Indeed? However, here is Pilate who had never heard a single word of the doctrine of God, even the Law was to him in disdain, so that everything that the Jews do he considers to be something trumped-up, and he adores his idols. Yet the name "God" affects him, and he is held back when it is spoken of. Is it on account of some majesty or some pomp which he sees in Jesus Christ? Not at all. It is only the name "God" which draws him to reverence. How much, then, some people will be condemned by this fear of Pilate, when they follow their beaten path and no progress can be made among them, although the name "God" is spoken of to them, and not only as a word in passing, but offering to teach them and to show them with the finger the testimonies of Scripture! If they condescend neither to think about nor to apply themselves with any diligence, must not the devil possess them entirely? Must they not know that they are as it were monsters, who have abolished every germ of religion, inasmuch as they have made themselves obstinate against God, as it were, defying all nature? That, then, is what we have to remember.

Though that may be, on the contrary we also see that all the fears which men have, and all sentiment and apprehension they have to honor God, will be, as it were, only a flash of lightning which passes before their eyes and immediately vanishes. For how did Pilate fear God? We see that it does not grip him at all, that he only shows such a great pride, that it seems to him that God is no longer anything. That, then, is how all those who are not governed by the Spirit of God will have on the one hand some fears by which they are seized, so that they will humble themselves for a time before

God, but they do not cease to raise their horns, then to forget, and to dull their consciences to do evil. As we see in Pharaoh that sometimes he is quite astonished. "And pray to God for me," he says. And when he sees the power of God so apparent, "Oh, it is the finger of God," he says, "one must be subject to Him." But soon after he is worse than ever. Thus, then, it was with Pilate. This admonishes us not to have any fears of God like gusts of wind, but to have a good root which remains firm in our hearts. For how is it that Pilate feared God? It is only to render him more inexcusable. That is why God awakens the sleeping consciences, which wish to reject every yoke, and He brings them back and incites them to think of themselves more closely, so that in spite of themselves they must recognize their poverty and feel their vices, although they wish to sleep in them. All the scruples, then, which condemners of God and all wicked men have — these are to be regarded as summonses which God issues to take away from them every excuse of ignorance. But then they slacken the reins, they throw themselves with abandon, and so they are in no wise held back — as we see in Pilate. At the beginning he is quite astonished, but soon afterwards he goes back to his natural self. *"And do you not know,"* he says to Jesus Christ, "that I have power to release you or to condemn you." Here let us note first of all, if He had been a robber, nevertheless, he would not have been able to move a finger unless God had given him the power. How is it, then, that Pilate dares to assume such unbounded license as to condemn and to set free according to his desire and by virtue of his position? For it would be better that the check be released from all robbers and that they had liberty to exercise their cruelty in the forests than for people to sit on such an honorable throne — people who take pleasure in power without thinking of their consciences and meanwhile throwing the world into entire confusion. Here we see (as I have shown) that there was no living root in Pilate, but only a gust of wind. So then, let us learn to so fear God that there may be a firm constancy in us to walk in His obedience, and that we may fight virtuously against everything that could turn us aside, and that always this check may hold us back: that it is not fitting to provoke the wrath of Him Who has all power over us. That, in summary, is what we have to remember.

However, also there is to consider how the glory which Pilate attributes to himself is nevertheless a great shame upon him. For his enemies could have reproached him no worse than this: namely, that he wishes to be held and reputed to have no discrimination between good and evil. Nevertheless he boasts of it. We see, then, inasmuch as the despisers of God imagine themselves to be raised, they must always feel themselves to be further cast down in confusion. God puts in them such a sense of disapproval that they boast of their iniquities in order to render themselves detestable both in heaven and on earth. What, then, is to be done? Let us learn to glory in the good, and let us consider what is lawful for us. For those who glory in their greatness, it is certain that they provoke God, inasmuch as they have often acquired their riches and their credit by unlawful means, by excess, by cruelty, and all kinds of extortions. When, then, they glory in that, it is, as it were, by defying God. He who has plundered from all parts will say, "I have done well." And there is the blood of poor people which he has sucked. He will say, "I have acquired it." And how? By frauds, wicked practices, pillaging one, gobbling up another, and having perverted all order. The other through ambition and unlawful means will have arrived at some dignity. Whereupon he wishes to be held in awe. This is manifestly to defy God.

Let us learn, then, (as I have already said) to glory in what God approves. It is true that although there might be some good in us, it is not lawful to usurp the praise which God reserves to Himself, and on account of which we must pay Him homage, inasmuch as He has given us everything. It is not proper, then, here to glory in ourselves, as if what God gives us belonged to us. But I say we must glory only in that it pleased God to adopt us for His children, and inasmuch as He gives us grace to walk in fear of Him, inasmuch as He gives us power to abstain from evil. In that we must glory. Then, if we are little and contemptible according to the world, let us pray that He may give us patience, and that we may prefer to be in such an estate than to be raised and meanwhile to enjoy ourselves like worldly people do, who make merry in such a way that nothing can restrain them. This, in summary, is how we have to glory, that is, that we may not wish to be more than God allows us, and that we may despise everything He disapproves of, although the world may applaud those who exercise tyranny and who practice every evil to excess. Let us leave, then, easily and willingly all such glories, not seeking anything else except to be recognized and confessed before God as His children. That, in summary, is what we still have to remember.

In conclusion it is said, "*Pilate, seeing that he was gaining nothing and that the tumult among the people was increasing, washes his hands and says, 'I am innocent of the blood of this man.'* " We have already declared that the innocence of our Lord Jesus had to be proved and it was testified to through the mouth of the judge himself. For when it is said that Jesus Christ suffered under Pontius Pilate and that He was condemned, it is not enough to have heard the account, but we must be fully aware that Jesus Christ not only is innocent, but that He is the fountain of all holiness and perfection. Why, then, is He condemned? There are here two different things, it seems. It is said that He is the Lamb of God without spot. Since He is the Lamb of God, He must be condemned for the sacrifice. The word "*Lamb*" implies that He is to be offered. And what does the Law pronounce of sacrifices? That they stand for sins and curses. That is why it is said that our Lord Jesus was accursed for our sakes, that is, that He received the curse which was due to our sins. This, then, is the quality and condition under which He is condemned, since God appointed Him as a lamb which must be offered in sacrifice. But also He had to be known without any blemish, and His purity had to come before our eyes, in order that we might understand our sins, as far as we have known that Jesus Christ is the mirror of all perfection; and that we might enter into examination of our faults to be displeased with them and to pass condemnation, which was prepared for us unless we had been delivered by Him. Now when Pilate took the basin and the water to wash his hands, it was far too frivolous a ceremony, as if he could be acquitted before God by that. But it was not to make his excuse before God when he tried to appease the fury of the people. For he did not protest before God that he was innocent, but he only said to the people, "Look to yourselves. As for me, I am innocent." As if he said, "You force me to this." But all that (as I have said) is not to excuse him. Also he is not performing at all the office of judge. For he ought sooner to die a hundred times than to swerve from his office. When he saw all the troubles of the world, he ought to have this magnanimity to do what he knew to be good and just. But when he sees the people to be so inflamed, he lets himself be carried away. However, it had to be, cursed as it was, that he testifies to the innocence of our Lord Jesus Christ, and that from his own mouth he justifies Him. Nevertheless, that does not excuse him from condemnation, but in that rests our consolation. For we know that if we should be brought before God today to appear before His throne, it would not be to receive condemnation; but since the fact that the blood of our Lord Jesus was spilled is the true purging of our souls, He receives us as pure and clean.

There, then, is where we must have our recourse. However, we see the word which is pronounced by the Jews. For they are flung headlong in such a way by Satan that they say, "His blood be upon us and upon all our children." Now they were the heritage of God, the people elected and chosen from among all the nations of the earth. Yet they renounce this dignity, and all the promises of salvation, this sacred alliance which God had established with their line. They are, then, deprived of all the benefits that God had previously distributed to them, inasmuch as they were descended from the race of Abraham. And the blood of our Lord Jesus had to fall upon them, indeed, to the confounding of them and all their descendants. As also He had previously declared to them, "Your iniquity must come to the full, and the blood of the Martyrs, from Abel the righteous even to Zacharias son of Barachias, who was murdered not long ago, must be brought upon you, and you must see that you were always murderers of the Prophets, and by this means you have fought against God and against His Word."[16] That, then, is how the blood of our Lord Jesus, which ought to be the salvation of all the world, and indeed especially of the Jews, since the birthright belonged to them, cried vengeance against them. But now let us learn to look deep inside ourselves, and to pray to God that it may come upon us in another manner, both upon us and, in particular, upon our children; namely, may we be washed and cleansed, seeing that we are abominable before God on account of our sins until we are washed and we suffer that the blood which was once poured out for our Redemption come upon us and that thereby we are sprinkled by the power of the Holy Spirit[17] (so says Saint Peter in his Canonical letter)[18] and may we be careful not to reject the grace which is offered to us by God, of which the Jews have been deprived because of their ingratitude, and have done nothing but provoke more and more His vengeance. May we, then, today be disposed to receive the purging of our Lord Jesus Christ, which cannot be apprehended[19] except by faith. May we pray to God that we may not have received this washing in vain, but from day to day may we be purified from all our blemishes. May it please our God to make the most of this purity which was acquired by our Lord Jesus Christ until we have arrived in His Kingdom, where we shall be freed from all corruptions of our vices.

Now we shall bow in humble reverence before the majesty of our God.

---

16 Matthew 23:34-36, Luke 11:49-51, 2 Chronicles 36:15-16.
17 1 Peter 1:2.
18 1 Peter. Calvin had some doubts on the canonicity of 2 Peter. See introduction to his commentary on the same.
19 Double meaning: (1) understood and (2) grasped hold of.

SERMON 8

Sixth Sermon on the Passion of Our Lord Jesus Christ *

Then the armed guards of the governor took Jesus into the praetorium and gathered before him all the band. And having stripped him, they put upon him a scarlet robe. And they plaited a crown of thorns, and they put it upon his head, and a reed in his right hand. And kneeling before him they mocked him, saying, "Hail, King of the Jews." And after having spit at him, they took a reed and struck his head. When they had mocked him they stripped from him the robe, and they dressed him in his clothes, and led him away to be crucified. And as they were leaving they found a Cyrenian man named Simon, whom they compelled to carry his cross. And having come to the place which is called "Golgotha," which is to say "the place of a skull," they gave him vinegar mixed with gall to drink. And when he had tasted it he would not drink it. And after they had crucified him, they divided his clothing by casting lots, that there might be fulfilled what is spoken by the Prophet, saying, "They divided my clothing among them, and they cast lots over my robe."[1] *And sitting down, they kept a watch over him there. They put also over his head their charge against him, written thus, "This is Jesus the King of the Jews." Then there were crucified with him two robbers, one on the right and the other on the left. And those who passed by reviled him, wagging their heads. And saying, "You who destroy the Temple and build it in three days, save yourself. If you are the Son of God, come down from the cross." Likewise also the chief Priests, mocking with the*

* From: *Corpus Reformatorum, Calvini Opera*, vol. 46, pp. 901-914.

1 Psalm 22:18. The American Standard Version (1901) and the Revised Standard Version (1946) omit all reference to this prophecy. However, Dr. Eberhard Nestle in his 16th edition of the Greek New Testament includes the reference in a footnote. "The Prophet" also presents a difficulty, since "the Prophet" without further qualifications usually refers to Isaiah.

Scribes and Elders, said, "He saved others, and he cannot save himself. If he is King of Israel, let him come down from the cross, and we will believe in him. He trusts in God; let God deliver him now if he is acceptable to God. For he said, 'I am the Son of God.'" Likewise also the robbers who were crucified with him reproach him.

— MATTHEW 27:27-44

Following what we have mentioned about this before, we must consider still better that the Kingdom of our Lord Jesus Christ is not of this world. For we see how He was in disgrace, they mocked Him, and instead of a Royal diadem He had a crown of thorns. Instead of a sceptre He had a reed. Then everything that could be imagined to heap shame upon a man, was done to Him. If we limit our attention to what is here narrated, it will be as it were an object of scandal to alienate us from our Lord Jesus Christ, and consequently from all hope of salvation. But we have to contemplate by faith the spiritual Kingdom which was mentioned above. Then we can conclude, although men mock the Kingdom of our Lord Jesus Christ that He never ceased to be prized according to His worth both before God and before His Angels. Indeed, we have to remember that the Son of God was thus treated in His person, in order to receive upon Himself all the shame which we deserve. For how can we stand before God while we are defiled in our iniquities? But since our Lord Jesus suffered them to spit in His face, He was willing to be buffeted on the head, He received all insults, that is how today we are recognized and avowed as children of God and therein consists our confidence. Indeed, also we have always to consider that God wishes to induce us to be more deeply touched by our faults, to hold them in horror and detestation, when we see that it was necessary that the Son of God, to make reparation for them and to acquire for us grace and absolution, so endured, and that the heavenly Father spared Him not at all. Seeing then, the confounding of our sins to be such in the person of the Son of God, we surely have to humble ourselves and to be entirely confounded in ourselves. However, we ought also to take courage, and to be grounded in such confidence that we may not doubt at all, when we shall come before God, that our Lord Jesus Christ acquired grace for us when He suffered Himself to be so vilified because of us. For He acquired for us glory and dignity before God and His Angels by this means.

Now it is here said that our Lord Jesus *was led to the place which is called "Golgotha,"* that is to say "the place of a Skull." The Hebrew word from which this is derived means "to roll,"[2] but they so used it because when a body has decayed, they find the skull dry, and it is like a ball which rolls away.[3] They called, then, this place "Golgotha" because many evil-doers were punished there, and their heads were seen there. Here we have to remember what the Apostle says in the Epistle to the Hebrews, that our Lord Jesus Christ was led outside the city, as was customary with sacrifices, that is, those that had been burned, and of which the blood was carried into the Sanctuary to wipe away the blemishes of the people.[4] It was said that such a sacrifice was as it were a curse. It must, then, be disposed of far away. Behold the Son of God Who was willing to receive this condition upon Himself, in order that we may know that in truth we are now set free and absolved before God. For we deserve that God reject us, even that He pour out His horrible vengeance upon us, while He looks at us as we are. There is, then no other means to acquire grace, except that we come to our Lord Jesus Christ, and that we have all our refuge in Him, since we are unburdened of such a load, when He was willing to be as it were cursed and detestable for our sakes, in order that we might find favor before God and that we might be acceptable to Him. For although already Pilate His judge had justified Him many times, yet He had to receive in His person everything that was required to redeem us. For He was our pledge, and in everything and by everything He had to answer for us. So then, after having known that our Lord Jesus was thus rejected, as not being worthy to be of the company of men, even, as it were, bearing such an

---

2 Heb. GALAL, to roll. So 9 times in Old Testament.
3 *une boule qui coule,* The rhyme is lost in English.
4 Hebrews 13:11, 12.

infection that He could not be endured; seeing, I say, that, let us learn to follow Him, and to renounce the world, as we are exhorted in this passage. And if we must be mocked, cut off as rotten members, and be held in detestation, let us endure it all patiently, yielding submissively, until the day come that our sorrows are converted into joy, that God will wipe away the tears from our eyes, and indeed, that what we now judge to be shame will be converted for us into glory. For it is certain that all that we endure for our Lord Jesus Christ is more honorable before God than all the pomp of this world. That, then, is what we have to remember on this point.

Now the Gospel-writer adds that our Lord Jesus was mocked by all those who passed by, and above all by Priests and Scribes and their kind. And what was the occasion of it? *"If He is the Son of God let Him come down,"* they say, "and let Him save Himself, for He surely saved others. If He is King of Israel, let Him show it." Here we see a terrible blindness in these miserable people, who were possessed by Satan, for not having any more feeling or insight. Behold the Priests who ought to be the Messengers[5] of God. For He had ordained them to this function, in order that His Word and His will might be known through their mouth. Behold the Scribes who are trained in the Law, and nevertheless they, supposing that they can crush our Lord Jesus, show that they tread under foot all Holy Scripture and all the religion of which they boasted. When the Messiah was previously spoken of to them, they certainly responded that He had to be born in Bethlehem. They ought also to have been warned and informed that the Redeemer Who was promised to them had to suffer such a death. This was not an obscure thing. The passage from Isaiah[6] was as clear as if one gave a recitation of what our Lord Jesus Christ endured. They ought, then, to have known that it was impossible to have a clearer picture of things than did the Prophet although he had spoken of them such a long time before. Then there are as in Zechariah so in Daniel the declarations that God must gather His

5 *les Anges.*
6 Isaiah 53.

people, and exalt His Church:[7] namely, that the Redeemer of the world should suffer every reproach and curse before the world. How is it, then, that they so defied the Son of God when He exercises His office, as it had been sufficiently declared by the Prophets? So we see that Satan carried them away, when they forgot everything they had previously known.

So let us be advised so to walk in the fear of God that, after having tasted His Word, we may receive it with reverence and obey our Lord Jesus Christ Who is presented to us there. For it is also in Him that we shall find entire perfection of virtues,[8] indeed, if we come to Him in humility. For if we presume to play with God our audacity must receive such a reward as we read here of these miserable men who were so carried away by their rage. Yet we have to profit from these blasphemies, learning from them to do the opposite. For since our Lord Jesus willed to be our King and our Head,[9] that is why He did not save Himself. The enemies of truth said, "Let Him save Himself if He is King of Israel.'" But He had to endure in His person to acquire for us salvation. Why, then, did our Lord Jesus not spare Himself? Why did He endure a death so bitter and so shameful, unless it was necessary in order that we might be delivered[10] through such a ransom.[11] We have, then, to defy all agents of Satan, and all his villains who vomited up such blasphemies as the Gospel-writer describes, and to be all the more sure that we really have a King Who preferred our salvation to His own life, and suffered everything that was required for our redemption, and had no other consideration except to redeem what was lost. For we would have been devoid of all hope if the Son of God had left us in our estate and condition. But when He was so swallowed up in death, that is where our deliverance lies. When He endured everything so patiently, that is the cause why God now extends His hand and His power to help us in time of need. Our Lord Jesus, then, had to be there, as it were, abandoned by God in order that

7 Daniel 12:1-3 and Zechariah 2:11.
8 *toute perfection de biens.*
9 *Chef,* leader, chief.
10 *delivrez,* released, rescued, set free.
11 Fr. *rancon* is derived from Lat. *redemptio* (*onis*).

today we may feel that He watches for our salvation, and He will always be ready to aid us in necessity when we require[12] it. However, let us also learn to arm ourselves against all temptations, when the devil comes to assail us and he wishes to make us believe that God has forsaken us and that He has turned His back upon us and that it is a disappointing thing to hope in Him. Let us know, then, when Jesus Christ is the true pattern[13] of all believers and He has shown us the way we must go, that it is sufficient reason for us to be patterned after Him.[14] He suffered that such blasphemies were poured out against Him, and yet He constantly resisted them in such a way that by this means the victory was acquired for us. Let us fight, then, today when the devil comes to lay siege against us, as it were, to overthrow our faith and to close the door upon us, so that we may not be able to have access to God, as if He had forgotten all about us. Let us follow our Lord Jesus Christ, and let us wait for the hour when God extends His arm to show that He is pitiful toward us and He is Father to us, although for a time He suffers that we are thus beaten down.

So much, then, for these taunts and mockings which were heaped upon our Lord Jesus. There are still others. "*He trusted in God. Let God save Him if God loves Him.*" That had already been typified in the person of David, for these very words[15] are recited when he complains that his enemies have taken occasion to shoot out their tongues at him,[16] and they almost put their feet on his neck,[17] in reproaching him for the confidence he had in God. Now it is certain that this is the most fatal plague that Satan can devise against us. For, the life of men consists in faith, and in the refuge which we have in God, leaning upon His promises. If we are robbed

12 *requerir* can mean either "require" or "request."

13 *patron*, patron, patron saint, employer, master, skipper, coxswain, pattern.

14 *configurez a luy*. *configurer* is no longer current in modern French. It suggests the exact matching of two or more patterns.

15 Psalm 22:8.

16 Psalm 22:7. Hebrew, YAPETEEROO BESAPHAH, they cause their lips to open. Probably they gaped.

17 This highly imaginative comment summarizes the attitude of the people. It has no literal basis, as far as I know.

of these, we are done, we are entirely lost and cast down. That is also why Satan tried to destroy the confidence which our Lord Jesus had in God His Father. It is true that Jesus Christ fought with a greater power than we are capable of. For He was not subject to any unbelief. Though that may be, yet He felt such fury as there was in these temptations. For as the devil had previously plotted such things, now he also doubles his efforts. He had said to Him, "If you are the Son of God, let these stones be changed[18] into bread, and eat, for you are a poor starved man.[19] And do you not see that you must experiment to see if you have any power or not?" Now in that Jesus Christ was not insensible, any more than when they reproach Him for the confidence He here had in God. So now, although we may not have the same power to resist, so that we may not come to grief, yet we ought to be strengthened in Him, knowing that it is for us and to our profit that He conquered such assaults and rose above them.

There are also those who say, "*He saved others and He cannot save Himself.*" We see once again how they were confounded. For was not the fact that He had saved others a certain and infallible mark of His Divine power? Jesus Christ had raised the dead. This was not unknown to them. He had given sight to the blind; He had healed paralytics, the lame, even demoniacs. Behold, then, Jesus Christ, Who unfolded the great treasures of His goodness and power in all the miracles which were done by Him.[20] Yet that is still an objection against Him. We see, then, how these poor madmen, unless someone restrains them, are their judges to deprive them of every excuse; so that, when they will come before the great judgment-seat of our Lord Jesus Christ, they will not be able to allege anything to cover themselves. For there they are, condemned by their own mouths. If our Lord saved others, it is certain that He could have saved Himself, unless He preferred others to Himself. What can be perceived there except an admirable goodness, that He wished

18 *converties.*
19 Matthew 4:3.
20 *par,* by or through.

to be cast into the abyss according to men in order to draw us out of the depth of the abysses, that He was willing to suffer everything we deserved in order to acquit us from it, briefly, that He renounced all temporal salvation, that is, He did not wish at all to bring His own life into consideration, He did not wish at all to spare His person, in order that we might have such a gage[21] and such a ransom. All the more, then, ought we to be confirmed in our faith. Seeing everything the devil plots to trouble us and to hinder us from coming to our Lord Jesus, ought to serve to make us all the more sure. May we know how to profit from all this. Now it is certain that the devil makes all his efforts to hinder us at this point. For knowing wherein rests our salvation, he applies every means in order to be able to deprive us of it. For he knows, if he can induce us to be scandalized in the person of our Lord Jesus Christ, that he has won his case. And we experiment with him too much. Besides, all the scandals which the devil raises up and puts before our eyes, to make us turn away from the Son of God, ought to serve us as confirmation. For when it is said that Jesus Christ saved others and does not save Himself, it is a proposition which, according to our human judgment, should be to make us conceive some disdain against the person of the Son of God, to reject Him, and not to put our hope in Him. But quite the contrary, let us know when the Son of God had no regard for Himself and He had no concern at all for His own life, it is because He held the salvation of souls so dear and so precious that He wished to employ everything to that end. Since it is so, we ought boldly to be founded upon Him to call upon Him and to be made entirely sure that it is not in vain that He suffered so for our sakes.

As for their saying "*Here is He who destroys the Temple and rebuilds it in three days,*" there is too villainous a malice in contriving that Jesus had said that He would destroy the Temple. But He had said, "Destroy this Temple and I shall rebuild it at the end of three days." It was not, then, referred to the destruction of the Temple, except by His enemies. And

21 ***un tel gage,*** specifically, a pledge to appear to do battle, indicated by throwing down a glove.

when they crucified Him, should they not have known that the thing already began to be fulfilled? For they were not ignorant of the fact that Jesus Christ had declared Himself to be the true Temple of God with respect to His human body. For since He is God manifest in the flesh and His Divine essence is united to His nature which He took from us, since, I say, all fullness of the Godhead[22] dwells in Him, it is very certain that His body deserves to be called "Temple," more than the one in Jerusalem and more than all the heavens. Now they destroyed it, inasmuch as He was among them, and He rebuilt it at the end of three days. Also they did not forget that; for they knew well afterwards what to say to Pilate.[23] But by that we see that if the devil possesses men he makes them so stupid that they can no longer distinguish between good and evil. They are full of such fury that they throw themselves with abandon against God, as if they wished to defy Him fully and with deliberate purpose. Let us see that, that we may be admonished to walk all the more in the fear of God, when we know how He worked by His admirable power to declare that it was not in vain that Jesus Christ had pronounced by His mouth, "Destroy this Temple and I shall rebuild it." For we see only confounding[24] in His death according to appearances and according to the common sense of men. But Jesus Christ repaired every thing by His resurrection. Since it is so, then, all the more ought we to be confirmed in the faith, and to defy Satan with all the gestures he can make to shake us and to cause us to doubt.

Concerning the saying *"They gave our Lord Jesus vinegar mixed with gall and myrrh to drink,"* it is proper to assume that this was done according to the custom of that time to shorten the death of evil-doers. All the same, Jesus Christ, having tasted it, did not wish to drink, because He knew that His hour had not yet come. They were accustomed, then, before evil-doers were raised on the cross, to give them this drink in order that the blood might be stirred up and they

---

22 *toute plénitude de Divinité.*

23 Matthew 27:63. "We remember that this deceiver said, 'After three days I will rise again.'"

24 *confusion.*

gave up their spirits sooner. For this kind of death was cruel enough, and they needed to be helped through it. In fact, we shall see later how the robbers had their bones broken and snapped in order that they might not languish any further. Though that may be, our Lord Jesus did not wish to drink this beverage, to declare that He was ready to receive in obedience the condition which was committed to Him by God His Father. It is true that this death was very hard for Him. For apart from its being dreadful, He had in it spiritual torments, of which we shall treat tomorrow, God willing. All that, then, might well have induced our Lord Jesus Christ to approach death as soon as it was possible for Him. But He wished to place Himself with entire obedience to endure until He might be delivered without any human means. That, then, in summary, is what we have to remember. But it is in these articles, when His clothing was divided among them and they cast lots over them, that the Scripture was fulfilled. David, a type of our Lord Jesus Christ, makes such complaints. It is true that this is by figure of speech, when he says that they have put gall in his drink, and vinegar, and they have divided his garments, and that in his affliction they still stung him and put him in further agony,[25] as cruel and inhuman people would still like to molest their poor victim who can make no resistance. David, then, uses such a figure of speech when he says that his wealth was divided among them.[26] Under that word he speaks of his wife, of his house, of all his goods, and of all his estate. But in the person of our Lord Jesus Christ this had to be seen with the eye. They gave Him, then, vinegar and gall, in order that it might be known that David was really the type of Him, and that He was the true Redeemer Who had been promised from all time. For why was the Kingdom raised in the house of David, unless with promise that it would endure longer than sun or moon? There was, then, this eternal Kingdom which today has been established in the person of the Redeemer. For these things, which were, as it were, in shadow and type in the person of David, had to have their perfection in Jesus Christ, as we see here.

25 Psalm 69:20, 21, and Psalm 22:18, rather literal.
26 Psalm 22:18.

Besides, as for the Gospel-writer's adding that even the robbers who were with our Lord Jesus mocked Him, it was said by only one, as it appears by St. Luke, who declares these things more at length. But it is a common enough manner of speaking, as when one says, "One speaks even to little children," Although there may be only one, the speaker takes the plural number. "There must be women among them." Yet there need be only one. In this way, then, it is said that our Lord Jesus was spited, mocked, and blasphemed by all, even by the malefactors. For when He was identified with two robbers, it is in order to aggravate all the more the shame of His death. It is true that this was the place where they were accustomed to executing evil-doers. All the same, they are not satisfied with such a shame. But He had to be considered worse and more detestable than all the robbers in the world, when they put one on each of His two sides, to say that He is the chief of them all. And in that, as says St. Mark, was verified what is said by the Prophet, "He was reputed[27] among the transgressors."[28] Now without this reputation, today in what place and condition would we be before God? For we cannot obtain grace without righteousness. God must hate us and reject us until we are righteous and purged of all spots and offenses before Him. And that it be so, can God renounce Himself? Can He strip Himself of His holiness, justice,[29] and integrity? Since, then, we bring before Him our stains, we must be abominable to Him. Now, how shall we now be justified before God, except inasmuch as our Lord Jesus Christ was reputed among the malefactors? We are, then, exempt from this class and God receives us, and we are as acceptable to Him as if we were entirely pure and innocent, inasmuch as our Lord Jesus suffered being in such shame and disgrace before men. That, in summary, is what we have to remember about the robbers.

---

27 *reputé,* reputed or accounted.

28 Mark 15:28. Isaiah 53:12. The American Standard Version and the Revised Standard Version relegate this reference to a footnote.

29 Calvin uses *justice* for both "righteousness" and "justice." I have generally translated it "righteousness" when the application was mainly individual and "justice" when the application was mainly social. Here it is an open question.

But we must insist to the end upon the account of St. Luke, that is, that one of the robbers rebukes his companion when he sees him so obstinate. "How now?" says he, "will there never be a time when you will be humiliated? For the condemnation and the punishment which you endure are for your misdeeds and for your crimes. You are a man plunged into every curse, and though during your entire lifetime you were so brutish as to take pleasure in your faults, so now you must begin to groan." For a man, however undone he may be, although he makes merry his whole lifetime, and thinks he will never come to account at all, he mocks justice, and even defies it, inasmuch as he trusts that he will remain unpunished, yet when he is captured, he must drop his cackling. "Now here you are," says he, "in great torment. You see that God and men are now bringing you to account. Also your conscience rebukes you that it is for your crimes that you endure. And must you still defy God?" Here is a sentence which well shows that this robber had been taught by the Spirit of God. Although we shall soon see it incomparably more, already in this word we can judge what kind of a teacher the Spirit of God is, when He gives such instruction to those who have been entirely led astray, indeed, made brutes; that they not only recognize their faults and prepare themselves so as to obtain grace, but they can speak just like learned doctors, and people who for a long time have been trained in Holy Scripture. For the principal remonstrance that we can make against a man so hardened and who still does not cease to storm against God when he ought to bend and come to repentance, is it not what this poor robber did? But though that may be, such an admonition profited nothing except to render inexcusable him who was so possessed by Satan. Even though it served no purpose toward him to whom it was addressed, it certainly ought to be useful to us today.

So let us learn to fear God, although He spares us. But above all if we are beaten by His rods, and He makes us feel that He is offended against us, then may we be all the more incited to groan, and may we also have constancy to endure patiently our afflictions, as we see that this poor robber did, and not to raise ourselves at all in pride and fury like the other. What is more, in these two we see, as it were, mirrors of all mankind. For we see the miseries with which we are surrounded. This life is, as it were, a depth of all privations, and these are the fruits of our sins. For we have been deprived of the blessing of God in the fall of Adam. It is true that although God by His inestimable goodness rises above this curse, when He always declares Himself Father in many ways and makes us feel His gentleness[30] and the love which He bears toward us and the care which He had for us, yet we have many marks of our sins, and high and low we ought to perceive that we are cursed by God. Death finally is common to all. When we shall have languished in this world, when we shall all have been subject to many maladies, to heat and to cold, when we shall have been tormented in one way and another, briefly, when we shall have endured infinite miseries, what will be the issue of it? We must return to corruption and ashes. However, we see those who are touched by God in such a way that the afflictions which they endure serve for their salvation and turn to their aid, as St. Paul speaks in the 8th chapter of Romans. Others grow worse and worse, and instead of humbling themselves and being touched with any repentance, only make themselves to fester still more, and increasingly provoke the wrath of God and light still more fire to be consumed by. We see that, then. So, let us cast our eyes upon these two robbers as upon mirrors of all the world. For from the greatest to the least we are all blameworthy before God. And if all together we shall endure, who will boast of his innocence? Who will be able to be absolved? Being then plunged into condemnation, we endure rightly for our sins. However, we do not all make equal confession of it. For there are those who grow from bad to worse, and their rebellion which they make against God is manifest. They gnash their teeth, they foam at the mouth in their rage and cruelty. And they do not wish in any wise to come to this condemnation. Or perhaps they take the bit in their teeth and show a wilful contempt[31] to say that God

30 Or "sweetness," one of Jonathan Edward's favorite attributes of God.
31 *contumace.*

will not get them anything at all and that they will have no master over them.

Now let us conclude that, when poor sinners recognize themselves, when they humble themselves, when they confess their debt, when they give glory to God, declaring that He treats them in all equity and uprightness, and that there is good reason why they are suffered to be so chastized, when, I say, poor sinners are drawn to such reasonableness, let us know that God has put His hand upon them, that He has touched them by His Holy Spirit and that in this one can observe an infinite goodness, when He so draws back from perdition and hell, those who were, as it were, devoid of all hope. Now, in summary we see in the person of this poor robber an example of faith which is as excellent as any there ever was. So much more ought we to be carried away and astonished by such a miracle which God performed. For in what estate is he? There he is near death, he endures horrible torments, he waits for someone to come and break and snap his legs, for himself to be dismembered there, who is still in a torment so bitter and dreadful that it is to make him lose sense and memory, he sees our Lord Jesus Who is also in the same desperate situation, indeed, with greater shame, and how does he speak? Not only does he recognize his faults to humble himself before God, not only does he exercise the office of teacher to convert his companion and to lead him back to the good way, but he makes a confession which deserves to be preferred to all others, if we consider well such circumstances. "Remember me," says he, "when Thou comest into Thy Kingdom."

How is it that he is able to conceive of a Kingdom in Jesus Christ? He there perishing on the cross, He is cursed both by God and by men. For this sentence of the law had been pronounced by the mouth of God, "Cursed is he who will hang on the tree."[32] And that was not done in a chance case, but God put there His only Son. When, then, he sees Jesus Christ to be there under the curse both before God and before men, indeed in the depth of despair from the human point of view, he cannot collect his thoughts to say that Jesus

32 Deuteronomy 21:23.

Christ is King, except it be in faith and in spirit. So then, he sees there things which could turn him away from the Son of God and which could make him conclude that it would only be an abuse and a mockery to trust in Him. Yet he calls Him King, seeing Him in His death. "Save me," says he, "Give me life. For if You will remember me, in that will consist all my bliss." Now when we shall have well pondered all these circumstances, it is certain that the faith which was in this robber was as excellent as was in any man who ever lived. However, let us not be ashamed to be his disciples, for in fact the death of our Lord Jesus Christ will not profit us unless we are, as it were, condemned in ourselves, in order to obtain salvation in Him. And we cannot be absolved before God, unless we have confessed that there is in us only iniquity and filth. Since it is true, then, that we are blameworthy before God, and that our own conscience judges and condemns us, let us not be ashamed to follow this robber, seeing that he can be to us a good teacher.

And even now that our Lord Jesus has ascended into heaven, that He has taken possession of the glory which was given to Him by God His Father, in order that every knee may bow before Him, let us not doubt that we are fully restored to His keeping, and conclude that there is wherein consists all our bliss, to know that Jesus Christ remembers us and that He governs us. Inasmuch as He has been ordained our Shepherd, He watches over our salvation, in order that we may be secure under His hand and under His protection. Besides, may we learn to bear patiently the miseries of this present life, and may that not turn us aside from coming to our Lord Jesus Christ. The robber was heard, as we see. Yet he did not escape death, which was very hard and terrible. So then, may we so esteem the spiritual grace which is given us in our Lord Jesus Christ, and which is offered us every day by the preaching of the Gospel, that it may be to make us rise above all the anguishes, quarrels, cares, troubles, and assaults which we could experience. May all our afflictions be sweetened, inasmuch as we know that all will turn out for our good and salvation, by the grace of our Lord Jesus Christ.

That, then, is what we have to observe. Besides, let us add to it the answer of our Lord Jesus Christ, when He promises to the robber that he will be with Him that day in Paradise. Although, then, our Lord Jesus was not yet raised from the dead, and He had not even fulfilled all that was required for our redemption and salvation, already He displayed the power and the fruit of His death and passion. It is true that the fulfillment was in the resurrection. But since it is conjoined to His death and passion, and since we know that, as He suffered in the infirmity of His flesh, so He is raised in the power of His Spirit. As He endured for our sins in order that we might be acceptable before God, also He is raised for our justification. When, I say, we know all that, with how much greater courage may we come freely to Him. May we not doubt at all, when it will please Him to remember us, and to hide us under the shadow of His wings, that we can defy Satan, death and all miseries, and glory in our infirmity. Although according to the world we are poor ill-starred creatures, may we never cease to rejoice in God, from the foretaste He gives us by faith of the heavenly glory and of this inheritance which He has acquired at such a price and from the hope of which we can never be cheated.

Now we shall bow in humble reverence before the majesty of our God.

SERMON 9

Seventh Sermon on the Passion of Our Lord Jesus Christ *

Now from the sixth hour there was darkness over all the land until the ninth hour. And about the ninth hour Jesus cried with a loud voice, saying, "Eli, Eli, lamma sabachthani?" that is "My God, my God, why hast thou forsaken me?" Some of those who were there, having heard that, said, "He calls Elijah." Immediately one of them ran, took a sponge, and having filled it with vinegar, put it on a reed, and gave it to him to drink. Others said, "Let him be; let us see if Elijah will come to save him." Then Jesus crying again with a loud voice, gave up the Spirit. And behold, the veil of the Temple was torn in two, from top to bottom; and the earth shook, and rocks were split. Tombs were opened; and after he was raised, many bodies of Saints who had been sleeping, arose; and having left the tombs, they came into the holy City and appeared to many. Now the Centurion and those who were there with him keeping watch over Jesus, seeing the trembling of the earth and the things which were done, were greatly afraid, saying, "Truly this man was the Son of God." —MATTHEW 27:45-54.

WE SAW yesterday that the mockeries and blasphemies of the enemies of God did not hinder the death and passion of our Lord Jesus from producing and showing His power in the midst of such contempt and ingratitude of the world. For here we see all those who were in some reputation and dignity among the Jews, who openly mock the Son of God. Yet that did not hinder Him from pitying a poor robber and receiving him into eternal life. It is not necessary at all that personality obscure or diminish the glory of the Son of God. If it is argued that a poor robber is not at all to be compared with those who rule the

* From: *Corpus Reformatorum, Calvini Opera*, vol. 46, pp. 914-928.

Church, who were teachers of the law; it is not proper, when we speak of the salvation which was acquired for us through the gratuitous goodness of God, to seek any excellence in our personalities, but rather we must come back to what St. Paul says, "This is a faithful teaching, that Jesus came to save poor sinners."[1] So then, when we shall consider the fruit of the death and passion of our Lord Jesus Christ, all men have to be humbled, and there will have to be found in them only poverty and shame, in order that God may by this means pour out upon them the treasures of His mercy, having no other consideration to provide for us, except inasmuch as He sees that we are cast into the depths in all miseries. Since then, this robber was a man disapproved of by all, and God called him so suddenly, when our Lord made effective for him His death and passion which He suffered and endured for all mankind, that ought all the more to confirm us. It is not at all, then, a matter of God's showing here how He extends His hand to those who seem to be worthy of it and who have some merit in them, or who were respectable and in general reputation among men. But when He draws from the depth of hell poor damned souls, when He shows Himself to be pitiful toward those on whom all hope of life had been foreclosed, that is wherein His goodness shines. That is also what ought to give us entrance to salvation. For hypocrites, although they profess to be somewhat restrained by the grace of God, yet close the door against themselves by their arrogance. For they are so inflated with pride that they cannot adjust themselves to our Lord Jesus Christ. So first may we be very certain that Jesus Christ calls to Himself poor sinners who have only confusion in their persons, and that He extends His arms to receive them. For if we are not sure, we shall never be able to take courage to come to Him. But when we shall be well persuaded that it is to those who are the most miserable that He addresses the salvation which He acquired, provided they recognize themselves as such, and they humble themselves, and they are entirely confounded, rendering themselves blameworthy (as they are) before the judgment of God; that is how we shall be assured, that is how we shall

1 I Timothy 1:15.

have easy access to be sharers of the righteousness which is here offered to us, and by which we obtain grace and favor before God.

Whereupon it is said, *"From the sixth hour until the ninth hour there was darkness."* I speak differently from our common language, for we would say twelve o'clock until three o'clock. But the Gospel-writer followed the common manner of speaking of that time. For when he says the third hour, it is not to say three o'clock, but it is at the first part of the day. There are here two things to note in summary. One is that they counted the hours differently from what we do today. For they counted the day from sunrise to sunset, and there were twelve hours in the day, whereas we measure the day by twenty-four hours, figuring from midnight to the following midnight. Clocks had to be managed differently, so that the hours were longer in summer than in winter. According as the days were longer or shorter, so the hours were long or short. The other point is that they divided the day into four quarters of three hours each, and each part was named by the first hour of the quarter. So all the time from sunrise to the second part of the day, was called the first hour. The second part, which extended to noon, was by them named the third hour. And the sixth hour began at midday and lasted until the third, or four hours later. The other part, which was the last, lasted until the sun set and day was ended. That is why it is said by one of the Gospel-writers that Jesus Christ was crucified about the third hour. And it is here said that this was about the sixth hour. Our Gospel-writer meant that from the sixth hour to the ninth hour there was darkness. For our Lord Jesus was crucified between 9 a. m. and noon, and He had been condemned about 9 a. m. by Pilate. And St. Mark means the end of the three hours, not the beginning, when he described the time that Jesus Christ was led to Golgotha. Now He was on the cross until the ninth hour, when already the end of the day was approaching. So it is most likely that our Lord Jesus did not remain in agony upon the cross more than three hours.

During which time it is said that there was darkness over all the land, that is, Judea. For the eclipse was not general through all the world. In fact that would have obscured the miracle which God wished to show. Because they might then have attributed this eclipse to the order of nature. On the other hand there are not many people who have spoken of it in the sense that it happened in other countries. Indeed, those who make mention of it are rightly suspected. But behold the country of Judea which is covered by darkness. And at what hour? For about the three hours after noonday, when the sun was not yet near his rest, as they say. But apart from the common order of nature there had to be darkness to cause fright and astonishment to all. Many consider that this was done as a sign of detestation, as if God wished to call the Jews to account, in order that they might have some feeling for such an enormous crime as they had committed, and as if He signified to them by this visible sign that even all creatures ought, as it were to hide themselves from such a horrible thing, when Jesus Christ is thus delivered to death. But we have to note that in a way the death of our Lord Jesus Christ had to be held as a dreadful crime, that is, with regard to the Jews. God has well detested their so villainous iniquity. For it surpassed all others. In fact, if we hate murder and such things, what will it be when we come to the person of the Son of God? That the men had been so mad as to wish to annihilate Him Who was the Fountain of Life, that they rose up to destroy the memory of Him by Whom we were created, and in the power of Whom we subsist!

Yet the death of our Lord Jesus did not remain merely a sacrifice of sweet savor. For we must always remember that it was the reconciliation of the world, as we have declared above. Besides, the darkness came in order that the sun give testimony to the Divine and heavenly majesty of our Lord Jesus. Although, then, for that minute He was not only abased and rendered contemptible before men, even emptied of everything, as St. Paul says; yet the sun shows that it does Him homage, and as a sign of that, it remains hidden. Since it is so, then, let us know that God, to render the wicked all the more inexcusable, willed that Jesus Christ in His death be declared sovereign King of all creatures, and that this triumph of which St. Paul speaks in the second chapter of Colossians began already, when he says that Jesus Christ triumphed in the cross.[2] It is true that he applies that in that He tore up the writ which was against us, and that He acquitted us before God, and by this means Satan was conquered; yet that was already shown by this eclipse of the sun. However, the Jews were convinced of their ignorance, even of a malicious and fanatical ignorance, as if it had been seen with the eye that Satan possessed them, and that they were, as it were, monsters made contrary to nature. That, in summary, is what we have to remember when it is spoken of the darkness which occurred.

It is true that we are enlightened today by the death and passion of our Lord Jesus Christ. For how is it that the Gospel shows us the way to salvation? How are we illumined to come to God, unless since there the Son of God is presented to us with the fruit and the power of His death? Jesus Christ is really, then, the Sun of Righteousness, because He acquired for us life by dying. But the Jews have been deprived of such a benefit. And in that the sun was obscured they were convinced that they were of all people reproved, and that there was no longer doctrine which would serve them, nor be useful unto salvation, since by their malice they had tried to extinguish and abolish everything that could give them hope. For it was entirely in the person of the Mediator, Whom they tried to destroy by their malice and ingratitude. It was quite right, then, that they were completely destitute of all light of salvation, in order that the wrath of God declared itself in a visible manner upon them.

It follows that our Lord Jesus cried, saying, *"My God, my God, why hast thou forsaken me?"* St. Matthew and St. Mark recite in the Syriac[3] tongue the words of our Lord Jesus, which are drawn from Psalm 22. And the words are not so pronounced by all the Gospel-writers as what the text of the Psalm bears. Even in this word "Eli," that is "My God," we see that St. Mark says "Eloi."[4] But this is by the corruption of language, as we have noted before this. For the Jews having

2 Colossians 2:14, 15.
3 A dialect of Aramaic, which also includes Chaldee, etc.
4 Mark 15:34. Hebrew, ELEE. The form in Matthew is a transliteration of the Hebrew. The form in Mark is probably a transliteration of the Syriac current at the time.

returned from Babylon, have never had a language entirely pure, as before. All the same this query and complaint is drawn from Psalm 22:1. God willed especially that this be recited in two tongues, to show that it was a thing of importance, and to which we ought to be attentive. In fact, unless we would wish to imagine (as do many fantastic people) that our Lord Jesus spoke according to the opinion of men and not according to His sense and His feeling, we surely must be moved by this, and all our senses must be rapt, when Jesus Christ complains of being forsaken and abandoned by God His Father. For it is a thing too dull and too foolish, to say that our Lord Jesus was not at all touched with anguish and anxiety in His heart, but that He had simply said, "They gather that I am forsaken." That shows that those who look for such glosses, are not only ignorant, but are altogether in jest. Besides, they never cease to blaspheme, like mastiff dogs, against God. And all those who speak thus, it is certain that they have no more religion than dogs and brute beasts, for they do not know how much their salvation has cost the Son of God. And what is worse, they mock it just like the villains which they are.

Then, we must hold it as a conclusive fact, that our Lord Jesus, being brought into such extremity and anguish, cried with a loud voice (yes, like those who are tormented to the limit), "My God, my God, why hast thou forsaken me?" In fact, we have said above that it would be a cold statement from the history of His death, if we would not consider the obedience which He rendered to God His Father.

This, then, is the principal thing we have to consider when we would be assured of our salvation. It is that if we have committed many faults and rebellions and iniquities against God, all of it will be buried, inasmuch as our Lord Jesus by His obedience has justified us and rendered us acceptable to God His Father. Now this obedience, in what did it consist, unless Jesus Christ, although death was to Him hard and terrible, nevertheless did not refuse to be subject to it? For if He had experienced in it no difficulty or contradiction, it would not have been obedience. But though our Lord Jesus by nature held death in horror and indeed it was a terrible thing to Him to be found before the judgment-seat of God in the name of all poor sinners (for He was there, as it were, having to sustain all our burdens), nevertheless He did not fail to humble Himself to such condemnation for our sakes, we know in Him a perfect obedience, and in that we have a good cause to glorify Him, as says the Apostle in the Epistle to the Hebrews, "Our Lord Jesus was heard in that he feared."[5] But though that may be, yet He had to sustain what was so hard and burdensome, indeed, entirely contrary to all human affection. It was necessary, then, that God His Father so trained Him in order that His obedience might be known.[6] We see, then, the Apostle, who specifies particularly that our Lord Jesus had to be astonished with fear. For without that we would not know what this sacrifice by which we have been reconciled is worth. In fact, St. Peter also shows that our Lord Jesus suffered not only in His body, but in His soul, when He says that He fought against the pains of death.[7]

It is true that Scripture will often say that we are redeemed by the blood of Jesus Christ, inasmuch as He offered His body as a sacrifice. That is also why it is said that His flesh is to us meat and His blood is to us spiritual drink. But that is said out of regard to our uncouthness. Because we are gross, the Holy Spirit brings us back to what is visible in the death of Jesus Christ, in order that we may have a completely certain pledge of our salvation. However, this is not to exclude what is shown in all the other passages, and even to derogate from the article that the death and passion of our Lord Jesus would not have served anything to wipe away the iniquities of the world, except insofar as He obeyed, indeed, abasing Himself even to so frightful a death. And He obeyed, not at all that His senses were taken away. But although He had to sustain great and extreme terrors, yet He put our salvation above every other consideration. This, then, is what we have to observe in this passage: That is, that the Son of God not only endured in His body such a cruel death, but that He was touched to the quick, having to sustain horrible assaults as if God had abandoned

5 Hebrews 5:7, an interesting verse to shed light on how God answers prayer.

6 Hebrews 5:8.

7 I think this is an interpretation of 1 Peter 3:18.

Him. For, in fact, He also sustained our cause, and He had to experience what condemnation there was upon poor sinners. By our sins we are, as it were, alienated from God, and He must withdraw Himself from us, and we must know that He has, as it were, rejected us. That is the proper thing for sinners. It is certain that Jesus Christ has never been rejected by God His Father. Nevertheless, He had to sustain these sorrows and He had to fight valiantly to repulse them, in order that today the fruit of the victory may come back to us. So we have to remember that, when our Lord Jesus was put into such an extremity, as if God His Father had cut off from Him all hope of life, it is inasmuch as He was there in our person, sustaining the curse of our sins, which separated us from God. For wherein rests our felicity, unless we are made alive by the grace of God, and enlightened by His brightness? He is the fountain of life and of every good, and our sins put, as it were, a long distance between Him and us. Jesus Christ, then, had to experience this. Let us consider now what someone might say. Is it possible that Jesus Christ experienced such terrors, since there is in Him only complete perfection? For it seems that it takes away from the faith which He must have had and from everything that we ought to believe of Him. That is, that He was without any spot of vice. Now the answer to that is very easy. For when He was tempted by Satan, it is certain that He had to have this apprehension that He was, as it were, on top of a tower and that He was subject to such an illusion according to His human nature. However, that took nothing away from His divine power. Rather we have occasion to magnify His goodness toward us, inasmuch as He thus abased Himself for our salvation.

Now it is said that He cried, "*My God, why hast Thou forsaken Me?*" In the first place it is very certain that Jesus Christ, insofar as He was God, could have no such apprehension. No, no. But when He suffered His Deity[8] had to give place to His death and passion, which He had to endure. That, then, is the power of our Lord Jesus which was kept, as it were, hidden for a time, until He had accomplished

8 *sa Divinité.*

all that was required for our redemption. Yet according to man, let us note that this complaint, this feeling and terror of which we now speak, in no wise detracted from the faith of our Lord Jesus Christ. For inasmuch as He was man He had all His confidence in God, as we have seen, and yesterday it was sufficiently treated. It was, then, the true pattern of a true, perfect, and entire confidence. It is said now that He was in such anguish that He seemed to be forsaken by God His Father. However His faith was always perfect, was neither beaten down nor shaken in any manner whatever. How, then, does He say, "Why hast Thou forsaken Me?" It is by natural apprehension. Behold, then, our Lord Jesus Christ Who according to the weakness of His flesh is, as it were, abandoned by God, and yet He does not cease to confide in Him. As in fact we see two parts in these words which are superficially contrary, and yet it all agrees very well. When He says "My God, My God" and He repeats the word in such a way, by that He shows the constancy of His faith. He does not say, "Where is God? How does He leave me?" But He addresses Himself to Him. He must, then, be entirely persuaded and assured that He will always find favorable access toward God His Father. Behold (I say) a certain and infallible testimony of the faith of our Lord Jesus Christ. When in the midst of the extremity and anguish where He was, He does not cease to call God His Father, and not in pretense, but because He was assured that He would find Him propitious in calling upon Him. Behold (I say) the faith of our Lord Jesus Christ which is sufficiently declared. Yet He repeats the word, because this fight is difficult, as if He would defy all the temptations which Satan prepared for Him, and He sought confirmation of faith that He might always persist in calling upon God.

Now He said further, "Why hast Thou forsaken Me?" Of course that was according to what He could conceive of as man. For He had to enter into that experience, not to be conquered by it. For St. Peter says, "It was impossible that He be held by the pains of death,"[9] that is, that He be seized

9 Acts 2:24.

like a poor man who altogether gives way and is crushed. "It was impossible," says St. Peter. And so the victory was in the midst of the fight. And that is to glorify all the more our Lord Jesus Christ. David had experienced this in part. For it is certain that in the midst of his afflictions, however great they were, he persisted to call upon God, indeed hoping in Him. But since he was frail man, his faith was very often shaken, as he confesses. But in our Lord Jesus, there was a special consideration (which was treated last Lord's Day), that is, that He had all His passions well controlled, because of the integrity that was in Him and there was in Him no natural corruption. As sometimes it will happen to us that our pains will proceed from a good cause, indeed, both our fears and our anxieties. But all the same there will always be vice mixed in it, since corruption is in all our passions. But in our Lord Jesus there was nothing troubled or disordered. It follows, then, that He was not so seized with anguish, that He did always have His hope fixed rightly on God, that He called only upon Him and remained firm and constant in that, knowing well that He would be Savior even to the end.

Whereupon it is said, "*Some of those who were near Him mocked Him.*" "He who calls Elijah, let us see if Elijah will come to help Him." One supposed that the guards, as ignorant of the Law, spoke thus. But this is too foolish an abuse, for they did not know who Elijah was. There is no doubt, then, that this blasphemy was pronounced by none others than the priests[10] who were trained in the Law. And are not they themselves deceived in what Jesus said? Not at all. For the Prophet whom they called Elijah is not named thus. The name, then, had not deluded them. For there is no doubt implied, seeing that the word "Elijah" is pronounced entirely differently from the word "Eli,"[11] that is, "My God." That could not cause any ambiguity. It is, then, by certain malice and impudence that the reproach that "He calls Elijah"

---

10 *sacrificateurs.*

11 These two words could not be confused in English. In French "Elie" (Elijah) and "Eli" (my God) are pronounced alike. Hebrew ELEE-AHOO (Elijah) has the first two syllables like ELEE (my God).

was put upon our Lord Jesus Christ. And if we find that strange, would to God that there were no such examples today. For one will see today the Papists who turn away and deprave by their calumnies what we teach, that is, what is drawn from the pure truth of God, and they knowingly blaspheme to render our doctrine odious to many ignorant people and people who do not hear what we preach every day. They deprave, then, falsely what we say and they take it entirely the wrong way, in order to give plausibility to their lie and entertain poor ignorant people with it. That is how the enemies of God, possessed by Satan, have turned aside by certain malice the words of our Lord Jesus Christ, and today among the Papists one sees the same thing. And not only is that perceived in the Papacy, but even among us there are belligerents who will say that we wish to make believe that Jesus Christ was devoid of all hope when we see that He sustained the anguish of death, that He was as it were cast into the depths, inasmuch as He was there in our name and He sustained the burden of our sins. But that in no wise takes away from the constancy of His faith, that it might not always remain in its entirety. And these rascals who make profession of the Gospel, never cease to knowingly blaspheme, by which they show that they are worse than those of whom it is here spoken. Seeing then that the devil today sharpens the tongues of his agents, and that each one by such brutal impudence comes to disgorge his venom against the purity of doctrine, let us not think it strange if our Lord Jesus was thus slandered. But may we bear patiently these blasphemies, praying to God (as it is said in the twelfth Psalm) that He may destroy these villainous tongues[12] which are so full of villainy and of execration, and which tend to blaspheme His Name and to obscure His truth.

Whereupon the Gospel-writer records that *there was there a vessel full of vinegar* (indeed, as we have already seen, which was mixed with gall) and that they took a reed, or better (as says St. John) a hyssop in order to have a long branch, and at the end of it they attached a sponge to make

12 Psalm 12:3.

it reach the mouth of our Lord Jesus. St. John speaks here more distinctly, for he says that Jesus Christ, knowing that all things were fulfilled, said that He was thirsty, and thereupon He pronounced once again *"It is done, all is fulfilled."* This, then, is what we have to note here, when this drink was given to the Son of God: namely, that He did not ask to drink because He was thirsty, for He had refused it, as already we have seen above. Why? For this drink was given in order to shorten the life. Now our Lord Jesus wished in everything and by everything to wait for the hour of God His Father in patience and rest. That, then, is why He did not wish to hasten His death, but rendered Himself peaceable and obedient, until all was fulfilled — indeed, although He had not yet given up the Spirit and He was not raised from the dead. For he means that until this hour He had shown a complete obedience, so that nothing now hindered Him from giving His soul to God His Father. This, then, is how we must take this passage: It is that our Lord Jesus declared that nothing more was lacking for our redemption except to depart from the world, which He was ready and prepared to do, and to surrender His soul to God. Seeing, then, that He had acquitted Himself of His whole duty as Mediator, and that He had done all that was required to appease the wrath of God toward us, and that the satisfaction for our sins was accomplished, He was willing to ask for this drink.

Now we have here a very noteworthy and excellent sentence, when it is said, "All is fulfilled." For it is certain that the Lord Jesus does not speak at all of any little or common things. But He intends that by His death we have all that we need to seek to have access to God and to obtain grace from Him. Not that His resurrection should be excluded by that, but it is as if He said that He has performed His office faithfully, and that He has not come to be a partial Savior, but that until the last moment He has executed the charge which was committed to Him, and that He had omitted nothing according to the will of God His Father. Since that is so, we are instructed to fully fasten our confidence in our Lord Jesus Christ, knowing that all parts of our salvation are fulfilled in what He did and endured for our sakes. That is also why His death is called a perpetual Sacrifice, by which the believers and elect of God are sanctified. Do we wish, then, to have certainty that God is Father to us? Do we wish to have liberty to call upon Him? Do we wish to have rest in our consciences? Do we wish to be made more fully certain that we are held to be righteous in order to be acceptable to God? Let us abide in Jesus Christ and not wander here or there, and let us recognize that He is wherein rests all perfection. Those, then, who wish other props, and who look from one side to the other to supply what must be lacking in the death and passion of our Lord Jesus Christ, renounce fully the power of which we are now speaking. Briefly they tread under foot the blood of Jesus Christ, for they dishonor it. Now in all the Papacy what is there except renunciation of the death and passion of our Lord Jesus Christ? For though they think to do good works, because they call them merits, by which they are confident that they acquire grace before God, it is certain that they disavow what was pronounced by our Lord Jesus Christ, "All is fulfilled." And since it is so, when they think to obtain salvation before God, and they wish to have remission of their sins, where do they go, except to their foolish devotions? For each one will perform his little duty at his post, so that all the so-called devotions in the Papacy are so many blasphemies to nullify what was pronounced when our Lord Jesus said, "All is fulfilled." What follows, then? That we may know that there is not a single particle of virtue or merit in us, unless we apply ourselves to this Fountain wherein is all fulness of it.

That, then, is how our faith ought to be fastened on our Lord Jesus Christ. Besides, may we know above all that when He was offered as a sacrifice it was to absolve us forever and to sanctify us perpetually, as Scripture says.[13] May we, then, have no other sacrifice than this One. It is true that in the Papacy, this diabolical abomination of the mass is called daily Sacrifice; and they say that Jesus Christ surely

13 Revelation 13:8, "the lamb slain from the foundation of the world." However, Calvin does not call undue attention to the book of Revelation.

once offered Himself as a Sacrifice to obtain for us the remission of our sins, but that it is still necessary that He be offered daily, which is blasphemy fully manifest, inasmuch as they usurp the office which was given to our Lord Jesus Christ, when He was ordained only eternal Sacrifice, indeed, with an oath that God adjures that it should be perpetual. When, then, mortal men take it upon themselves still to come to present and offer Jesus Christ to God, do they not rob the honor which God reserves to Himself alone, and which cannot be attributed to any creature? Since it is so, then, we see how these poor blind men, supposing themselves to keep appointment with God,[14] provoke His wrath and His vengeance, renouncing the death and passion of our Lord Jesus Christ. And so much more ought we to magnify the grace of God by which He has withdrawn us from such an abyss, that when we claim to approach Him, it is to defy Him openly. For we deprive ourselves of Him and of the fruit of His death and passion when we seek other sacrifice than that which He offered in His person. That, then, is what we have to remember.

Now it is said, *"Once again He cried with a loud voice and gave up the spirit."* And this cry was, *"I give back my soul* or My spirit *into Thy hands."* In that we see how our Lord Jesus Christ so fought against the pains of death, that from then on He was conqueror over it and He could gain His triumphs as having surmounted what was the most difficult. And this pertains to us, that is, we must apply it to our use. For we are assured not only that the Son of God fought for us, but that the victory which He acquired for us belongs to us, and that today we ought not to be in any wise frightened by death, knowing that the curse of God, which was terrible to us, is abolished, and that death, instead of being able to wound us like a fatal plague, serves us as medicine to give us passage into life. Now as previously by the example of David He said, "My God, my God, why hast Thou forsaken

14 *faire appointement avec Dieu.* The Latin idiom *a punctum* is behind the word *appointement.* Perhaps the phrase should be translated "supposing themselves to be in absolute agreement with God."

me?"[15] so now He takes the prayer made by David in the thirty-first Psalm, "I commend to Thee my spirit."[16] It is true that David said that, being in the midst of dangers. As if he said, "Lord, hold me in Thy protection; for my soul is as it were between my hands; it is there as it were fluttering. For I see myself exposed to all hazards; my life is as it were hanging from a thread. It does not remain, then, unless Thou takest me into Thy keeping." That is how David by this prayer constituted God as his Protector. However, he did not leave it until death itself to call upon God, and to be assured that always God is the Savior of His elect, not only to maintain and guard them in this world, but also when He withdraws them to Himself. For the principal guard that God keeps over us is that being withdrawn from this world we are hidden under His wings to rejoice in His presence, as St. Paul speaks of it in 2 Corinthians.[17] And our Lord Jesus also pronouncing this prayer declares that He dies peaceably, having conquered in all the combats which He had to sustain for us, and achieves already His triumphs in our name and to our profit and salvation. He fully declares by this same means that God is His Savior and that He keeps His soul as a safe trust. For that is what this request that He makes of Him implies, when He says, "My God, be Thou guardian of My soul, even after death."

When our Lord Jesus speaks so, it is as if He assured us all that we cannot fail in committing ourselves to our God, since He surely condescends to take charge of us, in order to sustain us, and that we shall never perish being thus under His hand. Now especially we have to note that Jesus Christ, saying, "My God, I commend to Thee My spirit," acquired the privilege which is attributed to Him by St. Stephen in Acts 7. It is that He was constituted guardian of all our souls. For how is it that Saint Stephen speaks in His death? "Lord Jesus, I commend to Thee my spirit."[18] This, then, is how St. Stephen shows the fruit of this request which was

15 Psalm 22:1.
16 Psalm 31:5.
17 Referring to "the hidden gospel," 2 Corinthians 4:3.
18 Acts 7:59.

made by Jesus Christ: namely, that now we can address ourselves to Him, and we ought to do it, declaring that since He was given to us as Shepherd by God His Father, we need have no doubt to be peaceable both in life and in death, knowing all will profit us and will be turned to our advantage. As St. Paul says, having Jesus Christ he will find gain in everything, that he will no longer lack anything in either life or death, for all will be useful to him.[19]

So then, let us learn now, when we shall be besieged by death, that Jesus Christ has taken away the sting which might prick us fatally in the heart, and that death will no longer be harmful to us, and that when our Lord Jesus gave His soul to God His Father, it was not only to be preserved in His person, but in order to acquire this privilege which is entirely preserved for us by virtue of this request; indeed, when we shall have our recourse to Him, as to the One under the protection of Whom we cannot perish, since He declares it. There is still this triumph of which we have made mention, which already profits us. For our Lord Jesus shows how precious His death is, when He so confidently departs to God His Father to lead us to Him and to show us the way to Him But the principal thing is that we may know that the fruit of it comes back to us, inasmuch as He tore up the writ which was against us, as He acquired for us full satisfaction for our sins, so that we can appear before God His Father in such a way that even death is no longer to do us evil or any harm. Although we still see in us many things which might astonish us, and we experience our poverty and misery, yet let us not cease to glory in Him Who was then abased for us in order to raise us with Him.

In fact, although on man's side there is only complete shame, yet when Jesus Christ was hanged there on the cross, already God wished at that time by the mouth of Pilate that He be declared King. So, although the Kingdom of our Lord Jesus Christ is vilified before the world, may we not, however, cease to hold it as the foundation of all our glory, and may we know that being in shame under His leading, we have

19 Philippians 1:20-24.

nevertheless whereof to rejoice; since our condition will always be blessed, because all the miseries, afflictions, and ignominies which we endure are more honorable and precious before God than are all the scepters, all the pomp, and things honorable, to which men are addicted. That, then, is how we must come to our Lord Jesus Christ, and cling in such a way to Him that we may know what the riches which He brings to us are worth, and above all when He leads us by His Gospel, may we reject all the conveniences and comforts of this world; indeed, may we hold them in detestation when they would turn us aside from the good way. Briefly, may our Lord Jesus obtain the honor which He deserves, and on our part may we also not be as reeds shaking with every wind, but being founded in Him may we call upon God, and in life and in death may the victory be given to us in which He has already triumphed. And while we are still here below may we give Him the honor of recognizing that it is He Who sustains us. This is what He will do when we shall really have our refuge in Him: He will do it, I say, not in a common manner but miraculously. For when we shall be cast down to the very bottom of the abyss of death, it is His office to withdraw us from it and to lead us to the heavenly inheritance which He has so dearly acquired for us.

Now we shall bow in humble reverence before the majesty of our God.

SERMON 10

Eighth Sermon on the Passion of Our Lord Jesus Christ *

And many women were there looking from afar, who followed Jesus from Galilee, serving him. Among them were Mary Magdalene, and Mary the mother of James and Joses, and the mother of the sons of Zebedee. And when evening had come, there came a rich man of Arimathea, named Joseph, who had also been a disciple of Jesus. He went to Pilate and asked for the body of Jesus. Then Pilate commanded the body to be delivered. And Joseph took the body and wrapped it in linen cloth, and he put it in his new tomb which he had carved in a rock; and having rolled a great stone to the door of the tomb, he went away.

— MATTHEW 27:55-60

WE HAVE seen above how our Lord Jesus declared the fruit and the power of His death in the poor robber, who surely seemed to be, as it were, a damned and lost soul. Now if all those who had previously been taught in the Gospel, and had had some taste of it, were alienated seeing the Son of God die, it would seem that the preaching of the Gospel had been vain and useless. Besides we know that the Apostles had been elected to the condition of being, as it were, the first-fruits of the Church. One could, then, have thought that this election had been a disappointing thing, and that they had been chosen to such office and estate. For this cause it is here declared to us that, although the Apostles had fled and in that was shown a villainous cowardice, St. Peter had even renounced our Lord Jesus and was, as it were, cut off from all hope of salvation, indeed, being worthy to be reputed as a rotten member; yet God did not permit the doctrine which

* From: *Corpus Reformatorum, Calvini Opera,* vol. 46, pp. 928-942.

they had previously received to be extinguished and entirely abolished. It is true that St. Matthew puts more faith in the constancy of women than of men. That is in order that we may learn to magnify all the more the goodness of God, Who perfects[1] His power in our weakness. That is also what St. Paul says, that God has chosen the weak things of this world, in order that those who suppose themselves to be strong may bow their heads and not glory at all in themselves.[2] If it were, then, here spoken of men and of their magnanimity, and that they had followed our Lord Jesus Christ to death, one would take that as a natural thing. But when women are led by the Spirit of God, and there is in them more boldness than in men, indeed, than in those who had been elected to publish the Gospel to all the world, in that we recognize that God was at work and that it is to Him that the praise ought to be attributed.

Now it is said especially, *"These women had followed our Lord Jesus, doing Him service."* Which is to better declare the inclination they had to profit by the Gospel. For it was no small excellence that they left their houses to traipse here and there, indeed, with great effort and even with shame. For we know what the condition of our Lord Jesus Christ was while He went about in the world. He says that foxes have caves and little birds are able to build their nests, but He has nowhere to lay His head.[3] We see on the other hand that these women had the wherewithal to feed themselves peaceably and at their comfort. When, then, they traipse so without being able to find lodging except with difficulty, they have to go without food and drink, they are subject to many mockeries, they are driven away and molested everywhere, and yet they rise above all that and bear it in patience, we can easily judge how God had strengthened them. However, at the death they still declare the hope that they had in our Lord Jesus Christ. For although they are bewildered, yet if they had supposed that our Lord had come to grief, they could have judged that He had completely failed. For

1 *faire valoir.*
2 1 Corinthians 1:19-31.
3 Matthew 8:20, Luke 9:58.

He had spoken to them of the Kingdom of God which was to be restored by His means. He had spoken to them of the perfect bliss and of the salvation which He would accomplish. And where are all these things? We see, then, how these poor women, although they had been bewildered and however much they are troubled, not knowing what would be the outcome of our Lord's life, nevertheless were held back by His authority. And yet He causes that in the end they could recognize and judge that He had not promised them anything in vain. They have, then, waited for the promise of the resurrection, although according to men they might have judged entirely to the contrary. However, we see how their faith was trained, in order that we might not be troubled beyond measure, if in appearance it seems that we are forsaken by God, and that all the promises of the Gospel are, as it were, abolished, but that we persist nevertheless. For these women give testimony against us, and to our great condemnation, if we fail in such combats. Would we wish a ruder example than what they have endured? However, they were victorious, indeed, by means of faith.

So then, let us arm ourselves when we are warned of the assaults which Satan makes against us, that we are armed to meet the blow, and we show that we are so supported by the power of our Lord Jesus Christ that although we may not perceive at first glance the fulfilment of what is said to us, we may not cease to rest in Him, and to bring to Him this honor and reverence, that He will show Himself faithful in the end. And we need to be thus proved to the limit. For otherwise we would be too delicate, and even our faith would be deadened, or perhaps we would imagine an earthly paradise, and we could not raise our senses high enough to renounce this world. As also we see it better in the person of the mother of John and James. We know that previously she had been driven by such an ambition that she had wished that our Lord might be seated on His Royal throne, and that He might have had there only pomp and bravery, and that her two sons might have been there as two lieutenants of our Lord. "Command, Lord," she says, "that one of my sons be at your right hand, and the other at the left." What a foolish woman! who is mindful only of glory and who wished to see an earthly triumph in her children. Now here is another and very different experience. For she sees our Lord Jesus hanged on the cross, in such shame and disgrace that all the world is opposed to Him, and He is even there, as it were, cursed by God. So we see this, when we shall be led into such a confusion that our spirits will be astonished with terror and anguish, but by this means God robs us of all earthly affections, in order that nothing may hinder us from being raised into heaven and to the spiritual life to which we must aspire. And we cannot do it unless we are purged of everything that holds us back on this earth. That, then, in summary, is what we have to remember concerning these women.

However, that is not to say that there may not also have been men, but the intention of the Holy Spirit was to put before our eyes here such a mirror in order that we might know that it is God who led these women by the power of His Holy Spirit, and He wished to declare His power and His grace, choosing instruments so feeble according to the world. The like is also seen in Nicodemus and in Joseph. It is true that St. Matthew, St. Mark, and St. Luke speak only of Joseph, who came to Pilate, and Nicodemus took courage, seeing he had such a leader. It is true that Nicodemus was a teacher of great esteem. Joseph was a rich man of property, indeed, also a member of the council. However, let us look to see whether there was in them such a zeal as to expose themselves to death for our Lord Jesus, and indeed if during His life they have left their houses to follow Him. Not at all. But when it comes to the death God moves them and incites them beyond all human expectation. We see, then, that God worked here a strange and admirable change, when He gave such boldness to Joseph and to Nicodemus, that they were not afraid of the rage of all the people, when they came to bury our Lord Jesus. Previously Nicodemus had come by night, fearing to be marked with infamy. Now he buries our Lord Jesus, indeed, when He has come to the extremity. God, then, had to give him a new courage, for he had hidden himself, and, indeed, no shadows had been dark enough for him, seeing his timidity and cowardice, unless God had corrected this vice in him. Briefly, we see how the death of our Lord Jesus profited, and that already He then displayed the graces of His Holy Spirit upon these poor people, who previously had never dared to make a declaration of their faith. Now not only do they speak by mouth, but what they do shows that they prefer to be held execrable before all the world and yet be disciples of Jesus Christ, than to lose what they had obtained; namely, the free salvation which had been offered them.

That is also why it is said that Joseph *waited for* the Kingdom of God. By this word it is declared to us that we are alienated from God and banished from His Kingdom until He gathers us to Himself for His people. We see, then, how miserable is the condition of men, until our Lord Jesus has called them to Himself to dedicate them to His Father. And if we are separated from this good, woe and confusion upon us! It was a great virtue then to wait for the Kingdom of God, because the Jews had corrupted it, and the occasions of it were great according to the world. For the Prophets had declared, when the people had returned from Babylon, that God would be in such wise their Redeemer that there would be a kingdom flourishing in all dignity, that the Temple would be built in greater glory than ever, that then they would enjoy all benefits, and that it would be a happy life, that all would have rest and that the only concern would be to enjoy God, and bless His Name, and give Him praise. That is what the Prophets had promised. But what is the condition of the people? They are consumed and gobbled up by their neighbors, they are stung, they are molested. Sometimes there is such tyranny that innocent blood is spilled throughout all the city, the book of the Law is burned, and they are forbidden to have a single reading of it under penalty of death. Such great cruelties are practiced that it is horrible to think of it. The Temple is full of pollution. The house of David — what has become of it? It has entirely fallen and the state of things continuously goes from bad to worse. So then, one must not be astonished, if in a people so rough and given to its appetites and affections, there were very few who retained the true religion and who had not lost courage; as we see also that the number of those who endured patiently and who were firm in the faith was very small and very rare. That is said of Simeon, it is said of Anna the prophetess, it is said of Joseph. But why? In a multitude so great, among the Jews in a country so populated, the Holy Spirit sets before us four or five as a thing which was not at all usual, and gives testimony that those people were waiting for the Kingdom of God. But it is in order that we may learn, when everything will be confused and in despair, to have our eyes fixed upon God. And inasmuch as His truth is infallible and immutable, let us remain firm until the end, and let us rise above all troubles, scandals, and perplexities of this world, and however we may groan let us not cease to aspire to what our Lord calls us to, that is, to wait patiently for His Kingdom to be established in us, and yet may it suffice us to have the Gage which He gives us of His Holy Spirit, by Whom He testifies to us of the free adoption He has made of us. When God declares that He holds us and regards us as His children, and when it is engraved on our hearts by His Holy Spirit, when we have daily the doctrine of the Gospel which resounds and rings in our ears, let us be confirmed in the faith and not fail at all, even though things are so confused that one could not imagine them any worse. That, then, in summary, is what we have to remember from this passage.

Now it is also necessary to note what St. John recites before our Lord Jesus was taken down from the cross: namely, that they pierced His side to see if He had already given up the spirit. For they had not hurried His death as they had with the two robbers. But seeing that it appeared that He had already passed away, they came to probe Him with a blow of a spear, and then they knew that He had died, and so the guards are satisfied. Now it is true that this, if the testimony of the Law were not added, would seem to us a somewhat cold statement. But St. John wished to give us proof that our Lord Jesus was the true paschal Lamb, since by the providence and the admirable counsel of God He had been preserved from every mutilation. For it is said in the

12th chapter of Exodus that they should eat the paschal lamb, but that the bones should not be broken, and that they should remain entirely whole.[4] Why was it important that Jesus Christ should not have His bones broken? For it was the common custom, as we see. They did not wish to spare Him, and He was even set in the midst of the robbers to be held, as it were, the most detestable, to be reputed the principal one among wicked men and criminals. We see, then, that God was here at work when He held back the hands of the guards, and even willed that His Son expired in order to be preserved, and that we might have here an evident sign that it was in Him that the truth of this ancient figure had to be fulfilled. Thus, then, we must notice that the Son of God was preserved from all breaking of His bones, in order that we might hold Him for our paschal Lamb, Who is to preserve us from the wrath of God, when we shall be marked with His blood. For we must come to this: that, if He is our Passover, we must every last one be sprinkled by His blood, for without that it profits us nothing that it has been spilled. But when we shall accept Him with this sacrifice, also we shall find there the remission of our sins, knowing that until He washes and cleanses us we are full of pollution. Then we are sprinkled by His blood, by this besprinkling which is made in our souls by the Holy Spirit. Then we are purified and God accepts us for His people, and we are assured; although His wrath and His vengeance is upon all the world, yet He regards us in pity and He owns us as His children. That, then, is what we have to remember from this passage when it is said that the bones of our Lord Jesus were not broken or snapped at all, in order that we may know that what had been declared by a figure in the Law has been verified in His person.

However, it is also said, "*Water and blood came out of His side, and he who saw it has given testimony of it.*" When we see that water and blood came out thus, it ought to remind us that it brings to us our purging and the agreement[5] to wipe away our sins, indeed, by His Sacrifice, as St. John

4 Exodus 12:8, 9, 46.
5 *l'appointement.*

speaks in his Canonical letter.[6] It is true that the blood will be able to congeal in death, as that is done by nature, and that with the blood water can come, that is, the most fluid, inasmuch as the color and the thickest part of the blood will have coagulated. But St. John declared, though that may be, that God wished to show wherein the death of His Son profits us: namely, in the first place that by the shedding of blood He is appeased toward us, as it is said that no remission of sins is possible without shedding of blood. For that is why from the beginning of the world sacrifices were offered. God surely declared that He would be propitious to all poor sinners who would have hope in Him; but He wished that sacrifices be added, as if He said that the remission of sins would be freely given to men, because they of themselves could bring nothing of their own, but that there would be the Mediator for recompense. That, then, is how the blood which flowed from the side of our Lord Jesus Christ is testimony that the sacrifice which He offered is the recompense of all our iniquities, so that we are acquitted before God. It is true that we must always feel guilty of that blood, that is, to humble ourselves and to bring us to a true repentance, and to take from us all presumption. But though that may be, we are made certain that God holds us acquitted and absolved by the Name of His Son, when we come to recognize our faults and offenses. And why? Inasmuch as the Sacrifice of His death is sufficient to wipe away the memory of all our transgressions. Now there is the water which implies purging. In order, then, that we may be washed from all our spots, let us recognize that our Lord Jesus wished that the water flowed from His side to declare that truly He is our purity and that we must not seek any other remedy to wash any of our stains from us. That, then, is how He came with water and with blood, and by this means we have all perfection of salvation in Him, and we must not wander about here or there, to be helped from one side and another.

Indeed, when we shall look more closely, we shall see that there is a striking resemblance between the blood and the wa-

6 1 John 1:7. Calvin does not comment on 2 and 3 John.

ter which flowed from the side of our Lord Jesus Christ, and the Sacraments of the Church, by which we have the proof and seal of what was done in His death. For having endured what was required for our salvation, having fully satisfied God His Father, having sanctified us, having acquired for us full righteousness, He wished that all that might be testified in the two Sacraments which He instituted. I say two. For there are no more which are instituted in His Word: namely, Baptism and the Lord's Supper. All the rest is only frivolous imagination which came from the audacity and temerity of men. Behold, then, our Lord Jesus Christ, Who displays the power of His death and passion as much in Baptism as in His Holy Supper. For in Baptism we have testimony that He has washed and cleansed us of all our pollutions, so that God received us in grace as if we came before Him pure and clean. Now let us recognize that the water of Baptism has not this effect. How can a corruptible element be sufficient for the washing and purging of our souls? But it is inasmuch as the water flowed from the side of our Lord Jesus Christ. Let us come, then, to Him Who was crucified for us, if we wish that Baptism may be useful to us, if we wish to experience the fruit of it, that our faith may address itself to our Lord Jesus Christ, Who wishes that we seek all the elements of our salvation in Him, without rambling and bending here and there. And then in the Holy Supper we have testimony that Jesus Christ is our Food. And under the bread He presents to us His body, under the wine His blood. This, then, is the full perfection of salvation, when we are thus purified, and God accepts us as if we had only integrity and righteousness in us; and so we are acquitted before Him of being any longer blameworthy, since our Lord Jesus Christ has fully satisfied for us. That, then, is how we must profit from the Sacraments, apply ourselves with all our faith to our Lord Jesus Christ, and not turning to any creatures at all. That also is how we are to be made sure of what was done by the death and passion of our Lord Jesus, and let our memory be daily refreshed by it when God shows us with the eye how much He valued it that from the side of our Lord Jesus Christ there proceeded blood and water.

So this in summary is what we have to remember concerning the saying that the side of our Lord Jesus Christ was pierced. Indeed also in this word, when it is said that the Scripture was fulfilled, may we recognize what has been said at greater length already, that is, that all has been governed by the secret counsel of God, and although the guards did not know what they were doing, yet God put into effect and execution what He had pronounced both by Moses and His Prophet Zechariah. We have already seen the testimony of Exodus. St. John adds as well from the Prophet Zechariah, "They shall see Him Whom they have pierced."[7] It is true that God uses that by figure of speech, for He defies the condemners of His Word who were hardened in every rebellion and malice. Or perhaps, he says, "It seems to them that they make war against men who preach My Word, and that they can hinder them by this means. Now it is against Me that they fight, and when they thus despise and reject My Word, it is as if they wounded me by blows of a dagger; and so they shall see Him Whom they have pierced." But that was truly fulfilled in the person of our Lord Jesus Christ; for even in His human body He was pierced. That, then, is how He was declared the living God Who had spoken from all time by His Prophets, since in His person all that had been promised is seen.

Now it is said consequently that Joseph, having obtained from Pilate permission that the body of Jesus Christ might be taken down from the cross, and that it be given to him for burial, had a clean winding-sheet and bought also some aromatic ointments (indeed, for a great sum, as it appears by St. John) of myrrh and aloes, and that he buried Him in a new sepulchre which he had made for himself (sic), which was hollowed out of a rock. In this sepulchre our Lord Jesus Christ already began to show the outcome of His death, that is, He soon was to come into the glory of His resurrection, and God willed to manifest it completely. This, then, is still an infallible testimony, that, among so many confusions of what we read in the narrative which could trouble us and

7 Zechariah 12:10.

shake our faith, we perceive that God always cared for His only Son as for the Head of the Church, and for His Well-Beloved, not only in order that we might be able to hope in Him, but that we might confidently expect, since we are members of His body, that the fatherly care of God will also surely be extended to us and to each one of those who hope in Him.

However, one might ask why our Lord Jesus Christ wished to be buried so carefully. For it surely seems that such sumptuousness as aloes, myrrh, and like things was superfluous. In fact, what good is it to a dead person that he is washed or anointed or a great parade is made in honor of him?[8] It would seem, then, that this was not in harmony with the teaching of the Gospel, where it is said that we shall rise at the last day through the inestimable power of our God. So it seems that all such pomp ought to be rejected and forgotten about. Consequently, one might judge that Joseph had a foolish devotion, which would tend to obscure the hope of the resurrection. But we have to note that the Jews had such ceremonies until our Lord Jesus Christ accomplished what was required for our salvation. And the sepulchre was for that time as the sacrifices, and washings, and lights of the Temple, and all like things. For that people, according as it was uncultured,[9] had to be treated like little children. It is true that by all the world the grave is considered to be holy, and God willed that this be engraved upon the hearts of men, even of Pagans, in order that there would be no excuse at all for men to become like brutes, to have no hope of a better life. The Pagans have abused it. But be that as it may, they will be reproached for this to the last day, that they had a great care in burying the dead, that there was no nation so barbarous that they did not always make much of that. They did not know the reason of it any more than of their sacrifices, but it was a sufficient condemnation, when they remained aloof from the truth of God and they corrupted the

8 Calvin desired for himself the plainest funeral service, that he be buried in a wooden box without ornament, and that no monument should be erected over his grave.

9 *rude,* rough, harsh, rugged, unpolished, uncouth. Lack of culture was one of the flaws Calvin saw in the Romanism of his day.

testimony that He gave them, in order to draw them to faith in the heavenly life. Be that as it may, the grave in itself has always been, as it were, a mirror of the resurrection. For the bodies are put in the earth as if in keeping for a time. If there were no resurrection at all, it would be just as well to throw them away in order that they might be eaten by dogs or by savage beasts. But they were buried honorably, to show that they would not perish at all, although they did go away in decay. Especially the Jews had some ceremonies. It is true that the Egyptians surpassed them in many ways, but they were only fanfares to make a great mourning party, to bewail themselves, to tear their hair. The Egyptians, then, did that, but the devil had bewitched them so that they perverted all order. As for the Jews, who made use of the grave, it was to confirm them in the faith of the resurrection.

So, following what I began to say, our Lord Jesus was willing to be buried according to ancient custom, because He had not yet accomplished all our salvation with respect to the resurrection. It is true that the veil of the Temple was torn at His death. And by that God showed that it was the end and perfection of all things, and that the figures and shadows of the Law no longer remained. However, that was not yet apparent to the world, and there was no one who was capable of recognizing that in Jesus Christ all the figures of the Law had come to an end. For this cause, then, He still wished to be buried. So much for one item. Now we know that in the resurrection of our Lord Jesus Christ life has been acquired for us, so that we ought to go right to Him, not seeking any other means to lead us than those which He has assigned to us. We have already said that He has given us two Sacraments to serve us as full confirmation. If the manner of burial which the Jews observed were necessary for us, there is no doubt at all that Jesus Christ would have wished only that it remained permanent in His Church. But it is no longer necessary that our attention be arrested by these earthly and puerile elements. It suffices us, then, to have a simple manner of burial, leaving these aromatic ointments, which do not typify the resurrection, which has been manifested in our Lord Jesus Christ. We would only separate ourselves from

Him, if we wished to have such base instruction. For we see that St. Paul says, "If our life is on high, there we must seek it in faith and spirit,"[10] and we must be joined to our Lord Jesus.[11] Let us reach out toward Him, let us not be wrapped up in anything which might distract, hinder, or retard us from being united to Him as to our Head, since it is said that His body was the Temple of God. That, then, in summary, is what we have to remember about the grave.

There is yet to consider that He was put in a *new* sepulchre, which was not done apart from the particular providence[12] of God, for He could well have been put in a sepulchre which had served for a long time. Also Joseph of Arimathea had his ancestors, and usually in such rich and opulent houses there is a common sepulchre. But God forsaw it from another viewpoint, and willed that our Lord Jesus should be put in a new sepulchre wherein no person had ever been laid. For it also was not at all without cause that He is called the first-fruits of the resurrection and the first-born from the dead. However, one might say that many have died and have been made sharers of life before our Lord Jesus Christ. Lazarus had been raised. And we know also that Enoch and Elijah were translated[13] without natural death, and were gathered into life incorruptible. But all that depends on the resurrection of our Lord Jesus Christ. We must, then, cling to Him as the first-fruits. In the Law the fruits of a year were dedicated and consecrated to God, when they brought only a handful of wheat at the altar, and a bunch of grapes. When, then, that was offered to God, it was a general consecration of all the fruits of the year. And when also the first-born were dedicated to God, it was to declare the holiness of the line of Israel, and that God accepted it for His inheritance, that He had reserved it to Himself being satisfied with that people, as a man will be satisfied with his patrimony.[14] Also when we come to our Lord Jesus Christ, let us recognize

10 Colossians 3:1.

11 1 Corinthians 6:17.

12 *une providence singulière.*

13 *ravis,* carried away, raptured.

14 *patrimoine,* inheritance.

that in His person we are all dedicated and offered, in order that His death may give us life today, and that it may no longer be mortal as previously. This, then, is what we have to observe with respect to the new sepulchre, that the sepulchre of our Lord Jesus Christ ought to lead us to His resurrection.

However, let us look at ourselves. For although everything which ought to help our faith was accomplished in the person of the Son of God, although we have testimony of it which ought to be sufficient for us, yet in our uncouthness[15] and weakness we are still very far from coming to our Lord Jesus Christ. And for this reason let each one of us, recognizing his faults, reach toward the remedies, and let us not lose courage. We see what Nicodemus and Joseph did. Now we have to consider two things for our example. The first is that they are not yet clearly enlightened concerning the fruit of the death and passion of our Lord Jesus Christ. There is, then, some crudeness and their faith is still very small. The other, that nevertheless in such extremity they fought against all temptations, and they came to seek our Lord Jesus dead to put Him in the sepulchre, protesting that they were hoping for the blessed resurrection which had been promised to them, and they aspired to it. Since it is so, then, when we experience some feebleness in us, may that still not hinder us from taking courage. It is true that we are weak, and God could reject us if He dealt with us in strictness.[16] But when we experience these failures, let us know that He will accept our desire, although it is imperfect. Besides, today, since our Lord Jesus is raised in glory, although we must still endure here many privations and miseries, and though it seems that daily He is crucified in His members, as truly the wicked, as much as is in their power, crucify Him; let us not fail on that account, knowing that we cannot be disappointed in what is promised to us in the teaching of the Gospel, and, although we must pass through many afflictions, yet let us look always to our Head. Joseph and Nicodemus had not at all this advantage which we have today: that is, to contemplate the

15 *rudesse,* implying that anybody who had any real culture at all would, of course, be a Christian.

16 *à la rigueur.*

power of the Spirit of God which showed itself in the resurrection of our Lord Jesus Christ. Yet on that account their faith was not entirely deadened.

Now, since our Lord Jesus calls us to Himself, and with a loud voice He declares to us that He has ascended into heaven, in order to gather us all together there, let us persist constantly to seek Him and to follow Him, and let us not consider it an evil thing to die with Him to be sharers in His glory. Now St. Paul exhorts us to be conformed to Jesus Christ, not only with respect to His death but also with respect to his burial.[17] For there are some who would be content to die with our Lord Jesus for a minute of time, but at length they get tired. For this reason I said that we must die not only once, but we must suffer patiently to be buried until the end. I call it death when God wills that we endure so for His name. For though we are not at first dragged to the fire or condemned by the world, yet, when we are afflicted, there is already a species of death which we must endure patiently. But, because we are not so soon humiliated, we must be beaten for a long time, and there we must preserve and persist in patience. For as the devil never ceases to plan what is possible for him to distract and debauch us, so all our lifetime we must not cease to fight against him. Although this condition may be hard and tedious, let us wait for the time to come when God calls us to Himself, and let us never cease to make confession of our faith, and in that let us follow Nicodemus, but not in his timidity. When he came previously to the Lord Jesus Christ, he hid himself, and he did not dare to show himself a true disciple, but when he came to bury our Lord Jesus, he declared and protested that he was of the number and of the company of believers. Since it is so, let us follow him today in such constancy. And although our Lord Jesus with the doctrine of His Gospel is hated by the world, indeed they hold Him in detestation, let us not fail to adhere to Him. Let us even recognize that it will always be all our happiness and satisfaction, when God will accept our service, and let us know that, if we must lan-

---

17 Romans 6:4, Colossians 2:12.

guish in this world, the fact that our Lord Jesus has come into the glory of His resurrection is not at all in order to be separated from us, but that at the proper time He will gather us to Himself.

Besides, one must not be astonished that our Lord Jesus was raised from the dead on the third day. For it is very proper that He had some privilege above the common order of the Church. In this was also fulfilled what is said in Psalm 16, "Thou wilt not permit Thy Holy One to see corruption."[18] The body of our Lord Jesus Christ, then, had to remain incorruptible until the third day. But His time was set and established by the counsel of God His Father. On our part we have no time assigned, except the last day. So let us wait until we have languished as long as it will please God. In the end we shall know that at the proper time He will find means to restore us, after we shall have been entirely annihilated. As also St. Paul exhorts us to that when he says that Jesus Christ is the first-fruits.[19] This is to retard the ardent zeal with which we are sometimes too much carried away. For we wish to fly without wings, and we are offended if God leaves us in this world, and that at the first sign of struggle He does not withdraw us into Heaven. We wish to be led there in a chariot of fire like Elijah. Briefly, we wish to gain our triumphs before having fought. Now to resist such cupidity and these foolish desires,[20] St. Paul says that Jesus Christ is the first-fruits and we must be satisfied that in His death we have a sure pledge[21] of the resurrection. So it is, since He is seated at the right hand of God His Father, exercising all dominion both above and below, although His majesty has not yet appeared, and though our life must be hidden in Him, that we are there like poor dead persons, and that while living in this world we are like poor lost people. Nevertheless it is proper for us to suffer all that until our Lord Jesus comes. For then our life will be manifested in Him, that is, at the proper time.

---

18 Verse 10.

19 1 Corinthians 15:20, 23.

20 *à telle cupidité et à ces fols appetis.*

21 *un certain gage.*

This, then, is what we have to observe with respect to the sepulchre of our Lord Jesus Christ, until we come to the last which will show us that not only has He satisfied for all our sins, but also that having obtained victory He has acquired for us perfection of all righteousness, by which we are today acceptable to God, to have access to Him and to call upon Him in Christ's name. And in this confidence we shall bow in humble reverence before His Holy Majesty, praying to Him that He may receive us in mercy, that however poor and miserable we may be, we may not cease to have our refuge in His mercy. Although from day to day we provoke His wrath against us, and though rightly we deserve to be rejected by Him, may we wait nevertheless for Him to show the fruit and the power of the death and passion which His only Son endured, by which we have been reconciled, and may we not doubt that He is always Father to us, especially when He will do us the favor to show that we are truly His children. May we declare this in fact, in such a way that we ask nothing except to be entirely His own, as also He has bought us at such a price, and rightly we ought to be fully reformed to His service. Inasmuch as we are so weak that we do not know how to acquit ourselves of the hundredth part of our duty, still He worked in us by His Holy Spirit, because always the weaknesses of our flesh carry with them so many struggles and fights that we can only drag ourselves along, instead of walking properly.

May it please Him to strip us of all this, and may we be joined to Him.

SERMON 11

The Resurrection of Jesus Christ *

Delivered Easter Day, on Which the Holy Supper of our Lord is Celebrated

Now on the evening of the Sabbaths, on the day which begins to shine for the first of the days of the Sabbath, Mary Magdalene and the other Mary came to see the sepulchre. And behold, there was a great earthquake. For the angel of the Lord came down from heaven, and came and rolled the stone away from the door and sat on it. And his countenance was as lightning and his clothing white as snow. And the guards, because of the fear they had of him, were terrified, and became as dead men. But the angel said to the women, "Fear not. For I know that you seek Jesus who has been crucified. He is not here. For He is risen, as He said. Come, see the place where the Lord was laid. And go away quickly, and tell His disciples that He is raised from the dead. And behold, He goes before you into Galilee. You will see Him there. Behold, I have told you." And they departed quickly from the tomb with fear and great joy, and they ran to tell the news to His disciples.. But as they were going to announce it to His disciples, behold. Jesus met them, saying, "All hail!" And they approached Him and grasped His feet and bowed before Him. Then Jesus said to them, "Fear not. Go, tell my brothers to go into Galilee and there they will see me." — MATTHEW 28:1-10

ONE MAY find it strange at first glance that our Lord Jesus wishing to give proof of His resurrection, appeared rather to women than to His disciples. But in that we have to consider that He wished to prove the humility of our faith. For we must not be grounded in human wisdom, but we must receive in absolute obedience what we know to proceed

* From: *Corpus Reformatorum, Calvini Opera*, vol. 46, pp. 943-954.

from Him. On the other hand, there is no doubt that He wished to punish the disciples, when He sent them women to instruct them, because the instruction which they had received from His mouth had been of no profit to them when it came to the test. For look how they are scattered. They desert their Master; they are confused by fear. And what good has it done them to be for more than three years in the school of the Son of God? Such cowardice, then, deserved great punishment, even that they might be entirely deprived of the knowledge which they had received before, inasmuch as they had, so to speak, trampled it under foot and buried it. Now our Lord Jesus did not wish to punish them severely, but to show them their fault by gentle correction He appointed women to be their teachers. They had been chosen beforehand to publish the Gospel to the whole world (they are really the first teachers of the Church), but since they were so cowardly as to be found thus bewildered, so much so that their faith was, as it were, deadened, it is entirely proper that they should know that they are not worthy to hear any teaching from the mouth of our Lord Jesus Christ. Notice, then, why they are sent back to women until they have better recognized their faults, and Jesus Christ has restored them to their position and privilege, but by grace. Besides (as I have said), all of us in general are urged to receive the testimony which is sent to us by God, even if the persons who speak are of little importance or if they have no credit or reputation in the eyes of the world. As in fact, when a man is elected or appointed to be a notary public or a public officer what he does will be received as authentic. One would not say this or that to contradict him. For the office gives him respect among men. And will God have less pre-eminence than earthly princes, if He ordains only those whom He pleases to be His witnesses, from whom one receives whatever He should say without contradiction or reply? Certainly it must be so unless we want to be rebels even against God Himself. This, then, we have to remember in the first place.

Besides, let us note also, although our Lord Jesus Christ appeared to women and they held the first degree of honor, He Himself gave sufficient testimony to His resurrection, so that, if we do not close our eyes, stop up our ears and by certain malice will to be hardened and stupid, we have an abundant certainty of this article of faith, as also it is of great importance. For when St. Paul refutes the incredulity of those who still doubted if Jesus Christ was raised, he mentions not only the women, but he mentions Peter and James, then the twelve Apostles, then more than five hundred disciples to whom our Lord Jesus appeared. How, then, can we excuse our malice and rebellion if we do not give credit to more than five hundred witnesses who were chosen for that not on man's part but from the sovereign Majesty of God. And it was not only just once that our Lord Jesus declared to them that he was living but many times. Thus, what the Apostles have doubted and their incredulity ought to serve us for a greater confirmation. For, if at first appearance they had believed the resurrection of our Lord Jesus Christ, one might allege that it would have been too simple. But they are so slow that Jesus Christ has to reproach them for being blockheaded people with no faith, for having minds so heavy and thick that they understand nothing. When, then, the Apostles were so unready to receive this article of faith, that ought to make us all the more certain. For, that it was then brought to them as by force is good reason now for us to follow. As it is said, "You have seen, Thomas, and you have believed, but blessed are those who believe without seeing." Now, then, when it is thus spoken that our Lord Jesus appeared to two women, let us think of what is said from the other passage from Saint Paul that we may know that we need not stumble at those who speak to give credit to what they say according to the importance or condition of their persons, but rather we ought to raise our eyes and our senses on high to subject ourselves to God, who well deserves to have entire superiority over us and that we be captives under His Word. For if we are not teachable it is certain that we shall never profit from the teaching of the Gospel. And it ought not to be ascribed to foolishness when we receive what God declares and testifies to us. For when we shall have learned by obedience to profit in His school and in the faith, we shall know that the perfection of all wisdom is that we be thus obedient to Him.

Now let us come to this story which is here narrated. It is said that "Mary Magdalene with her companion came to the sepulchre the first day of the sabbaths," that is, the first day of the week. For the Jews keep Saturday, which they call Sabbath, as the day of rest, as also the word signifies, and then they name the days following in all the week, first day after Sabbath, second day, etc. Now because they count the beginning of the day as at sundown, it is said that the Marys bought aromatic ointments after the sabbath was finished and made their preparations to come the next day to the sepulchre. And they were not only two. It is true that St. John names only Mary Magdalene. St. Matthew names two of them, and we see by St. Luke that there were a large number there. But all this agrees very well. For Mary Magdalene did the leading, and the other Mary is here named explicitly because she followed most closely. Meanwhile, several have come to anoint the body of our Lord Jesus, but notably it is here said that they have come to see the sepulchre to know if there would be access and entrance. That is why two are here specially marked.

St. Matthew adds that the angel appeared to them while the two were there. But because only one spoke the word, that is why he is thus specially named. Finally as they go away, they meet our Lord Jesus Who sends them to His disciples in order that all may be assembled in Galilee, wishing to show them there His resurrection, and this, because the city of Jerusalem had deprived itself by its wickedness from such a testimony. True it is that the Fountain of Life was still there, for out of it proceeded the Law and the Word of God, but meanwhile our Lord Jesus did not wish to reveal Himself to His disciples in that city, when the wickedness was still so recent there. On the other hand, He also wished to conform to their hardness of heart. For they were, as it were, seized with astonishment so that the sense of sight would not have been enough unless He had taken them apart, and had shown Himself in such a way that they would have been fully convinced.

Now we see again here how the women who are named are not yet permitted to worship our Lord Jesus Christ as their Master, although they were troubled by His death. Consequently, we can well judge that the Word of God was always implanted in their hearts. For although their faith was feeble, they seek our Lord Jesus at the sepulchre. There is also in them a certain ignorance which cannot be excused. For they should already have raised their spirits on high, waiting for the resurrection which had been promised them — to which the third day was especially assigned. They were, then, so occupied that they did not understand the principal thing—namely, that our Lord Jesus had to obtain victory over death to acquire for us life and salvation. I say that is the principal thing, because without it the Gospel would be nothing (as says St. Paul) and our faith would be entirely destroyed. Thus these poor women, however much they may know the Gospel which has been preached to them to be the pure truth, nevertheless, are so troubled and confused that they do not understand that He was to rise, and thus they come to the sepulchre with their aromatic ointments. There is, then, a fault which is to be condemned. But their service is nonethe-less agreeable to God, for He excuses their astonishment until He has corrected them. In that let us see when our Lord approves what we do, still we must not put that to our credit to say that we have merited it, while, altogether on the contrary, it is of His abundant grace if He acknowledges that which was not worthy to be offered to Him. For there will always be occasion to condemn our works when God examines them strictly, forasmuch as they will always be tainted with some spot. But God spares us and does not refuse what we come to offer Him, whatever weakness or fault there may be, seeing that all is purified by faith and we know that it is not without cause that we are acceptable to Him in Jesus Christ. This, then, we have to observe.

However, let us recognize also that there surely must have been another fragrance, much better, much stronger, in the sepulchre of our Lord Jesus Christ, than that of these ointments of which mention is made. We have already mentioned that the Jews were accustomed to anoint the body in order to be confirmed in the hope of the resurrection and of the heavenly life. It was to show that the bodies do not decay to such an extent that they cannot be preserved until the last day, and so that God may restore them. But the body of our Lord Jesus Christ had to be exempt from all such decay. Now the spices could not effect that, but, because it had been declared that God would not suffer that His Holy and Godly One should see corruption, that is why by a miracle our Lord Jesus has been preserved from all decay. Besides, because he has been exempt from corruption, we are now certain and assured of the glory of the resurrection, which has already appeared to us in His Person. We see, then, now, that the fragrance of the sepulchre and of the resurrection of our Lord Jesus Christ has permeated even to us, so that we may become alive by it. Now what follows? That we may go no longer to look at the sepulchre as these women, by whose ignorance and weakness we are served, but that we may soar upward, since He calls us and invites us there, since He has shown us the way, and He has declared to us that He has entered into possession of His heavenly Kingdom to prepare us a room and a place there when by faith we shall find Him there.

But we must also note what St. Matthew adds: The angel, says he, appeared, who frightened the guards so that they became as dead men. The women were likewise frightened, but the angel after that administered the remedy. "As for you," said he, "Fear not, for you seek Jesus Who was crucified. He is risen, as He said." Here we see how God accepts the affection and the zeal of these women so that He corrects, however, what He does not approve of. I mean that He corrects it through the mouth of the angel who is there in His name. We have said that it is by singular kindness that God receives our service when it is imperfect although He might have it in abhorrence. He receives from us, then, what is of no value as a father will receive from his children what otherwise would be regarded as rubbish and jest. Behold, I say, how generous God is toward us. But, on the other hand, it is true that He does not wish men to take pleasure in and to make light of their faults. Therefore, the angel corrects this fault on the part of the women. Although their intention is good, still they are condemned for their particular fault. Therefore, St. Luke records that they have been more harshly rebuked. "Why seek ye the living among the dead?"

But here we have to observe that the guards, as men who are unbelieving and wicked, who had no fear of God or religion, were seized with fear, possibly even, as it were, with a spirit of frenzy. The women, to be sure, are afraid but they immediately receive consolation. Behold, then, how terrible the majesty of God is to those to whom it appears. That is why we feel our weakness when God declares Himself to us, and while at first we were puffed up with presumption and we were so bold that we no longer thought that we were mortal men, when God gives us any sign of His presence, we must necessarily be crushed, and know what our condition is, that is, that we are only dust and ashes, that all our virtues are only smoke that floats away and vanishes. This, then, is common to all, whether good or bad. Besides, when God has thus terrified unbelievers, He leaves them there as reprobate men, because they are not worthy of experiencing His goodness in any way. Therefore, also, they flee His presence, they are angry and gnash their teeth and are so enraged that they lose all sense and reason, becoming men entirely brutish. The faithful, after having been frightened, rise up and take courage, because God consoles them and gives them joy. This fear, then, which the faithful feel in the presence of the majesty of God is none other than a first step in humility in order that they may pay Him the homage which is His due, and that they may submit to Him, knowing that they are nothing, in order to seek all their good in Him alone.

This, then, is why the angel says, "Fear not." This word is worthy of notice. For it is even as though he had said, "I leave this rabble in their confusion, for they are not worthy of any mercy, but now I turn to you and bring you a message of joy. Be, then, delivered from this fear, because you seek Jesus Christ." Since that is true, let us learn to seek our Lord Jesus, not (as I have said) in such hardness of heart as these women of whom it is here spoken (as also there is no longer any occasion to go to search for Him at the sepulchre), let us come by faith straight to Him without pretense. And in so doing so let us be sure that this message belongs to us and is addressed to us. We must come boldly and without fear, but not without respect (for we must be touched with fear in order to adore the majesty of God). But, anyway, let us not be frightened as if we were altogether overcome with distrust. Let us know, then, that the Son of God will adapt Himself to our limitations when we come to Him in faith, and we shall even find in Him cause for consolation and joy, inasmuch as it is for our profit and salvation that He has acquired lordship and dominion of the heavenly life.

However, the women went away with great joy and great fear. Here again the weakness of their faith is shown. I have said that the purpose toward which they aspired was good, but they did not take the right road, as we learn from the fact that they are cowardly, and that they cannot make up their minds to believe or not to believe the Resurrection. Although they had heard it spoken of many times, still they cannot conquer their feelings to come to a final conclusion that it is no longer necessary to look for our Lord Jesus at the sepulchre. Note, then, the origin of this fear. Thus we see that it is a mistaken sentiment. It is true (as I have suggested) that we must fear God to yield reverence toward His majesty, to obey Him and to be entirely abased, so that He may be exalted in His glory; to keep every mouth shut, so that He alone may be recognized righteous, wise, and all-powerful. But this fear mentioned here is, in the second place, evil and to be condemned, for it is caused by the confusion of these poor women. Still, though they may see and hear the angel speak, it seems to them almost like a dream. Now by that we are warned that God works in us so often when we do not perceive whether we have profited or not. For there is so much ignorance in us that, as it were, clouds prevent us from coming to perfect clearness, and we are entangled in many fancies. Briefly, it seems that all the teaching of God is almost useless. Nevertheless, we find some apprehension mixed with it which makes us feel that God has worked in our hearts. Even though we have only a little spark of grace, let us not lose courage. Rather, let us pray to God that He may add to this little which He has begun, and that He may make us to believe and that He may confirm us, until we are brought to perfection, from which we are still very far. Even though the fact that the women had been thus occupied by fear and joy were condemned as a fault, we see that God always governed them by His Holy Spirit and that this message which was borne to them by the angel was not entirely useless.

Now we have to pass on. Our Lord Jesus appeared to them on the road, and said to them, "Fear not, but go, tell My brothers to gather together in Galilee and there they will see Me." We see still better in this passage how the Son of God draws us by degrees to Himself until we are fully confirmed, as is needful for us. It was surely enough that the women heard the message by the mouth of the angel, for he bore marks that he was sent by God. His countenance was like lightning. It is true that the whiteness of a robe and like things do not express vividly the majesty of God. However, these women had a very sure testimony that this was not a mortal man who spoke, but a heavenly angel. This testimony, then, might well have been sufficient for them, but, even so, the certainty was so much greater when they saw our Lord Jesus, whom they first recognized to be the Son of God and His unchangeable truth. This, then, is to ratify more plainly what they had heard before from the mouth of the angel. And that is also how we grow into faith. For from the beginning we know neither what power nor efficacy there is in the Word of God. But if one teaches us, and well, we learn something, and yet it is almost nothing. But little by little it makes its impression on us by His Holy Spirit and in the end He shows us that it is He Who speaks. Then we are resolved so that not only do we have some knowledge, but we are persuaded in such a way that when the devil schemes everything he possibly can he is not able to shake our faith, inasmuch as we have this conviction: that the Son of God is our teacher and we lean upon Him, knowing that He has entire mastery over us and that He merits entire sovereign authority. We see that in these women. It is true that God does not work in all the same way. Some from the very first will be so attracted that they will perceive that God has exerted an extraordinary power on their behalf. But often we shall be taught in such a way that our rudeness and weakness will be plainly seen, so that by it we are so much more admonished to glorify God and to recognize that it is from Him that we have everything.

Let us now consider the word that we have quoted, "Go, tell my brothers to meet me in Galilee." We see that the Son of God appeared here to Mary and her companion not only to reveal Himself to seven or eight, but He wished this message to be published to the Apostles, that it might now be communicated to us that we should share in it. In fact, without that, of what profit would this story of the Resurrection be to us? But when it is said that the Son of God has so manifested Himself, and that He wished the fruit of it to be communicated to all the world, that is how we gain so much better a conception. So, then, let us be assured that our Lord Jesus wished that we might be made certain of His resurrection, because in that also rests all hope of our salvation and of our righteousness, when we truly know that our Lord Jesus is risen. Not only has He purged us of all our filth by His death and passion, but He could not remain in such a state of weakness. He had to show the power of His Holy Spirit and He had to be declared Son of God by rising from the dead, as St. Paul says, both in the first chapter of Romans, and in other passages. Thus it is that we must now be assured that our Lord Jesus, being raised, wishes us to come to Him and that the road might be opened to us. And He does not wait for us to look for Him, but He has provided that we might be called by the preaching of the Gospel and that this message might be spoken by the mouths of His heralds whom He had chosen and elected. This being so, let us recognize that today we share in the righteousness which we have in our Lord Jesus Christ, to reach the heavenly glory, since He does not wish to be separated from us.

And that is why He calls His disciples His brothers. Surely this is an honorable title. And so it was reserved for those whom our Lord Jesus had engaged as His servants. And there is no doubt that He has used this word to show the brotherly relation which He wanted to sustain toward them. And so He is also united to us, as it is better declared by St. John. In fact, we are driven to what is said in Psalm 22, from which this passage is taken: I will declare Thy name to my brothers, which passage the Apostle, applying to the Person of our Lord Jesus Christ, included not only the twelve Apostles in calling them brothers of Jesus Christ, but bestows the title on all of us in general who follow the Son of God, and He wishes that we share such an honor. That is why, also when our Lord Jesus says, "I am going to My God and to your God, to My Father and to your Father," it is not spoken for a small number of people, but it is addressed to the whole multitude of believers. Now our Lord Jesus, although He is our eternal God, does none-the-less in His capacity as Mediator abase Himself to be near us, and to have everything in common with us, that is with regard to His human nature. For, although He is by nature the Son of God and we are only adopted, and that by grace, still this fellowship is permanent, that He Who is the Father of our Lord Jesus Christ, through Him is also ours, to be sure, in different aspects. For we need not be raised as high as our Head. There must not be any confusion here. If in a human body the head were not above all the members, it would be a freak, it would be a confused mass. It is reasonable also that our Lord Jesus should keep His sovereign position, since He is the only Son of God, that is, by nature. But this does not prevent our being joined to Him in brotherhood, so that we can call upon God boldly in full confidence of being answered by Him, since we have personal and familiar access to Him. We see, then, what this word means, when our Lord Jesus calls His disciples brothers, namely, that it was so that we have today this privilege in common with them, that is, by means of faith. And that does not take away from the power and majesty of the Son of God, when He unites Himself with creatures so miserable as we are, and He is willing to be, as it were, classed with us. For we should be all the more filled with joy, as we see what goodness He displays, as we see that in rising from the dead He has acquired for us the heavenly glory, to acquire which for us He also had abased Himself, yes, was even willing to become as nothing. Now, since our Lord Jesus condescends to acknowledge us as His brothers so that we may have access to God, let us seek Him, and come to Him with full confidence, being so cordially invited. That is, as one might even say, He uses not only speech to draw us, but He adds also the visible Sacrament, so that we may be led as we are able to follow. And in fact, however weak and slow we may be, still we cannot excuse our slackness if we do not come to our Lord Jesus Christ. Here is the table which He has prepared for us. And to what purpose? It is not to satisfy our bodies and our bellies, although even in that God declares that He has a fatherly care for us, and our Lord Jesus Christ shows that truly He is the life of the world. If we take daily our rest and food, even in that our Lord Jesus declares to us His goodness. But He shows a special consideration in this table which is set for us here, for it is to show us that we are brothers of our Lord Jesus Christ, that is to say that as He united us to Himself (as He says in the 17th chapter of St. John) He has also united us to God His Father, and fully declares to us that He is our meat and drink, that we are fed with His own substance to have all our spiritual life in Him. And that is more than it would be if he called us His brothers a hundred times.

So then, let us realize the unity that we have with our Lord Jesus Christ, that is, He is willing to have a common life with us, and that what He has may be ours, even that He wishes to dwell in us, not in imagination, but in fact; not in an earthly, but in a spiritual manner; and in any case, that He so works by the power of His Holy Spirit that we are united to Him more than are the members of a body. And just as the root of a tree sends its substance and its power through all the branches, so we draw substance and life from our Lord Jesus Christ. And that is also why St. Paul says that our Paschal Lamb has been crucified and sacrificed, so nothing more now remains but that we keep the feast and that we take part in the sacrifice. And as in old time in the Law when the sacrifice was offered they ate, now also we must come and take our meat and spiritual food in this Sacrifice which has been offered for our redemption. It is true that we do not devour Jesus Christ in His flesh, He does not enter us under our teeth, as the papists have imagined, but we receive bread as a sure and infallible token that our Lord Jesus feeds us spiritually with His body; we receive a drop of wine to show that we are spiritually sustained by the blood of our Lord Jesus Christ. But let us observe well what St. Paul adds, that just as under the figures of the Law it was not permitted to eat bread that was leavened and of which the dough was bitter, now that we are no longer under such shadows, we must put away the leaven of malice, of wickedness and of all our corruptions, and have bread or cake (says he) which has no bitterness in it. And how? In purity and sincerity. When, then, we come to approach this Holy Table, by which the Son of God shows us that He is our meat, that He gives Himself to us as our full and entire nourishment, and He wishes that now we participate in the sacrifice which He has once for all offered for our salvation, we must see to it that we do not bring to it our corruptions and pollutions to be mixed with it but that we renounce them, and seek only to be fully purified, so that our Lord Jesus may own us as members of His body, and that by this means also we may be partakers of His life. That is how today we must make use of this Holy Supper which is prepared for us. That is, that it may lead us to the death and passion of our Lord Jesus Christ, and then to His resurrection, and that we may be so assured of life and salvation, as by the victory which He has obtained in rising from the dead righteousness is given to us, and the gate of paradise has been opened to us, so that we may boldly approach our God, and offer ourselves before Him, knowing that always He will receive us as His children.

Now we shall bow in humble reverence before the majesty of our God.

SERMON 12

First Sermon on the Ascension of Our Lord Jesus Christ *

We have made the first discourse, O Theophilus, of all the things that Jesus began to do and to teach, until the day when he was received into heaven, after by the Holy Spirit he had given commandment to the Apostles whom he had elected. To whom also he showed himself alive (after he had suffered) by many proofs, appearing to them, and speaking of the Kingdom of God, during forty days. And having gathered them together, he commanded them that they should not depart from Jerusalem, but that they should wait for the promise of the Father, "Which," he said, "you have heard from me." —ACTS 1:1-4

BECAUSE our faith must be founded upon God and upon His truth, St. Luke here declares that Jesus Christ did not send His Apostles to teach what seemed good to them; but He put His Word in their mouths, and He gave them certain instruction in it, in order that they might bear a faithful message; indeed, of which we would have no occasion to doubt. So then, when today the Gospel is preached to us, we ought to be assured that it is the charge which God committed to His Apostles, and that we must receive it all as coming from Him; as in fact it proceeds from Him. Yet in order that we may have greater reverence for the Gospel, it is said not only that Jesus Christ gave it, but that it was *by the Holy Spirit.* For although Jesus Christ is true natural Son of God, also He is man, and has assumed our flesh and our nature. Now under shadow of that (as the world is wicked) they tried to find pretext to despise this doctrine or not to hold it as so important. That is why St. Luke pronounces

* From: *Corpus Reformatorum, Calvini Opera,* vol. 48, pp. 585-596.

that what the Apostles have to teach proceeds not only from Jesus Christ, but it has also proceeded from the Holy Spirit. We see now that the charge to preach the Gospel is Divine, and that it did not come from men, but from God Who established it.

However, we must also note that the summary of the Gospel is comprehended in these two words: namely, what Jesus Christ *taught* and what He *did*, so that to be Christians, we must be instructed in this doctrine which was brought to us by Jesus Christ, and also that we may have complete confirmation. For not only has He spoken, but He has accomplished all things necessary for our salvation. Besides because the principal thing He did for our salvation is His death and His resurrection, consequently that is what is spoken of. St. Luke, then, says that Jesus Christ *"after having suffered, showed Himself alive to His disciples,"* indeed, with many proofs. And not without cause; for when the promises of God will have been recited to us, our faith will always be in suspense, until we are assured of His grace. Wherefore we cannot be without the pledge which He gives us; namely, that Jesus Christ suffered for our redemption, and bore the pain due to our sins. We see, then, that St. Luke does not speak here in vain of proofs which were given to make us certain that Jesus Christ rose from the dead. For this is what St. Paul says in I Corinthians 15. "If Jesus Christ is not raised, our faith is futile, the Gospel is preached in vain, we have no more hope than beasts."[1] By that we see that the end of our hope is that Jesus Christ was raised from the dead. In fact, it is the victory which He acquired. Yes, to show us that He is master both of life and of death.[2] St. Paul says that Jesus Christ died for our sins,[3] and if He had remained in death, what hope could we have in Him? But behold His resurrection, which is the triumph He achieved over death, in order that we could hope in Him. St. Peter, to show us the confidence which we ought to have in Jesus Christ, af-

1 A paraphrase of 1 Corinthians 15:14..
2 Romans 14:9.
3 1 Corinthians 15:3.

firms nothing else than His resurrection.[4] Let us note, then, that when St. Luke says that Jesus Christ showed Himself alive, he speaks of a thing that was required for the assurance of our salvation. Wherefore, if we wish to have the principal thing of Christianity, we must accept this resurrection, by which He has acquired for us life and salvation, and by which He showed Himself to be the true Son of God.

Besides, let us learn also, since St. Luke says that Jesus Christ gave such proofs that He was raised, not at all to leave in doubt what has been so well proved by God. If, then, now we are not entirely persuaded of the resurrection of Jesus Christ, that comes from our ingratitude. For He did not intend that His resurrection should not be sufficiently indicated to us. Also St. Luke uses a word which signifies an argument which leads to such a great proof.[5] In fact, we see how the gospel-writer labored on this. For when it comes to narrating the resurrection, they bring forth all the circumstances, and then they recite so many testimonies, how He spoke, how He was touched; and they declared that it was not an apparition or vision, by which they could be troubled later. This, then, is what we must recognize, that since they so labored the point, we must not have any doubt about it, but it is proper for us to hold their account as entirely certain, since they have such proof. And yet upon this point where St. Luke says that Jesus Christ showed Himself alive after He had endured death, and there had been such certain proofs, let us learn that we must have a foundation for it which can never be shaken. Also that, since He was victorious by His death, He now has His hand stretched out to lead us to salvation. And whenever we wish to have certainty of our faith, we must not come to any creatures, but we must behold as in a mirror, that just as Jesus Christ was raised and conquered death, He opened heaven in order for us to enter by His leading.

He adds that showing Himself *He expounded the Kingdom of God* with His friends. By which we have to note that the

---

4 1 Peter 1:3.

5 *l'approbation quant et quant. Quant et quant* is from the Latin *quantus quantus,* sometimes used for *quantus-cumque.*

commission, which was given to those from whom we have the doctrine of the Gospel, was not by a word nor for a minute of time, but that for a long time they were instructed, as it was fitting. And having received a complete teaching, and an authority to distribute it, they have faithfully announced it to us. That is what must be noted in his word. Now it says that Jesus Christ showed Himself to His Apostles, and that showing Himself He expounded the Kingdom of God to them. But one must know what St. Luke means by the Kingdom of God. He does not mean by this Kingdom of God the life eternal, as is commonly taken, and as one could here superficially take it, to say, that the Kingdom of God is what we wait for by hope. But St. Luke takes it for the spiritual government by which Jesus Christ keeps us in His obedience, until He has entirely reformed us to His image, and, having robbed us of this mortal body, He places us in heaven. That is what St. Luke wishes to say. But to see it more clearly, let us consider the opposite of the Kingdom of God, that is, the life of men who are given to their corrupt nature. In fact, if Jesus withdrew Himself from us, leaving us to go as we would wish, we would be outside the Kingdom of God. For the Kingdom of God presupposes a reformation. But we bear only miseries and corruptions in this world. Briefly we are wandering beasts and the devil rules over us, and he subjects us just as he wills. That is what man is until God has reformed him. So then, let us be apprised by that, to know what we are until Jesus Christ reforms us. What then? Do we wish a greater evil than this, that Satan possess us so and be our master? So we see (I say) what we are, until God, according to His infinite goodness, has extended His hand to us, indeed, to introduce us into His Kingdom, and be subjects to Him and to His justice. However, we see also how we ought to esteem this grace when it is given to us; and when Jesus Christ draws us to Himself. This is the felicity of men: that God be their King. It is true, although kings desire kingdoms to gain glory, nevertheless when there will be a Prince who will be endowed with excellent graces, each one will consider himself happy to be under his subjection. But when Jesus Christ rules over us, we have a King Who is not only endowed with many and excellent graces, but Who rules over us for our profit. In fact, do we bring Him any profit on our part? For we can neither add any more nor take away from Him. So we see that what I have said is very true, that we are blessed when God establishes His Royal throne in our midst to govern us.

This, then, is what we are taught in the second place: namely, to prize and esteem such a benefit when God gives it to us. Now the means is by His Gospel. Also that is why Jesus Christ spoke so often of the Gospel, calling it the Kingdom of God.[6] For if we do not adhere to it, we are rebels against God and are excluded from all His benefits. For we cannot be sharers in it until we are reformed. That is what the Gospel does by calling us to Jesus Christ, and by showing us how we must be regenerated by His Holy Spirit. Since it is so, then when the Gospel is preached to us, it is in order that we may be reformed to Jesus Christ; and that everything that is of us may be cast down, and that Jesus Christ may raise us by His grace. It is not, then, without cause that the Gospel is called "the Kingdom of God." In fact, as without that the devil has dominion, on account of which he is also called "the king of this world," so when Jesus Christ causes His Gospel to be preached in a country, it is as if He said, "I wish to have dominion over you and to be your King." But that is not to say that all those who are in the country where the Gospel is are subjects to God. For we see also how among them some raise themselves and show the iniquity which was previously hidden in them; others despise the doctrine, and there is no fruit at all of the Kingdom of God in them. But even so, Jesus Christ always has some company wherever the Gospel is preached. Why so? For He is not King without subjects. However, we can conclude that it is an inestimable benefit when God presents to us His Gospel. For what do we wish more than when Jesus Christ says to us, "Here am I. I take you into My charge, in order that you may be under My wings and under My protection"?

6 i. e., Matthew 4:23, 9:35, 24:14, Mark 1:14. "The Gospel of the Kingdom" can also be translated "the Gospel, which is the Kingdom."

What do we wish more than that? Now by the Gospel we have testimony that all that is given to us. That, then, is certain that when Jesus Christ so introduces us into His Kingdom, and receives us to Himself, it is furthermore to clothe us with immortality and incorruption, in order that we should enter into this glory which He has promised us. When, then, we receive this Gospel, it is that we may enter into this Kingdom of God.

But what? It is only an entrance! We must march further in it. It is what He does when He withdraws us from this wretched captivity of sin; and we have the liberty which He promised us. So, then, it is not all to have entered, but we must follow further, until we are fully united to Jesus Christ. In fact, we see that, although God has illumined us by His Holy Spirit, and though we desire to walk in His fear, and to know His goodness to put our confidence in it, yet there is still so much miserable infirmity in us, that we have to fight against many temptations; and we are often conquered. What of it, then? Is it enough to have entered? Not at all; but we must recognize that our life is a road[7] upon which we must always march until we have come to our Lord Jesus Christ. So the Kingdom of God must increase more and more, until we are stripped of sin. For we experience sufficiently every day how necessary it is that we be united to God as we ought. It is, then, a sign that God does not reign here as He ought. For if He reigned here, there would be neither nerve nor vein which did not unite us to Him. On the contrary we see so much rebellion when we wish to do what God teaches us. Seeing, then, that there is still such a resistance in us against God and His justice, it is a sign that He does not have dominion over us peaceably. For all that we have, indeed, even to the end of our nails, ought to lead to this — that the glory of God appeared and shone everywhere. On the contrary, from the top of the head to the feet, we see all resistance in us. That is how we can see that the Kingdom of God is not fully accomplished. Yet we are admonished to march forward until God is to us all in all: namely, that He fills us

---

7 *une voye,* a way. Lat., *via.* Cf. Acts 22:4, 24:14, 22.

so with Himself that we are emptied of ourselves, even that we are divested of this body, and that we are raised in this glory which He has promised us.

The words, then, that Jesus Christ spoke to His Apostles, of the Kingdom of God, lead to this — that we renounce ourselves and all that is ours, that Jesus Christ raise His throne there, that He lead us, that we be entirely conformed to His justice, and that we seek only to follow Him as our sovereign King. Now I say that all this is addressed to us. Why? Because the Apostles have been taught not only for themselves, but for us. Let us note, then, that when the Gospel is announced to us, it is in order that we may leave this world; namely, all the wicked affections that we have in us, and all the vanities which hold us here below. We must be entirely changed and God must give us a new life. This is how we ought to profit by the Gospel that it may be truly the Kingdom of God, and that it may have such authority over us as belongs to it. However, let us recognize that God does not call us to Himself to hold us in a static condition, but that He may urge us on always, until He has led us to perfection; making known in us that the present life is, as it were, a sea full of all miseries. That is how Jesus tends to lead us into the heavenly Kingdom after we have entered into the Kingdom of God in this world.

He adds, that *He forbade them* to depart from Jerusalem until they had received the promise of God. All this is narrated for the building up of our faith. For we see how necessary it is that this point be assured and made certain to us; namely, that the doctrine of the Gospel was not invented by men, but that God sent it from heaven. This, then, must be put beyond all doubt. How will it be, unless it be well shown us and made very sure that Jesus Christ so sent His Apostles that they were not led at all by their own impulse, by their counsel, or by their will; but that God sent them, and dictated to them their lesson, and that they had intelligence of this doctrine, not by their senses, but by the Holy Spirit? One must note, then, that St. Luke says here, that He often expounded this doctrine to them, in order that they might be so much better informed on it and they might not go astray. Beyond that he says they would have to be illuminated by the Holy Spirit, in order that they might be emptied of all human wisdom, and that it might be known that their doctrine was a work of God. Let us note that, then, in order that our faith may be always fixed upon God, as an anchor, to be firm. For among creatures we shall not find anything which does not flow like water, and our faith will be poorly founded there. But when it shall be in God, we are not at all subject to wavering, but we shall remain firm. That is why it was forbidden to the Apostles to depart from Jerusalem until they had received the promise. In that we see their obedience, for according to the reason of men they could have replied, "How is this? Are we not Apostles of God? Have we not authority to preach His Word? Do we not know how to execute our office?" They had some reason to say this. For what purpose had God instituted them in this office, unless they were to perform it? But they knew that it was He Whom they must obey. Woe to the man who wishes to advance and get to work before God drives him to it. On the contrary, when God sends him; he must not strive at all, but say, "Lord, here am I, use me." That is how St. Luke shows that the Apostles were rendered obedient to Jesus Christ when He forbade them to leave Jerusalem until they had received the promise of God. By that we see that the grace of the Holy Spirit had already worked in them. For a little before that they were bewildered, they left their Master, they no longer knew what the assistance of God was, and His safekeeping. They let themselves be scattered by Satan. But why? Then God exercised toward them the grace of hearing His voice, now He needs only make a gesture with His finger, and they obey. If He forbids them something, they do not attempt it. But on the contrary, when He commands them to march, there is neither resistance nor difficulty which holds them back.

So then, we see that God must work in us to bring us to such subjection. For otherwise, when He will say "Hold back" we will wish to march, and when He will wish us to begin to march forward, we shall fall back. That is how we are by our nature. We have such a good example of it in the Jews. For if we read how they behaved themselves, even after having been delivered from Egypt, we find in them a great ingratitude. For when God commands them to march against their enemies, and promises to them that He will give them victory, they are not willing to march, but they murmur against God, "Indeed, where are we going? It seems that He wishes to destroy us, and sends us like sheep to the slaughter-house." Behold, their rebellion. On the contrary, when God says to them, "Do not move," they wish to march, and no one can hold them back. "And why?" they say. "We are losing time. Shall we not march?" That is how men wish to march when God forbids them, and when He says, "March," there is no one who wishes to move a pace. Briefly, it seems that men wish to struggle hard to contradict God. This is how they are. Their boldness is like a frenzy, they are strong, as a lunatic will be strong enough, even to murder both himself and others. For when God wishes to restrain them they are furious, and they wish to kill everyone On the contrary, when God incites them to march, they are so cowardly that there is not a single finger which He can move. Yet we have to pray to God that He will exercise grace towards us, that like the Apostles we may be stopped when He commands it, and that we may march when He speaks.

That is why He has given to each one His office and His charge. When He ordained families, He declared what authority the man had over the woman and over his family, and what obedience the woman owes to her husband, and children to their parents. So He gave the Law to each one. So it is when He ordained government. He shows to the Magistrates what is their office, and how they ought to use the authority which is given to them. To the Ministers of His word similarly, He has given them their lesson in writing. That is how Jesus Christ has so well regulated us, that if we look to Him we shall not attempt anything except what He commands us. We see that St. Paul says that everything that is done without faith is sin.[8] Now if God had left us in doubt about what we have to do, we could do nothing but

8 Romans 14:23.

sin continually. And yet He has given us our rule of what we have to do, and of what we have to leave undone. Let us consider, then, how to rule ourselves by Him, without attempting anything from our foolish heads.

Besides, we see that the Apostles remained in Jerusalem, since Jesus Christ has told them to do so, indeed, although they knew that God had ordained them in this calling. And even though Jesus Christ had given them the Holy Spirit by breathing upon them, yet they knew that they were not yet equipped as they needed to be, but they wait for the promise of the Father. This promise (as we shall see later) was the Holy Spirit. Why did they wait for it? It is for us. We see, here, then, that Jesus Christ having ascended into heaven always cares for us, and that from there He assists us; and He is not so removed from us that He does not keep us company by His grace to govern us. That is why St. Luke says that He was received on high after, by the Holy Spirit, He had given commandment to the Apostles whom He had elected. It was not, then, that He went away without thinking of us. What then? He gave charge to His Apostles, and showed them how they should conduct themselves after having received the Holy Spirit. Now we have here a pledge that never shall we be destitute of His assistance, provided that we cling to Him. Besides, it is a great consolation for us that Jesus Christ, having ascended into heaven, has all authority in His hand, and is above all creatures, being established lieutenant of God in order to govern everything both above and below. Now to better profit from that, let us note that Jesus Christ, being so exalted by God that all creatures are put in subjection to Him, is however our Head, and that this great dominion and empire which He has profits us, indeed, if we are His members. But He cannot be our Head unless we have true union with Him. This, then, is wherein consists all the assurance of our salvation. It is, that since Jesus, having ascended on high, has dominion over everything, indeed, so that even the Angels are subject to Him, they and all creatures will serve us by that token. On the contrary He keeps the devils locked up, so that they are nothing except by His leave. We are, then, assured that they can do nothing against us. Why not? For they can do nothing against Him. Besides it is necessary to join this glorious power with the knowledge that He is here with us. Not that it was here for a time, but that His power extends to us, as it is spread through heaven and through earth. Now He gives us testimony that He is with us when we listen to His Word. For He has promised it and He is not at all like man to use a lie. That is also how we are certain of His presence, and that by His Holy Spirit He will maintain us. Otherwise what would happen? We could do nothing else but fail, for we are too frail to do anything else. On the contrary we see the devil who is armed with all kinds of ammunitions against us. It is, then, very needful that God give us strength by His Holy Spirit in order that we may be able to resist him. That is how being far from Jesus Christ, with respect to His body, we are near Him with respect to His power.

And this is what He shows us in the Supper; and we have to apply this doctrine. And to do this we must not approach Him like many, who come here just like beasts, but let us know what is here given to us. When we see that God gives us nourishment for our bodies, that is already a blessing. But we do not come here to eat and drink ourselves full. Why then? To signify to us that we ought not to seek here our physical life. For, as says St. Paul, we have houses to eat and to drink in,[9] and so we do not come here to nourish our bodies. What then? We have testimony that Jesus Christ wishes here to nourish our souls. And our souls — will they be nourished by bread and wine? Not at all. There is nothing by which they can be nourished other than by Jesus Christ. For they must be preserved to life immortal, which even the Angels cannot give us. For as they have not always been, so they could come to an end. Let us conclude, then, that there is only one Father of Life: namely, Jesus Christ. Now we come to seek Him at the Supper, and each one in coming here must have stopped at this goal to say, "I come here to seek testimony that Jesus Christ is my life,

9 1 Corinthians 11:22.

and that being incorporated in Him I shall live eternally." But how shall we come to seek Him in the Supper? If we come here according to the way the Papists come here to seek the body of God, we are mistaken. For it is the most execrable idol there is to think that this bread that we take here is the body of Jesus Christ. We must, then, seek Him on high, and knowing that He is in heaven let us not doubt at all however that He is with us by His grace, so that just as we see and touch the symbols, likewise Jesus Christ truly accomplishes in us what the symbols signify to us: namely, that He dwells in our souls. Although naturally by our sins we are dead in our souls, He wishes to make us sharers of this life eternal. As, then, He says to us, "This bread signifies to you My body," also truly He accomplishes it in our souls. And as our bodies are sustained by bread, also our souls, having Jesus Christ for spiritual nourishment, are maintained by the power of God; and He dwells in us by His grace. But it is not all to have this understanding. For our affections must ascend to heaven, or otherwise we would not be at all united to Jesus Christ. There are many who well know that Jesus Christ is not here inside this bread and wine, but yet where is their heart? The heart of some will be plunged in covetousness, others will be inebriated by ambition, the heart of others will be entangled in all villainy. There are clowns who will not think of anything else but their nimbleness. Others will be drunk, and will have their heart only in the kitchen. Others will be full of blasphemies, murmuring and of all villainy. These are what St. Paul to the Colossians calls earthly members. "If you wish (says he) to approach Jesus Christ, you must leave your earthly members."[10] What? Must we leave our feet and our hands? Not at all, but our fornications,[11] gluttonies, envies, malice, and all other pollutions. Do we wish, then, to seek Jesus Christ on high? We must be rid of all these earthly members. For what relation would there be between us and Jesus Christ. We must not mix Him at all with our pollutions, but we must come to Him in order that He may withdraw us from them. That, then, is how we must not only know that He is in heaven, but also we

10 Colossians 3:5.
11 *paillardises.*

must leave our earthly members, which separate us from Him, and we must be raised on high. How? In true chastity, in sobriety, in true charity, in temperance, in diligence, in patience, in every other virtue. These are the wings to raise us to heaven, although properly speaking we need not have wings to fly there, or ladders to climb there; but that Jesus Christ leads us there and raises us by the graces which He distributes, as those which I have named. This is how we must apply this doctrine to the Supper, so that, when the bread and wine are presented to us, we must learn to seek all good in Jesus Christ, that we may be united together, and that each one must lay aside his own affections. If I feel myself to be distracted from Jesus Christ by any means, I must tear all that away from me, so that I may be truly raised to Jesus Christ — not that we can be raised to Him in perfection, but we must try to come closer and closer to Him. In fact, the Supper is given to us to this end; and we receive it not only once in our lives, but often, to signify to us that we must walk in this world until He has withdrawn us to Himself and delivered us from this body.

After this holy teaching we shall bow in humble reverence before the face of our God.

SERMON 13

Second Sermon on the Ascension of Our Lord Jesus Christ *

Jesus, having gathered his disciples together, commanded them that they depart not from Jerusalem, but that they wait for the promise of the Father, "Which," he said, "you have heard from me, that John indeed baptized with water, but you will be baptized by the Holy Spirit from here in a short time."
— ACTS 1:4-5

WE HAVE discussed before the obedience of the Apostles, in that they waited patiently for this promise which was given to them by the mouth of Jesus Christ, and that, although already they had been constituted in the office as Apostles, yet they did not presume to meddle with preaching, until after they had been confirmed by the Holy Spirit. That, then, is obedience with humility, in which they knew that they must be led by God. Now we have to discuss what is added, that when Jesus Christ speaks to them of the promise of God His Father, He says, *"You have heard from Me before."* As if He said to them that they must not expect from God what seemed good to them, but what He has promised. In sum, here we must receive a doctrine, that our faith ought not to be founded in what we shall have thought by ourselves, but in what has been promised to us by God. As St. Paul says, "Faith comes by hearing,"[1] not by hearing the propositions that men can bring forward by themselves, but by hearing the Word of God only. In fact, because we are inclined to diverse temptations, it is very needful that we be founded upon God and that He even should have spoken to us. But indeed He will not descend from heaven to speak to us. It is true. But we must be certain that the doctrine

* From: *Corpus Reformatorum, Calvini Opera*, vol. 48, pp. 596-604.

1 Romans 10:17.

which is preached to us is from Him, as also Jesus constituted Himself a witness by speaking to the Apostles. "What I announce to you," says He, "is what I have learned from My Father. And you must not distrust Me at all, for I am a faithful witness." As, in fact, we see that Jesus Christ did not at all exceed His office. So, in all that we expect, let us look neither here nor there, but let us content ourselves with His Word. Besides, since the Name of God is often abused, let us consider carefully whether it is He Who will have spoken to us. Now we have not Jesus Christ to speak to us in person, yet He ratifies what is contained in the Law and the Prophets. The doctrine, then, must not be doubted at all. Why not? For it is proved. That is why, in following this doctrine, we cannot fail. On the contrary, it is in vain for us to say "We are Christians," when we have only a frivolous opinion. Now let us consider what is the faith of the Papacy. They will say well, "I believe this and that." But if they are asked, "Why do you believe it?" they will say it is because someone has told them so. "But who has told you?" "They were our predecessors." That is why there is no certainty in their faith, but only a frivolous opinion. Yet we have to consider the grace that God has exercised to draw us out of the Papacy. For we are not maintained upon a supposition, but we have this infallible truth which He has given us, upon which we must be founded. It is true that this cannot be unless it be ratified by the Holy Spirit in our hearts. For otherwise it would be in vain to say, "God has spoken; this doctrine comes from Him." Until the Spirit of God has worked in us, to show us that the promises of God are authentic, we shall only be unsettled. But as Jesus Christ is the faithful witness of His Father, also He confirms us by the Holy Spirit, and we ought to pray that He may do it more and more.

This is what we have to discuss now. For Jesus Christ had promised the Apostles that He would send them the Holy Spirit, as we can see in St. John 14 and 15, where the promise is declared that Jesus Christ said to them, "When I shall ascend into heaven, I shall send you the Holy Spirit."[2] Now,

2 John 14:16, 26, 28, 15:26. "I go unto the Father" in 14:28 refers to the ascension.

then, He confirms this statement, in order that they may wait for Him constantly. He adds, *"John baptized with water but you will be baptized by the Holy Spirit."* It is a confirmation of the promise that He gives them here. As if He said. "It is My office to baptize, not with water but by the Holy Spirit. This office was not given Me in vain by God My Father. You must, then, feel the experience and the fruit of it." For this is a point we must know, that nothing was given in vain to Jesus Christ. Now He does not need it for His own use. But it is for His members, in order that all of us may draw upon His fulness and grace for grace. So let us conclude that, since this office is attributed to Jesus Christ, to baptize by the Holy Spirit, we must have the experience of Him in us and we must be sharers of such a benefit. Otherwise He would have an unsteady title, and it would not have the truth in it at all. And it would be blasphemy to say that. We must, then, recognize that Jesus Christ performs such a baptism in us. That is what He here proposed to His Apostles. Now Saint John the Baptist had already remonstrated against the Jews that baptized only with water. And the reason he had to say so was that they attributed too much to him by taking away from Jesus Christ. He rejects that, then, and says that what he is doing is only to administer the visible signs of water, and that to confer grace upon Baptism does not belong to him, but is the office of Jesus Christ. "Behold," he says, "I administer water to you; but He Whom you do not yet recognize, that is, He Who has this power to wash spiritually, I am not worthy to loosen the strap of His sandal. For although I have come before, I must decrease and we must fix our attention upon Him to magnify Him." This is the word of John the Baptist; and now Jesus Christ uses it, as saying, "This should not be to you anything new, for you have heard long ago that the privilege of baptizing into the Holy Spirit is reserved for Me alone."

One might here ask a question: namely, why does Jesus Christ mention John the Baptist rather than someone else? The reason is plain, since the greatness of John the Baptist, if men had abused it, would have hindered Jesus Christ from being duly magnified. And if He had spoken of someone else, it might still have seemed that John compared very favorably with Jesus Christ. He chose, then, the most excellent, in order to show that we must not stop at the creature, but that it is to Him that we must give all our attention. Also we see that whereas men try to build themselves a reputation among men, John the Baptist instead took great pains to abase himself, in order that people would not attribute to him more than what belonged to him. And after having said many words, he concludes that he must be decreased, and that Jesus Christ must be exalted. He does not say that in hypocrisy, but he says it in truth. Would to God that this teaching had been better retained by the world. But why? We tend always to this wicked superstition that we look to creatures, and these are to us so many veils to hinder us from looking to Jesus Christ. That is why so many idols have been made in the world, as there is an infinite number of them. As many holy persons as there were in the world, that many idols have we prepared, indeed, although the graces of God which have transcended them are to us arguments to address ourselves to Him, and not to stop at them. When the Papists wish to magnify their saints, they say that it is written, "Praise God in His saints."[3] I permit myself to say they are beasts, in taking this passage thus, seeing that the Prophet, saying "Praise God in His holy *place,* or in His sanctuary," means heaven, as if he said, "Praise this Divine Majesty ruling in His celestial throne over all creatures." But still they magnify the saints among them, so that (as they say) you would not be able to tell God from the Apostles, or perhaps, He is there put, as it were, in a class with others. Now this diabolical proverb which is held among them, "One would not know God apart from the Apostles," will be a testimony against them that they have torn up the glory of God like dogs and have given a piece of it here and another piece there,

3 Psalm 150:1, reading from the Vulgate (1573), *"Laudate dominum in sanctis suis."* Hebrew, QODESH, "place of separation" or "sanctuary" occurs in Psalms 20:2, 63:2, 68:24, 74:3, 77:13, 102:19, 114:2, 134:2, 150:1. Hebrew, QADOSH, or QADDISH, "those separated" or "saints" occurs in Psalms 16:3, 34:9, 85:5, 89:7, 106:16. In all fairness it must be remembered that the Vulgate was translated before modern Hebrew vowel points made possible the careful distinction of nouns derived from a common verb.

and have thus distributed it to whomever it seemed good to them. Whereas Jesus Christ alone ought to be exalted, and the Prophets and Martyrs annihilated in comparison with Him, they have done entirely the opposite.

So then, seeing that we are inclined to the vice of exalting creatures and robbing Jesus Christ of His glory, let us hold all the more firmly the saying that *"John baptized with water"* to show that, if we have to do with any grace, we must come neither to Peter nor to John, but to Jesus Christ, of Whom it is said that He received the grace of God, not at all in part, but in fullness, to show that we must address ourselves to Him alone. Besides, some have taken this as an occasion to say that the Baptism of John was not perfect. But this is an abuse. For the intention of John, when he spoke thus, was not to declare the truth of the Sacrament which he administered, but only the difference between his person and that of Jesus Christ. Although, then, the Sacrament of Baptism administered by John, and that which Jesus Christ administered, are the same Sacrament, and tending to the same end, yet John declares that he has not power to give worth to Baptism, but this belongs to Jesus Christ. There is, then, no doubt at all that it is the true Baptism which he administers, for we do not look at the sign but at the truth, and yet the sign is conformable to that of Jesus Christ. But the principal thing that we have with respect to Baptism consists in two points: it is that we are stripped[4] of the old Adam, renewed and united to Jesus Christ, and that we are purged of all our spots when God pardons us of our sins. That is the sum of Baptism. Now let us see if John did all that. It is certain. For he came preaching the remission of sins, and administering Baptism to this end. Further, in baptizing he preached repentance, which implies what we have said, that we be put to death with respect to our selves, and that this corruption that we have from Adam be abolished, in order that the justice of God rule in us. So when we shall have examined this quite well, we shall find nothing else here. But why? It is very necessary to distinguish between

4 *despouillez,* despoiled, skinned, robbed.

the person of the minister and the person of Jesus Christ. True it is that when one speaks of Baptism in itself, it is the washing away of our sins. Why so? Because by this we are confirmed that we have entered into Jesus Christ, in order that we may be purified and that we may live by His power. Scripture speaks thus. As we see that when Ananias baptizes St. Paul, he says to him, "Come and wash away your sins."[5] But also it is not only a matter of the sign when one speaks of Baptism, but of the truth there signified: namely, of being acceptable to God through the remission of sins, of being renewed by His Holy Spirit, in order that we may live no longer to ourselves. And why do we say that all that is comprehended in Baptism? Because the commission of Jesus Christ is without doubt and certain; and He accomplishes inwardly what it signifies outwardly. Otherwise it would be playing a farce upon a stage, if reality were not joined with the sign. This, then, is how God joins reality with the sign, in order that we may know that, just as the visible sign signifies, so we receive the graces there signified. So it could be said of the Supper. When we receive the Supper, as the minister distributes to us the bread and the wine, Jesus Christ makes us partakers of His body and His blood, in order that we may be truly His members; and by this means it is said that the Supper is the communication of the body and blood of our Lord. But when it comes to treating the part that mortal man does, then we must consider what power he has. When I baptize, is that to say I have the Holy Spirit up my sleeve to give it? Or the body and blood of the Lord to give it to whomever it seems good to me? It would be climbing too high to wish to attribute to mortal creatures what belongs to Jesus Christ. Let us not, at all, then, take away from the office of Jesus Christ, which is to baptize by the Holy Spirit. Just as I take water to baptize, Jesus Christ accomplishes what I signify, and He accomplishes it by His own power.

This, then, is what John says, "I baptize with water, but Jesus Christ baptizes by the Holy Spirit." This is what is here treated, and will be again in the eleventh chapter.[6] Be-

5 Acts 9:18, 22:16.
6 With reference to Acts 11:16. This sermon exists in manuscript at Geneva.

sides, now we must speak in like language: namely it is not up to us to perfect the things which we signify. Yet nevertheless we must be certain that God accomplished what is signified by the sign, and that, just as the washing away of sins is signified by water, so He accomplishes it by His blood. This is how we must distinguish the person of Jesus Christ and the person of the minister, in order that each may be in his degree and in his measure, and that it may be known that all perfection comes from this Fountain. Besides, it is certain that, when John said that Jesus Christ baptized in spirit and in fire, it is not restricted to a single appearance of the Holy Spirit in this form. For this promise is still fulfilled now, and it will take place until the end of the world. Let us note, then, that when the Holy Spirit was sent visibly to the Apostles, it signifies to us that the Church will always be ruled by the Holy Spirit, and that He will fill us with His graces to the extent that He dwells in us. It is true, that we shall not have Him in perfection, since we need to be kept in humility. And if we had Him in perfection, what would happen? We would no longer care to call upon God, and we would not think we needed Him at all. We must, then, always want His benefits, in order to be solicitous to ask Him to bestow more upon us. However, let us recognize that we are all baptized in the Holy Spirit and in fire; and that Jesus Christ does not permit His sacraments to be in vain, that is, to believers. It is true that although a man may be baptized into the name of God, yet, if when he comes of age he is seen to be inclined to every evil, it could be said that he is not renewed at all, since he is of such brutish nature. But that is not to sav that the Sacrament has not its property and nature. For Baptism of itself implies that we are renewed. And if we are not, the fault is in us: namely, since we will not allow that Jesus Christ accomplish in us His grace; and being unbelievers, we close our hearts against Him, so that there is no entrance at all for the grace which He wishes to bestow upon us. So then, the Sacrament will always have its power, but we do not receive the fruit in us, because it has no entrance except by faith.

Now we have to note that the reality of Baptism is not in the water but by the Holy Spirit. Further, that the Holy Spirit is given us through Jesus Christ. This is what we must surely note: that, if we wish that Baptism may be profitable to us, we must not stop at the water, as if our salvation were enclosed in it, but let us recognize that the Holy Spirit must do the whole thing. Besides, as we see, this doctrine has been poorly received in the world. For it seems to the Papists that the grace of God is attached to it, and they make it a charm like sorcerers, and attribute to the water the power of the Sacrament. And that is why they condemn the infant who has not been baptized. And to prevent this danger, they are not satisfied to confer the power to baptize upon all men irrespective of condition, but also upon women, for fear, they say, that infants may die without being baptized. So they think that the reality of Baptism is in the water, and by this means the blood of Jesus Christ is rejected. As for us, let us learn that the reality of Baptism is not in the water, but in the Holy Spirit. Yet the sign is not useless. For it testifies to us that our souls are washed. But to have the reality we must come to the Spirit, as we have shown. Further, the Holy Spirit is given through Jesus Christ, in order that we may not come to seek the Spirit in the water or in men, but that we may look on high. And this is still a point which the world has abased. For who looks at Jesus Christ, when it is a matter of having something for our salvation? No one. For it seems to us that men have full mastery, as if Jesus Christ had resigned His office and He were no longer in heaven at all. That is how dull-witted men are. However, Scripture raises our heads (by a manner of speaking), to raise us on high. For there we hear Jesus Christ admonishing us, "Consider that it is I Who baptize you." It is true that it is said that God sends the Holy Spirit, but Jesus Christ also sends Him. For when the Father sends Him it is in the name of Jesus Christ and at His request. Further, Jesus Christ, speaking of Himself, declares that He will send Him. And in fact He is the same God as the Father. And then, since having been made man He is our Mediator, all power has been given to Him in heaven and on earth; so that He is, as it were, the arm and the hand to distribute to us the graces of God. Let us note also why it is that John speaks of Baptism by Spirit and by fire, and uses these two words. For it is the same thing. When he says "by fire," it is as if He refines us to take away our impurities, as when they melt gold and silver, it is to purge it; indeed, we see that places full of impurities are purged by fire. The Holy Spirit has not, then, this title in vain, seeing it belongs to Him to purge us of all our pollutions. But it is also to signify to us that, when we come into this world, we bring only pollution, and that the longer we live, the more we amass pollutions and impurities. As Jeremiah speaks of it,[7] saying that man does not know himself. For there is such a sink of all wickedness in us, that God alone can know it. Surely we can throw an anchor to the bottom of the sea, but only God can sound our hearts. So, we are infected before God, and stinking like lepers, even so infected as to be horrible. But what shall we say? This is a consolation, when we see that Jesus Christ wishes to purge us by His Holy Spirit, as in fact we have testimony in Baptism that He wishes to make us new creatures, purging the infirmities that are in us. But just as all superfluities are taken away from that which is purged by fire, let us recognize also that, when God wishes to reconcile us to Himself, what is ours must be taken away. Further, let us note that as long as we shall remain in ourselves we shall perish, and although always we wish to remain in our entirety, God must diminish us to save us, and to make us acceptable to Him. And that is done by His Holy Spirit. We see, then, wherein we must glory: namely, in God. It is true that man may well have some presumption to magnify himself before men. But when it will come before God, what we esteem highly will be rejected. Let us learn, then, that there is nothing but evil in us, and the good that will be there will be when He shall have purged us by His Holy Spirit.

Besides, when he adds "It will be very soon," it is to give us greater courage. Not that we ought to murmur or be dis-

---

7 Jeremiah 17:9.

couraged, if God wants to show us His help. For we have no right to set the time for Him. In fact, the time that He takes is always very short. Why so? For He never ceases for a minute of time to help us. For example: When we are in affliction we call upon God. It is true that we shall not be delivered immediately all at once, but most often the evil will grow. Yet God assists us, for He consoles us — which we shall sufficiently perceive if we are willing to consider it. For what man can sustain even the least evil, unless God assists him? That, then, is a proof of His assistance, when we do not fail. As St. Paul says, "If we are afflicted and we do not become impatient we know the assistance of God."[8] That, then, is why God does not deliver us immediately. Yet He does not let us languish long. For the longest time that we can speak of it is our life. God promises assistance against assaults and deliverance. However, we have to fight against the temptations of our flesh as long as we are in this world. It is true. But if we consider the shortness of our life shall we find the term long? Not at all. For even a thousand years are only a day in God's sight. If then, we consider that, then it will hardly cost us much to endure all our life. That is why He says that it will be very soon.

So, let us learn to profit from this passage. Not only to recognize that Jesus Christ spoke to His Apostles, but to recognize that this word is addressed to us. It is true that we do not receive the Holy Spirit in the form of fire. Yet this office was not given in vain to Jesus Christ, and we have the power of it. Also, He did not take away Baptism when He left us. But since He left the sign, it is full proof that He will always be present to make this sacrament effective through His Holy Spirit. But also we must recognize that we are full of all pollutions, in order to come to Jesus Christ that He may cleanse us of them. It is true that we shall not have this opinion of ourselves, but God must, through the admonitions which He makes of it, draw us to Jesus Christ to seek the truth of Baptism. But above all let us not be so foolish as to think that creatures can help us, but let us come straight

8 A summary statement of Romans 5:3-5.

to Jesus Christ, recognizing that He is our all. It is true, when it is said that He baptizes, if we consider that He is far from us and raised in this sovereign majesty above all creatures, it will seem that we have some occasion to mistrust. But since He is our Brother, we have access to Him to address Him there. May we be confident, then, that He will keep His promise, and that everything that He said by His mouth will be certain and indubitable, and that besides the time will not be long. And yet, when we shall have endured for a day, that we be ready to endure for a month, and that we may look to this Kingdom which changes not. Then it is certain that we shall go not only a step, but that we shall continue to walk, until we shall have arrived at the goal which is proposed to us.

Following this holy teaching we shall bow in humble reverence before the majesty of our God.

SERMON 14

Third Sermon on the Ascension of Our Lord Jesus Christ *

Now when they had assembled they asked him, saying, "Lord, wilt thou reestablish at this time the Kingdom of Israel?" And he said to them, "It is not for you to know the times or the seasons which the Father has placed in his own power.[1] *But you will receive the power*[2] *of the Holy Spirit coming upon you; and you will be witnesses to me in Jerusalem, and in all Judea and Samaria, and unto the end of the earth."* — ACTS 1:6-8

IF WE could consider the infirmity that is in men as long as they are destitute of the grace of God, we should have profited much. Under the word "infirmity" I include all the vices and imperfections which are in men; as those who are weak and easily conquered by all temptations, like the rudeness of their spirits, as being corrupt and perverse. When, then, we shall have considered these things, we must pray to God to take it into account and to remedy such miseries to which we are subject. That is why I say that we shall have profited much when we shall have considered these things. Yet we have to note what is declared in this passage by St. Luke. For he shows how crude the Apostles were after having been taught for three years and having heard from the mouth of Jesus Christ all that pertained to their salvation. We shall see, here, then, that they are still new scholars, as if they had never heard a single word. Why? until God has corrected this ignorance, men will always be just this awkward, which ought to greatly humble us. Let us recognize, then, that we shall have to have heard all that has been

* From: *Corpus Reformatorum, Calvini Opera,* vol. 48, pp. 605-613.

1 *puissance.*

2 *vertu.*

said to us. It is as if one said it to a tree-trunk until God has taken away this crudeness which is in our corrupt nature. Otherwise we shall not understand what He says to us, for His word exceeds our capacity.

That there was such ignorance in the Apostles, we can see in these words which they utter. For the question they ask Jesus Christ is foolish and of no profit. It is only a superfluous curiosity when they ask if He will reestablish at this time the Kingdom to Israel. Afterwards, when they say *"at this time,"* they show by this that they would be very willing to triumph immediately without any labor. Instead of being called to labor in the Gospel, and to plant it through all the world, they would like very much not to suffer, but to be immediately filled with all benefits. Here is a double fault. Afterwards, when they say *"Kingdom,"* they still are at fault in this. For they attribute an earthly kingdom to Jesus Christ. and it seems to them that He ought to rule in the manner of princes of this world: and they think that, since they are nearest to Him, then they will be exempt from every pain and every evil and they will triumph by having great offices and estates. And when they add the word "to Israel," still they are at fault, because they restrict to Israel the grace that God had promised to the whole world. We see, then, that they do not say a single word which does not contain an error.

Besides, Jesus Christ rebukes them in the response which He gives them, and although He does not repel them by saying "You are at fault," nevertheless the words which He uses show well enough that He says them to reprehend them. When he says *"It is not for you to know the times or the seasons which the Father has placed in His own power,"* He reprehends them for this foolish curiosity which, when they should have asked what was necessary or perhaps useful, their minds fluttered about things curious and of no value. For we must be satisfied with what it pleases God to declare to us; so that there is nothing better than to ignore what God does not teach us in the Scripture. That, then, is how He reprehends them for this curiosity.

Besides, when He says to them, *"You will receive the power of the Holy Spirit coming upon you,"* He shows them by this that it is foolish for them to wish to ascend so high as to wish to inquire into the secrets of God. For they are not capable of that, until they have received this power from on high. They surely had received some grace of the Holy Spirit, but He shows them that they surely needed more of it; and that it was not time to triumph, but that it was time to go to battle; afterwards they would see what would happen. Then He says, "You will be to Me witnesses in Jerusalem, and in all Judea and in Samaria, and throughout all the earth." As if He said, "It seems to you that I ought to triumph in the manner of earthly princes, but My Kingdom is spiritual." So He corrects their last error, concerning what they asked about the Kingdom of Israel, when He says that the Gospel must be carried even into Samaria. For there was great enmity between the people of Judea and of Samaria, although they were neighbors, and though they somehow agreed on certain principles of religion, as one could say today between us and the Papists. For we have some family-tie, inasmuch as we have the Gospel, and they say as well that they have it. So the Samaritans had the same Law as the Jews, but they had perverted everything, as the Papists have now, and yet the hate was still greater. Here Jesus Christ says to His Apostles that the Gospel must be preached to those of Samaria. We see, then, how Jesus Christ reprehends them very sharply for their error, and leads them back to the right road.

Besides, we must apply all this to our own use. In the first place, if the Apostles were so crude, as is easily enough perceived, this vice was not only in them, but it is also in us. Let us consider, then, as in a mirror, that what is preached to us is not all, but God must enlighten us and give opening to the Word, that it enter us, and that He open our minds, in order that we may be able to comprehend His will. Otherwise we shall hear in vain, for all that will pass away without profit. Yet we must pray to God that He may direct His grace toward our comprehending His will. Otherwise we shall remain in our stupidity. That is what we have to note in the first place from this passage.

Now with respect to the faults which are to be found in the question of the Apostles, we must consider them with the response that Jesus Christ makes to them, and in which He rebukes and corrects them. In the first place we see that men are inclined to curiosity. We experience it in ourselves. Let us see if we are accustomed, as is proper, to inquire into things which are necessary for us. Not at all. But if they are even spoken of to us a second time, it seems to us that it is nothing but a headache. And if there is a difficult matter, which is even very necessary to understand, if two words of it are spoken to us, it seems to us that it is enough. This is our inconstancy, that we cannot fix our minds upon things necessary. But when someone tells us fables, lies, and things of no profit, oh! we shall never be tired of listening to them, we spend the whole day that way. We would even be willing to soak our ears in them all night. We see, then, that the human mind is so frivolous that it is not concerned at all about things which are necessary. It destroys things which are good and profitable to it — it gets a kink in it (as they say) just speaking of them. This is surely where it would be well to employ all our life: namely, in considering the grace which God has exercised toward us, by sending us Jesus Christ to make us wise. For it is a wisdom which extends everywhere, both above and below and on all sides. It is what St. Paul says to the Ephesians, when he speaks of the length, breadth, height, and depth,[3] that is, as far as your mind can extend, employ yourself in knowing more and more the love that God has shown us by giving us Jesus Christ His Well-Beloved Son. That is where we ought to employ all our life. And yet if one speaks to us about it for a half-hour, it seems that it is too long. By which we see that our minds wander, and that they ask only to wander to things useless. They delight here and feed there. And if it is a matter of our wishing to confirm things that we ought to hold sure, or perhaps, if someone wishes to warn us of things which are to happen to us,

3 Ephesians 3:18.

we cannot give ourselves to that, for immediately our mind is diverted, and it wanders here and there and makes castles in Spain; and he who has wealth thinks of his possessions and his riches. On the contrary, he who has nothing at all will remain there insensible as a brute beast and he will not think of what is said. That is how we are all tainted with this vice, and there is no one who is not convicted of it before God. So, seeing that the Apostles were curious to know things which in no wise pertained to them, let us not condemn them at all on that account. But let us recognize that we have good reason to condemn ourselves. Since we see that this is such a common vice, each one must learn to withdraw his mind from such fancies, and we must not willingly be given to such errors, but we must apply our minds to understand what it pleases God to offer us of knowledge of His counsel and to hold ourselves to that.

Likewise let us weigh carefully this word: *"It is not for you to know the times or the seasons which the Father has placed in His own power."* When He says this, here is a word which ought to check us to withdraw us at once from all curiosity. Indeed, although our nature goads us to go ahead, we must, nevertheless, draw back, and recognize what Solomon said, "He who is a searcher of the secrets of God will be oppressed by the glory."[4] If we are such searchers and curious, we shall surely experience that this was not said in vain. Let us recognize, then, that it is not for us to go beyond such a limit. But let us consider what it is that He forbids us to inquire into: *"What the Father has placed in His own power."* One could here ask a question: namely, has not the Father placed in His own power winter and summer, and the order of times and seasons? Yes, it seems, then, that He wishes to say that it is not our right to inquire into this. No, in fact, for this is not all that the Father has in His own power of which Jesus Christ said to His Apostles that it was not for them to know. But it is of things which He reserves to Himself in part and of which the knowledge is forbidden to us. Now He has declared to us things which

4 I think this is a summary statement of Proverbs 25:2-8.

are according to the order of nature and how it must be cold in winter and hot in summer. But if sometimes we see great cold waves in summer, let us recognize that this comes from our sins which pervert the order of nature; and that for the enormity of these we surely deserve that all be perverted, but nevertheless God does not cease to remedy it. So then, since God has declared this to us, He has not reserved it to Himself alone. For He does not wish at all that we imagine His power as an excessive power, but what He wishes to be unknown to us, He holds back so that it does not reach us. Following this, then, Jesus Christ said, "It is not for you to know that which the Father has placed in His own power." As if He said, "Be satisfied with what I declare to you and abide by it. For if you wish to enter into dispute, and to inquire into what He wishes to be hidden from you, you will only be confused, since He spared nothing in order that all that is expedient for you to know might be declared to you." If, then, we wish to go beyond this, it is as if we wished to defy Him. This is what we ought to note from this passage: namely, men must learn to control and restrain themselves, not at all to wish to inquire into that which God wishes to be hidden from us, and to be diligent to recognize and to inquire to know[5] what He wishes that we shall know.[6] But beyond this let us not be at all anxious to wish to inquire: And why is this? and why is that? Let us guard against such curiosity as against a deadly pest. Each one who will not do this will only do violence to his nature. For we are inclined to such follies by our nature, as to leave the principal thing that is necessary for us, and yet to amuse ourselves with what is neither necessary nor useful, but only a foolish curiosity, as each one shows in his place. As for example, here we have the Gospel, which is a fountain of all wisdom, and to teach us to confide in God, and to have our refuge in calling upon Him by means of it, and in order that we may fight against our carnal affections, to be entirely conformed to Him and to obey Him. That is what our Lord claims even by all Scripture. Now it seems to us that it is too little to know this,

5 *scavoir.*
6 *nous cognoissions.*

and everyone wishes to go poking into things that God wished to be hidden from us. We wish to control our Lord, and it seems to us He would have done better to do otherwise. This is what happens to us. Yet I said that if we wish to practice this teaching and not be curious at all, each of us must hold his nature in check, since it drives us into such imaginations. Then man is not satisfied to consider God in the creation of the world, although there is enough wherewith to be satisfied in considering the works of God. But what happens? Men leave the works of God, even those which He has done for our redemption (which is a work exceeding all length, breadth, and height), and wish to inquire why God has made such an effort to create the world, since it is still less than seven thousand years since the world was created. But let us note that before God created the world, He appointed hell to put such curious people in. And with good reason. For besides being a reprehensible curiosity to enter into such thoughts, is it not audacity to raise ourselves against God by raising ourselves against His work, as if it did not seem good to us? That, then, is why we must be satisfied with things which God has put in our understanding. For though we applied all our life to contemplate them, yet we would not have time enough to comprehend the least part of them. And may each one know that he must obey what Jesus Christ has pronounced, that He must not inquire into what the Father reserves to Himself: namely, things which are not declared by His Word.

By this we see that He shows us our incapacity, which He confirms still more in what follows, saying, "*But you will receive the power of the Holy Spirit coming upon you,* and then you will be more capable of understanding what God declares to you." By this Jesus Christ admonishes us that it is temerity when we wish to inquire further than God declares to us. For it is as if we wished to fly above the clouds, although we have no wings; since if we recognized our limitations we would take heed not to go as far as we are accustomed to doing. And we must note carefully that He says, "*the power of the Holy Spirit coming upon you,*" which is as if He said, "Poor beasts, recognize what you are. For what is your mind to comprehend things so high? How can they enter it? So learn soon to humble yourselves and to know your ignorance, and learn to pray to God." In sum, we have here a general warning that, although God does allow us our natural senses, yet we are extremely brutish. And it would not take much to make us block-headed, and we would understand nothing by the Scripture, although it were expounded in minute detail. This intelligence, then, must come from God Who gives it to us through His pure goodness. For although we have Scripture and it is expounded to us, it is as if the sun shone and we were all blind. What remains, then, except that we pray to God that He may relieve our ignorance?

Let us come to the second error. It is that they wished to triumph at once and then to live wishfully without any pain. Now this vice is in us all, for there is no one who does not desire to reign with Jesus Christ in that eternal salvation which He has promised us. However, when someone speaks to us about bearing His cross, and of entering into combat against Satan, against the world, and even against our own nature, we surely would like to withdraw ourselves from the task. Further, we ought to be careful to note this passage: namely, that if we wish to be sharers in the benefits of Jesus Christ, we must now put our hand to the work.[7] Do we wish to be victorious with Him? Let us fight, since we are in time of war. If we wish to be sharers in all His benefits, we must endure the hardship which He will permit to come upon us in this world. This is what St. Paul says, "If we are sharers in His sufferings we shall also be sharers in His consolations."[8] See, now, that Jesus Christ is seated at the throne of glory, all is placed in His hand. But before He arrived there, how did He go about in this world? What afflictions did He endure? He was so afflicted that it seemed that His life was wretched. For during all the time that He lived, He never had anything but affliction, and at the end He endured the most cruel death that it was possible to in-

7 "No man, having put his hand to the plough, and looking back, is fit for the kingdom of God." Luke 9:62.
8 Romans 8:17.

vent. What is more, it seems that He is forsaken by God when He permits that He be thus condemned by the world. This is what we must consider, that if we wish to enter into this immortal glory, we must bear His cross in this present world. Now we would be very glad to attain in one leap, but we do not wish to take a step through hatred, scorn, and afflictions. But after all? Nevertheless it must be done. For we shall not change the order which God has set up — it is inviolable. We certainly want to realize what is done in paradise, but we do not wish to keep on the road, which is that God did not put us here below except in order that Jesus Christ may be served by us in this world, in order that we may be sharers in His glory, after we shall have fought with all our might against the assaults which will have been made against us to turn us away from Him. But to wish to realize what is done in paradise, and not to stay on the road — this is mockery. We must, then, consider to what it is that God calls us, and we shall find that we are called to fight, and that there is such a great difficulty to rise above combats, that we shall not have the leisure to amuse ourselves with inquiring into things which serve us nothing, things vain and curious; but we must find sufficient this Word which shows us the road we ought to take.

There are here two things by which Jesus Christ corrects the curiosity of His Apostles: namely, He declares to them that they ought to discern what they have to do. Here He is, I say, to correct the vice to which we are inclined: namely, let us consider what God teaches us by His Word. For when we shall be attentive to it, this will take away from us the vice of being too curious and too bold. There are, then, firstly, the promises that Jesus Christ gives them, *"You will receive the power of the Holy Spirit,"* as if He said, "Be satisfied with what God wills to send you." Let us learn, then, when our nature makes us itch to go out of bounds, to hold to the promises of God, and let us recognize: Here is where we must stop. Let us be satisfied, then, with this and may it be all our food and refreshment. Then there are also the commandments of God, to know to what He wishes to employ us in. When we shall know this we shall not have leisure to wander across country, but we shall find that the road is long enough, indeed that it would be necessary to fly, if we were concerned to do what He commands us. It will be easier to understand when we know that the Word of God is the medicine to correct this curiosity. How so? Here are the promises that we have, with respect to the present life, that God promises to assist us. Jesus Christ also has taught us to ask for our bread. But what? This is not the principal thing. For He surely extends His hand upon brute beasts and nourishes them. This, then, will be too little a thing for us to consider; but the principal thing is that we taste His mercy, by knowing that He has pity on us poor sinners, and that He does not wish that we should perish in our follies, rather He extends His hand to withdraw us from them. Let us have confidence in this, then. Afterward He calls us to life eternal with Jesus Christ, and promises us that we shall be united with Him. When, then, we have these promises, each one must give himself to spiritual exercise evening and morning and this must be our wisdom. Then, we have His commandments, to which we must cling without polluting ourselves in superstitions; and each one must deny himself, to live in all love and charity with one another, in sobriety, in chastity, in humility, and all honesty. Each one must be pure and clean of all inclination to luxurious ease. This is a general rule. Further, each one has here his particular lesson. The father of a family ought to understand what love he ought to have toward his wife. The wife ought to know that she is subject to her husband, and both of them must be admonished of what instruction they owe their children. Afterwards, magistrates have here their lesson. Ministers of the Word of God likewise have theirs. Briefly, it is a perfection of doctrine followed in all respects, where each one is instructed sufficiently, so that no one can ignore his duty. That is what we have to note. And if each one applied himself as he should, it is certain that he would not have leisure to wander across country. Besides, if we are such vagabonds, it is a certain sign that we have never understood the principle of our salvation, and how we ought to be disciples of our Lord. And by this we can reprehend these curious people who ask questions, and we can say to them, "My friend, since you ask such questions without purpose, you have not yet learned what your Baptism is. For you would know that you must deny yourself. But now you would like God to let you wander here and there. Study your questions, then, and then they will be disputed for a hundred years." Furthermore, we ought to be attentive to think. Here. Where God calls us. Namely, may we know wherein is the confidence of our salvation. Afterwards, may we pray to Him that He may have pity on us, and also that we may learn to correct our lives. That is where all our senses ought to lead. And when it is a matter of our being distracted to think here and there, we must consider how to do our duty of paying attention to our consciences. Then Jesus Christ is our physician Who will surely know how to provide the remedy.

Following this holy teaching we shall bow in humble reverence before the face of our God.

SERMON 15

Fourth Sermon of the Ascension of Our Lord Jesus Christ *

Of remarks made by the Angels to the Disciples and Apostles

> *And when He had said these things, He was lifted up as they were looking at him; and a cloud removed him from before their eyes. And as they were looking at him going to heaven, two men in white garments presented themselves before them, and said to them, "Men of Galilee, why do you stand still, looking into heaven? This same Jesus, who is raised from among you into heaven, will come just as you have seen him go."* ACTS 1:9-11

WE ARE going to expound what St. Luke here tells: namely, that the Apostles saw our Lord go up into heaven. Now it is not enough that we know the account, but we must note that he cites it as one of the principal articles of our faith. And it is certain that the articles of our faith are not useless, but necessary to our salvation. However, we shall never profit well from the Ascension of our Lord unless we know that it really happened. And for this reason St. Luke says that the Apostles saw Him ascend. And he adds that they stayed there until they were advised that it was no longer necessary to remain there, and that they must return to Jerusalem to take up their duty as He commanded them, and to do it until He shall return on the last day. That is why He tells us of the Ascension of our Lord so as not to leave it in doubt. True it is that it is said, "Those will be blessed who believe and have not seen." For this reason it is more necessary that we believe in this Ascension than if we had seen it. For since the Apostles have seen it and recite it to us, we ought not to doubt it.

* From: *Corpus Reformatorum, Calvini Opera,* volume 48, pp. 613-622.

We come now to where St. Luke says, "A cloud removed Him from before their eyes." One might here ask a question as to why the heaven did not open so that the Apostles might see the condition of our Lord and His glory. But it is not without cause that they lost sight of Him by a cloud. For our Lord knows the range of our mind, and is kind enough to correct the haughtiness of our spirit, that we may be restrained. For even if the sight of the Apostles had extended into the heavens we might have taken that as an occasion to exalt ourselves, as we see we are too prone to it. We are very much inclined to that, even to let our imaginations wander and to observe no modesty, to wish to know the secrets of God, even those which He wishes to be hidden from us. It was expedient, then, that this cloud intervened. For by that it is shown to us that we ought to humble ourselves and not have in us this arrogance to wish to transcend the heavens to inquire into the facts of God. That is the instruction which we must take from this passage.

Now it is said that "two angels appeared," but St. Luke calls them "men," according to the common practice of Scripture. For, since angels are by nature spiritual, we cannot see them unless they show themselves to us in some visible form. That is why our Lord has willed that from the very beginning that they should appear in the form of men, but so has He willed that always there might be in them some sign to recognize that they were angels. For if we recognized them only as mortal men, we would not give them the honor which belongs to them, and that would take away from the understanding which we ought to have to give faith to their message. Thus God has always marked them so that they might be recognized. That is why it is here said that they were clothed in white robes, as also when Jesus Christ was raised from the dead they appeared in white garments. In that our Lord wished to show that it was necessary that men receive them in reverence, listening to what they would announce, without having any doubt about it. That is why St. Luke says here that they were clad with white robes. But we must note the circumstances. For there is not one circumstance lost that God wishes to have omitted, since we know that His wisdom extends everywhere and that it is infinite. Besides, if the angels are majestic when they appear to men, what will God be when He appears in His glory? For the brightness of the majesty of the glory of God is not only as the brightness of the sun, but more than a hundred thousand suns if they were in the world. Thus, then, when we see that the angels ought to be so precious to us, and that we ought to hold them in such great reverence, we must consider that, if we are told of the majesty of God, if we think of it, we must hold it in great reverence, and we must recognize that we are nothing, but all majesty is in Him. That is what is indicated to us when we are told of the majesty of angels, even though they are shown to us only in human form.

Now as to what they say: "Men of Galilee, why do you stand still, looking into heaven?" It is commonly thought that the Apostles were here called Galileans as a reproach, since we see that the Galileans were not of high reputation among men. According to their opinion, then, it is as if the angels said, "Poor, blockheaded people as you are, do you not recognize that just as He has gone up to heaven, so He is coming back again?" But we see no probability that this was said in this sense. However, let us recognize that the angels called the Apostles Galileans because they were so reputed, even as Jesus Christ bore this name. When they wished to accuse the Disciples of belonging to Jesus Christ, they asked them, "And you, are you not Galileans?" Again, after the death of Jesus Christ the wicked used this word, as we see that a wicked man whom they called Julian the Apostate said, being at the point of death, "You have conquered me, O Galilean," cursing there Jesus Christ and defying Him, even while he felt himself to be conquered by Him. Thus the Apostles are here called Galileans, because they were considered to be people from that country.

Besides, not without cause they are here reprimanded by the angels. For they well knew that Jesus Christ was to go up to heaven, for many times He had told them, and He even said to them, "It is expedient for you that I go away, for if I do not go away, I shall not send Him to you." Then must have forgotten, then, even though they remained thus looking on high to see what would happen. For, as I have said, He had indicated to them that it was expedient that He go away, and He had told them that He must reign and that they should serve Him here meanwhile. He had also told them that He had to be seated before God His Father to intercede for His faithful ones. But they show that they have scarcely remembered what had been so often shown to them. However, their ignorance ought to serve as a warning. For it is not only for them that this is said, but it is for us also. Let us note, then, what is said to them by the angels so as to recognize the benefit we receive from the Ascension of Jesus Christ.

When it is said that He will come just as they have seen Him go up, that is to show us that we need not look for Jesus Christ here below until He comes to judge the whole world. And now when we look for Him it must be by faith which surpasses all human intelligence. That is the first point in this passage, which is well worthy to be observed. For since by nature we are always inclined to lower things, it is very difficult for us not to be inclined to some superstition when one speaks of the Ascension of our Lord Jesus Christ. In truth, we see what has happened here. Although He has gone up to heaven, and it is written that when He returns to earth it will be just as He was seen to go up, still those who call themselves Christians have never ceased looking for Him here below. Thus it has come to pass that they look for Jesus Christ in bread and wine, and they wish to hide Him in a box, and they wish to carry Him here and there, and to play with Him as with a doll. How come such superstitions, unless our nature is as ready to lower things as a stone? And when I say that we are inclined to lower things, we want to drag down God all the time, with all that we know of Him, and we would like Him to be like us. We see, then, by experience that men have always wished to have Jesus Christ with them in the flesh, but we see, on the other hand, that the angels, wishing to rid us from such speculations, said, "Men of Galilee, why do you stand still, looking into heaven?" True it is that in looking for our Lord it is very necessary that we raise our spirits to heaven, but we must not look for Him according to our senses and our understanding; thus faith must now control. Do we not know that faith surpasses all human sensibility? For it is not a faculty which men have inherited, but it is a grace which God gives them in correcting their nature. We must, then, seek our Lord, but not with the eyes, nor with the ears, nor with the feet, nor with the hands, but faith must supply all that is lacking in us. Thus, when we have heard this passage, we shall be sufficiently armed against these whims with which the whole papacy is shot through, where they say of a piece of bread "This is God," and they think they can lock Him up as a doll. We shall be, I say, sufficiently armed for the encounter with them when we know that it is said that we must not seek for Him according to the natural senses of man, but only by faith. Further, we are admonished not to give rein to our superstitions, and not to think that we can have God with us bodily. Since this vice has always been with man, it is all the more necessary to be wise in this case. We know that the Jews said to Aaron, "Make us gods." That is how men want to have God with them to handle Him and do with Him as they like. Let us always remember, then, this passage to arm us for the encounter with this vice. For although Jesus Christ be declared to us, and He be our Brother, we cannot comprehend Him except by faith, and we must not imagine Him according to our fancy when He presents Himself.

Besides, since we know that Jesus Christ has gone up into this heavenly glory, let us note why He is there: In the first place, that He may remind us of what is said, that He has not entered a holy place made by the hand of man, but He is in heaven, and that up there He is interceding for us before God His Father. And that, when we presume to pray to God we shall be rejected unless Jesus Christ is there in our name. Since He is there, He is our Intercessor and presents our prayers there and causes us to be answered, as if we had the privilege of saying what we have to do and to pour out our heart before God. That is what we have seen in the Epistle to the Hebrews, that as the high priest entered the sanctuary for all men, also, since Jesus Christ is in heaven, we must be certain that He is there to intercede for us. For the high priest, when he entered the holy place, carried on his head (sic) the names of the children of Israel, and before him he carried twelve stones which signified the twelve lines of descent of the people to show that, although he entered all alone, yet it was for all. Also, since Jesus Christ has entered into heaven and He bears us there, although we are only brute beasts, and also He bears our names before God to show that He has us in His heart; we need not pray to God in doubt, but we may be assured that our prayers will always be acceptable to Him, since we pray through Jesus Christ. And if this were well understood, there would not be so many superstitions in the papacy. Why do they have so many patron-saints? Why do they have recourse to the Virgin Mary? Because they have never understood why Jesus Christ has gone thus into heaven. For if they had understood that He went up to be our Intercessor, they would not have said that they are not worthy to offer their requests to God and that therefore they must have other advocates. But they might have understood that since Jesus Christ is there in our name we can have access there without having patron-saints and advocates. So, this is what we must recognize in the first place.

Further, He has ascended so that, being seated at the right hand of God His Father, He may govern the world, and He may govern it in such a way that He always helps those who believe in Him, and He has special care for them. If Jesus Christ had always remained with us, beyond the fact that we would be more given to superstition, He would not have this power through which all things are subject to Him. True it is that He could have had it, but we do not speak of Him without following the order which He has given in His Gospel. And really, it would be folly to dispute whether He could otherwise have done this or that. For His power is infinite. But even as He said after His Resurrection, that all power is given to Him by God, and also it is our belief that He is seated at the right hand of God the Father Almighty. Is that to say that He has a throne there and that He just sits there? No, not at all. But He is present there at the right hand of God as God's Lieutenant. If we dared to stand before this glorious majesty of God, we would be crushed down and confused, but to have access there we have Jesus Christ, to Whom all things are subject in heaven and on earth. Now, although Jesus Christ has all power eternally, still we say that He is sitting at the right hand of God until we have said that He has gone up into heaven. Therefore, He has preeminence in every respect after His Ascension.

Now we shall note that this kingship of Jesus Christ is for us, for there was no need to make it for Him, since He is eternal with the Father. But what follows? He is at the right hand of God in this nature which He assumed with us. This is so that we may be assured that, since we are in His protection, no evil can happen to us. True it is that He will permit us to be hampered by our flesh and to be surrounded with many miseries. But what of it? He is always ready to stretch out to us His hand, and we must be certain that, although we suffer for a time, the end of it will be for our salvation. That is what must be understood when His Ascension is spoken of. Thus, since He has gone up there, and is in heaven for us, let us note that we need not fear to be in this world. It is true that we are subject to so much misery that our condition is pitiable, but at that we need neither be astonished nor confine our attention to our selves. Thus, we look to our Head Who is already in heaven, and say, "Although I am weak, there is Jesus Christ Who is powerful enough to make me stand upright. Although I am feeble, there is Jesus Christ Who is my strength. Although I am full of all miseries, Jesus Christ is in immortal glory and what He has will some time be given to me and I shall partake of all His benefits. Yes, the devil is called the prince of this world. But what of it? Jesus Christ holds him in check, for He is King of heaven and earth. There are devils above us in the air who make war against us. But what of it? Jesus Christ rules above, having entire control of the battle. Thus, we need not doubt that He gives us the victory. I am here subject to many changes, which may cause me to lose courage. But what of it? The Son of God is my

Head, Who is exempt from all change. I must, then, take confidence in Him. This is how we must look at His Ascension, applying the benefit to ourselves.

Let us now attend to what the Angels said. "*You will see Him coming from heaven* as you have seen Him going there," — to signify that we must not wait for Him except when He will come on the day of Judgment. All this ought not only to wrest all superstition from us, but it ought to draw us to Him in heaven. We have already said that we must see Him only by faith. Since it is so, let us consider what St. Paul says to the Colossians. "Since Jesus Christ is dwelling in heaven, Who is your Head, in Whom you have all your life, you must have your heart and your mind there, although in your bodies you are here."[1] Since we know that Jesus Christ is on high, we must learn to renounce the world, to be united to Him. It is a long distance from Him to us, and we shall be separated from Him, unless we take the means that St. Paul gives us, which is to put off these earthly members, which he explains afterwards, and says that they are luxuries, avarice, gluttony, pride, envy and all such things.[2] Do we wish, then, to be sharers in this ascension? We must not be separated from Him. But how shall we be joined to Him? We must put off these earthly members and things which hold us here below. Some are given to luxury, others to vengeance, others to gluttony, and others to other vices. Although faith raises us on high, our affections must follow it, in order that we may renounce all the world and all things which could hinder us from being united to our Head. This is why it is said that He will come just as He was seen to go to heaven — in order that we may learn to unite ourselves to Him through the affection of our hearts. Beyond this the Angels do not pretend to speak, neither of the robes that Jesus Christ had, nor of other things; as many fanatics seek things which are neither required nor useful to salvation, but the Angels have said this to show that He will come visibly. As if they said to the Apostles, "It seems to you evil that your Master is

1 Colossians 3:1, 2, 4:1.
2 This list does not quite coincide with Colossians 3:5, though the list is typically Pauline.

taken away from before your eyes, but this will do you no harm at all, for you will see Him come back in this glorious immortality where He is now." The Papists have other subtleties of little children, by saying that their God is in their mass, and that they have Him with them to play with Him just as it seems good to them. They say that it is true that Jesus Christ will come in visible and open judgment, but that now He comes privately and secretly. It is true that He comes daily to us. It is not for nothing that the Scripture says that we are visited by God. Also we well say that the Gospel is to us testimony of His presence. But we must note how it is that He dwells with us. St. Paul says that it is by faith. We must not, then, daydream, but we must understand what St. Paul is talking about, saying, "Know you not that you are the temple of God in which He dwells?"[3] Just as God is through all and in all things invisibly, Jesus Christ communicates Himself to us. And when we are united to Him, our souls are nourished by the substance of His body (although He is up there in heaven), but this is done by the power of faith and by the Holy Spirit. For Jesus Christ does not descend corporally. Wherefore the Papists are too ignorant in saying that He comes privately,[4] and that He gets mouldy under the bread and under the wine.

Since we know what this word signifies, let us apply it to our use. We have said that the Angels had promised to the Apostles, that, although they had seen Him ascend into heaven, He would come back. Of what profit would it be to us that He has descended to suffer death and passion, if we had no hope of ever seeing Him again? But when we have the promise that He must come back to gather us and to unite us to Himself, that is wherein we ought to be consoled. So, this was said not only for the Apostles, but it was said for us. And we must learn to be consoled in this, that although we are separated from Him by a long distance, yet He will appear for our redemption. Yet we ought to raise our heads, and by that surmount all the annoyances that could happen to us. Indeed, by this we can well judge whether or not we have

3 1 Corinthians 3:16.
4 *par cachets,* or by bits.

faith in Jesus Christ. For when we are told that He will come again,[5] if we rejoice in it, and we experience a desire for His coming into our hearts, it is a sign that we have true faith in Him. On the contrary, if we fear this day, and if we have the feeling that we would willingly turn it away, if it were possible, it is a sign of our unbelief. Now it is surely seen that faith is very rare in all the world. For we ought to be consoled when His coming is spoken of to us, since it is the day of our redemption, as says St. Paul in Romans 8.[6] And they do very little about it. If, then, we are sorrowful when His coming is spoken of to us, is it a sign that we do not hope that Jesus Christ may be our Redeemer? It is true that our redemption has been accomplished by His death, but yet when we shall be stripped of this body, then we shall be stripped of the servitude of sin. That is why death ought to be desirable to us. So, since the universal redemption will not be until the last day, we must also surely groan, as all creatures groan, waiting for this day, since they are subject to corruption because of the sin of man, and they desire to be delivered from it.

So then, heaven and earth, and all other creatures desire that Jesus Christ may appear, in order to restore all things. Will it not be a great shame upon us if we have no more desire for His coming than have the insensible beasts? For we have not only the understanding which God has given to us as mortal men, but we have the spirit which He has given us to desire His advent. And it is a sure sign of unbelief when we do not desire this day at all. And if we do not raise our heads always and whenever this word is pronounced to us, we show sufficiently that we have no faith in Jesus Christ. Besides, although believers receive consolation from this sentence, also the wicked must feel a fear inside themselves of His coming. And although they do nothing but mock it, yet they have a dread that seizes them in the heart, and it is that our Lord may turn them away at His judgment. And it is

---

5 *revenir,* come again, or come back.

6 Many modern interpretations of this chapter do not refer it to the second coming. This fact, I think, reveals the lopsidedness of much of what now passes for Christianity.

not without cause that many understand Jesus Christ only as their Judge; for they were not willing to receive Him when God wished to give Him to them as Redeemer. It is true that many do nothing but laugh now. So they will have to experience Him Whom they have defied. As there are some who, if today Judgment is spoken of to them, will respond, "Well, perhaps. Time will tell, but it may come." As my mockers, who last Wednesday mocked in this place, who are not satisfied to be worthless and do defy God in the taverns, but will come here to act like monsters by their impiety and by their impudence; and to show that they are as shameless as harlots, coming to mock God and His Word even in His Temple and in the presence of His faithful ones. Now, Whom do they mock now? They will experience, I say, Him Whom they have defied. For He will come, He will come. And He has not ascended into heaven to endure that the wicked mock Him without His taking vengeance. But He has His register to note in it all their mockeries. And since they are not willing to come to account voluntarily, they must come to receive their judgment with the devils their fathers and their brothers. Now, since this doctrine is given to us for our instruction, let us learn to humble ourselves in time, and to do homage to Jesus Christ; since He is the Prince of Angels and they obey Him, let us be in this their companions. And since we are thus assured that He is before God for our sakes, let us not fear to pray to Him. Besides, let us be consoled if today we endure much pain, and let us wait for the day of God, on which the Lord Jesus has promised to come in order to unite us to Himself.

Following this holy teaching we shall bow in humble reverance before the face of our God.

SERMON 16

First Sermon on Pentecost *

Of the Descent of the Holy Spirit upon the Apostles, Delivered on the Day of Pentecost, on which is celebrated the Holy Supper of the Lord.

> *And when it came to the day of Pentecost they were all of one spirit in the same place. And suddenly there was a sound from heaven, as if a mighty wind were raised, which filled all the house where they were seated. And parted tongues as of fire appeared to them and rested on each of them. And all were filled with the Holy Spirit, and began to speak other languages, just as the Spirit gave them to speak.* — ACTS 2:1-4

WE ARE by nature so inclined to unbelief that the truth of God must be sealed in our hearts in an authentic manner so that we may receive it and be entirely decided about it. True it is that God stamps it on the heart of every believer by His Holy Spirit, and that is also why He is named the Seal of the Gospel. But those who were to proclaim this teaching through all the world must have been sealed in the first place, and God must have governed them in such a way that now we are assured in full certainty of the teaching which they have published to us, that we do not receive it from them as from mortal creatures, but that God is the real author of it. For we know that our faith would have too weak a foundation if we had only the authority of men. We would be, then, always shaky unless our spirits were raised above the world and were founded in God, knowing that it is from Him that this Word of salvation has proceeded which is daily preached to us. And that is why this account has been set down for

* From: *Corpus Reformatorum, Calvini Opera*, volume 48, pp. 623-636.

us in writing, so that whenever we read or hear the Word of God, this comes before us, that men have not invented what is contained in the Old and New Testaments, but God by a visible sign has testified, even as there was need, that men were organs solely of His Holy Spirit. As for Moses and all the Prophets — they have had the approval of being sent by God, so that if their teaching is held in doubt by us, that must be imputed to us and to our ingratitude and malice.

Now it is said to us that before the Apostles had published the Gospel to all the world God made His Holy Spirit descend upon them, so that we might know that they have put forward nothing of their own, but that they have faithfully delivered that which was commanded to them by God. We see, then, how this account ought to serve us. For if we were not assured that the Apostles were as new creatures and that God had given them a certain mark to show that they were approved and authorized by Him, what would become of our faith? It would be only a fleeting opinion. We could say, "I think so; so it seems to me," but that we should be entirely persuaded to have a proper firmness and constancy -- it would be impossible. For what is man? Since there is nothing but vanity here below, we must put out our anchor even as far as heaven, as also the Apostle says in the Epistle to the Hebrews. And then we can sustain all whirlwinds and tempests, and the world and the devil can gain no hold on us, however they may plot. But our faith will be always firm and will not give way when we hold this basic principle: that God is He Who leads us onward, Who calls us to Himself, and that the teaching which is preached to us is His pure and infallible truth. This, then, is how we must summarize what we have read: that when there arose a great disturbance like a rushing wind, God wished to show by a visible sign that He had chosen the twelve Apostles to carry the message of salvation here and there. It is true that for the time being there were only eleven, but the number of twelve was not allowed to remain forever broken, because in the place of Judas, Matthias was sent. And that is how the number was repaired that had been formerly destroyed; and this interruption was only for a little time, as St. Luke records later.

There are, then, the twelve Ambassadors of our Lord Jesus Christ, who had already been chosen and marked by Him. However, they had to be furnished with gifts which were required for a charge so difficult and so lofty. They must, then, be fashioned from on high, and God had to work in them in a strange and admirable manner which surpasses all humman capacity. Now with respect to a wind and disturbing whirlwind which was there, it was to show that the Holy Spirit descended upon the Apostles not only to make them sharers in His gifts, but also in order that all the world might be disturbed by it. For it had been said by the Prophet Haggai,[1] "'Yet a little while and I will shake heaven and earth,' says the Lord." Now that was fulfilled in the preaching of the Gospel. We see, then, when the Holy Spirit descended, that it was not only for a little handful of people, but in order that this might reach all the ends and extremities of the world. For otherwise this narrative would be very cold to us, if we were not well persuaded that it was for us and for the building up of our faith that God sent once for all His Holy Spirit. Besides, God could surely have sent the Holy Spirit in a more gentle manner. But let us note that this impetuosity was to beat down all pride of the flesh, and on the other hand, to wake us up, since we are too drowsy and slow. There are two very great vices in us, which hinder us from feeling the power of the Spirit of God, to throw in our lot with the Gospel. One is that we are haughty and full of presumption. Now all that must be put down and in humility we must learn, both great and small, to do such homage to God, that we be emptied of everything, and that we consider our life as coming from Him and from His pure grace. It is needful, then, that this pride which is rooted in our nature be reproved, even in a violent manner, because we are too hardened in it. On the other hand, each one feels in himself an earthly sluggishness, so that we are preoccupied and wrapped up in this world. Briefly, we are almost stupid, so that we can taste neither the Word of God nor the power of His Holy Spirit, unless we are awakened, as it were,

1 Haggai 2:6.

by force. That then is what is here narrated means, that a whirlwind was raised, like an impetuous wind. Now in the first place we see that the descent of the Holy Spirit was to move all the world and to make all mankind tremble, so that God might be adored with common accord and that men might be subject to Him. However, we must be awakened, since we are too stupid, and we must also be led to obey God, being stripped of all presumption, knowing well that there is only all misery in us, that we are only mud and rottenness, indeed, even that there is only corruption in our souls until God has renewed us.

Besides, when the Holy Spirit descended in such a form, that is, in *parted tongues and as of fire*, it was to better express how God wished to work through the preaching of the Gospel. If a man speaks, his voice is dispersed in the air and it is a dead thing. Now it is said that the Gospel is the power of God unto salvation to all those who believe.[2] How so? Can a sound which flies into the air and which is dispersed lead us to the Kingdom of heaven?[3] Nobody by himself knows how to create even a little fly. It is necessary that the image of God be repaired in us, that we receive this incorruptible seed to reach the heavenly glory, to be companions of Angels, to be transfigured even into the glory and immortality of our Lord Jesus Christ, and to be sharers in His Divine nature, as St. Peter speaks of it.[4] And can this be done by the voice of a man? Certainly not, but it is then said especially that the Holy Spirit is joined in the same place with the word which is preached. For why did He take this figure of tongues? It is certain that there is always some likeness between the visible signs and the truth[5] which is represented by them. We must, then, see why the Holy Spirit appeared in the form of tongues. It is to show that he would be in the mouths of the Apostles, and that He would give to them what was required to execute their office and their commission, and

2 Romans 1:16.
3 *de cieux*, plural, as in the Greek in Matthew 7:21, 10:7, 11:11, 12, 13:24, 13:31, etc.
4 The primary reference is to 1 Peter 1:23. Calvin interprets the meaning of being born again of incorruptible seed.
5 or reality. Fr. *verité*, Lat. *veritas*, and Gr. ALETHEIA.

indeed, that He would make their labor profitable that it might not be useless. For also, in the first place, we know that even the most clever man to be found would not know how to pronounce a single word unless he were governed by the Holy Spirit. By this God shows us our condition, since we would not be able to open our mouths to say a single word to His glory, which would be appropriate, unless He had given it to us. It was, then, very necessary that the Apostles were governed by the Spirit of God, or else they would have become mutes. We see also what crudeness there was in them, for they might have had much more active and keen spirits, except that God by their crudeness wished to show us, as in a mirror, our condition unless we are illuminated by His grace. It is true, when the Apostles went about with our Lord Jesus, they held Him to be their Master, they were subject in all modesty to His doctrine; yet what did they know about it? We see that they were poor beasts, so that, considering how little they learned in such a good school, we must be ashamed of their slowness. But that serves us well. For there they are! Changed in a minute, so that the grace of God has all the brighter a luster, since we see that they speak of the secrets of God so loudly as being wonders, and everyone is astonished by it, and previously there was nothing. Further let us consider what their virtue and constancy was. They had all been weakened. It seemed that their faith was dead and extinct. There was Peter who was, as it were, the leader, who so shabbily renounced his Master, and yielded like a slave of Satan. It was very necessary, then, that God put down His hand. For from man's side there was no possible remedy. So, let us note that not without cause the Spirit of God appeared under the form of tongues, to show that by this means the doctrine of the Gospel was approved and sealed by God, in order that we might receive it in all reverence and humility, and that there might not be any dispute at all about where it came from; since God displayed His arm and declared that He was the author of it.

Besides, it is not without cause that the tongues are parted and of fire. For we know how the human race was divided in itself as well as being alienated from God. And the plot that was made to build the tower of Babel[6] was the reason why men were barbarians to one another, so that there was no longer any communication. But it seemed that God dispersed them, as it were, in spite. How then were the Apostles, having always been isolated as foolish and unlearned people in this corner of Judea, able to publish the Gospel to all the world, unless God accomplished what He had previously promised: namely, that He would be known by all tongues and by all nations? It is true that it is said that all will speak the Hebrew language in order to join in a true faith, but the truth is better declared to us when it is said that all believers, from whatever region they may be, will cry, "Abba, Father," invoking God with one accord; although there may be diversity of language. That, then, is how the Spirit of God wished to display His power in these tongues, in order that the Name of God might be invoked by all and that we might together be made partakers of this covenant of salvation which belonged only to the Jews until the wall was torn down. By that we see the wonderful goodness of our God, when He changed evil into good. For if we seek the reason why there are different languages in the world, we must come to the conclusion that it is on account of a curse from God. Yet here appeared His goodness and fatherly mercy, when the message of life was brought into all tongues. That is how God converted evil into good. All the more have we to magnify and bless His Holy Name, knowing that difference of languages did not hinder Him from declaring through all the world that He wished to receive those who previously were estranged from Him, and to gather them all, as it were, into His bosom, until they are received into the inheritance of heaven.

So much for one item. But it would not be enough that the Gospel be preached, and that God by this means might be known by all the world, unless this doctrine had more and more power to touch hearts to the quick, and to draw men into obedience. That is also why the tongues appeared like fire. For in the first place we need to be purged, since there

6 Fr. *Babylone.*

are only corruption and filth in us. If one scans all our affections and desires, he will find that there is stench everywhere. We have to be made over,[7] and God must purge us in a strange fashion. Then, on the other hand, we are as cold as we could be. We need, then, to be set on fire with the love of God. Instead of being all wrapped up in the things of earth, He must raise us on high, which He does by means of His Word.

Now we see, in summary, how this account serves us today. In the first place, to the end that we might receive the doctrine of the gospel as a certain and infallible truth it bears the mark of God and it is sealed by His Holy Spirit and is an excellent witness of our adoption. That, then, is how we are brought into obedience, seeing how God has given approval to His Gospel, both to be assured in order that our faith may no longer be variable, and that we be not always liable to change our words and our opinions, but that we walk always without swerving from the good path, until we have finished our course. That is how in the power of the Spirit of God our faith will be victorious over the world. For if it were a matter of limiting ourselves to the wisdom of men, where would we be? But when we have as a foundation the Spirit of God, that is how we are never shaken. However, we have to think of ourselves, in order that God may today make us partakers of that which we have just now declared, that is, that we invoke Him with true accord (I say, although we are separated by tongues) and then that we be renewed by the doctrine which is preached to us, in such a way that we know that there has to be fire to change us, and to cleanse both our senses, and our spirits, and our hearts of all corruptions of this world. For although the elect of God are made submissive by means of the Gospel, yet on the other hand we see that the enemies of truth become more proud and more rebellious, so that it puts the world into combat, as experience today shows. For as long as the Gospel was not preached all the world was without care and at rest. There were neither arguments nor disputes. And why not? The devil reigned without contradiction. But when our Lord

7 *recuite,* cooked again

Jesus Christ appeared with the pure doctrine of the Gospel the skirmishes got closer and closer. And we see today the combats among those who are called Christians. All the more ought we to pray to God that He may make us to experience why the Holy Spirit descended upon the Apostles and that He may give us the grace that with entire obedience we may render testimony that it was to gather us, where as previously we were scattered, and that we may be joined together under our Lord Jesus Christ, that we may be members of His body and that truly He may be our Head.

Besides, to succeed in it, we have to pray to Him that He may give us such a firmness that there may be only fire, instead of the coldness which is in our hearts, that also He may remake us so that we may cast off all the corruptions of our nature, that we may be so renewed that we are separated from the world. We shall see often how the word of God is a fire; indeed, but it is of another kind, to consume all who contradict; as the Prophet Jeremiah speaks of it, showing that even to the people of Israel it came thus, that they were, as it were, straw and stubble to be burned by the Word of God, because of their malice and rebellion. And today, how many are there who are made inexcusable since they fight against God, like enraged beasts, who foam at the mouth, and perhaps other things, who are mockers and profane people, who defy God, attributing neither authority nor honor to His Holy Word? Now it is true that such people will not render the Word of God useless or without power, but that they will have to experience it as a consuming fire, to be reduced to ashes and completely crushed. Let us learn, then, to note why God wished that His Holy Spirit appeared in tongues of fire. It was so that believers might know that they needed to be touched to the quick, even in such a manner that God change them and renew them. That, then, is what we have to bear in mind, in summary, to properly apply this account to our use.

Furthermore, let us note the two principal parts of faith, and then let us come to ourselves to know what we would be unless God cared for us. In faith there is first knowledge or certainty, and then there is firmness and constancy. Now when God speaks we are deaf to what He says, because we are already preoccupied with this world, and even all the wisdom contained in the Gospel will be foolishness to us until God has enlightened us. In the first place, then, God must open the way for us to know Him and to cling to this truth, or else we shall be deaf to His word, we shall be stupid and without any comprehension. So much for one item. For the second, we need to persevere against the assaults which Satan stirs up against us, and against so many skirmishes; for those we must be armed and equipped. Now how shall we be thus armed until God extends His hand? Only the power of the Holy Spirit can suffice for that. When, then, we shall have been taught a hundred times by the Gospel, yet since we are fickle and unsteady, we shall be soon turned away from it, unless God confirms us in it. Even today, when there are so many perils and threats, poor believers cannot open their mouths to call upon God, unless death is right next to them; they cannot make confession of their faith, unless fire is kindled to abolish all memory of our Lord Jesus Christ. When then there is such a resistance, and those who ought to maintain the Christian faith are inflamed by Satan to ruin everything, if it were possible for them, must not God be at work here? Yet we are today invited by the experience, and warned of what need we have to practice what is contained in this account, and beyond that to call upon God and to pray to Him that, since He wished to give testimony when the Gospel came into the world, inasmuch as He was at work there by the power of His Holy Spirit, we also may experience Him, each one in his place. Since we must be persuaded and resolved that the word which is preached to us does not proceed from men, also it is not to be interpreted through anyone's cleverness, as St. Peter shows. For he connects these two points. (1) Since the Holy Spirit of God has spoken by His holy Prophets, (2) we also on our part, when we wish to understand what is declared by their doctrine, each one must put away his natural senses, and must not bring here his speculations, saying, "so it seems to me; thus I presume"; but we must come with soberness and modesty, asking God that He may govern us and introduce us by His Holy Spirit into the understanding of His Word, of which He is author. So much, then, for one item.

Since today we see that the devil has refilled the world with so many sects, that there are many heretics who do not cease to upset all purity of the Gospel and even that there are so many despisers of God, and mastiff dogs who no longer have either faith or religion in them; all the more do we need always to present ourselves to God in order that He may enlighten us by His truth, and that we may be so united to our Lord Jesus Christ that nothing may be able to separate us from Him. On the other hand, may He give us a Spirit of power and of constancy until the end; in order that, however much the enemies of truth may be animated, we may persist nevertheless, and that Satan by this means may be conquered. And we ought not only to have concern for ourselves, but we ought to think with concern for others. It is here very easy for us today to make confession of our faith: we do not see the fires kindled like our poor brothers, we do not experience the storms which fall upon their heads;[8] yet we surely must be united in one body. For why are we assembled, unless in order that we may have true brotherhood together, since God through His infinite goodness has adopted us for His children, and He daily testifies to us that He wishes to be our Father? It is, then, very fitting that our solicitude should extend to those who are, as it were, in the snare of wolves, who experience new troubles daily; that we may have such pity for them, that we may pray to God that He may help them and that He may strengthen them for the battles, according to their need; that He may never permit them to remain confounded, but, though Satan may plot from all sides to ruin their faith, that nevertheless they may persist until the end. Even we need to be admonished of how things are today; for if ever there was persecution prepared, it is now;[9] especially, is there a place where the rage of the enemies of God flared up for a whole week, so that they have more occasion than was ever seen to execute their cruelty against poor

---

8 Geneva was rapidly becoming a haven for persecuted refugees from many parts of Europe.

9 Ignatius Loyola, founder of the so-called "Society of Jesus," Roman order established for the systematic extermination of the Protestants, lived 1491-1556. So successful were his wicked devices that there are hardly any Spanish Protestants left today.

believers.[10] Also it is seen how these miserable tyrants are possessed by Satan, and that there is such a frenzy in them that there is no longer any hope of bending them in any manner whatever. Now our poor brothers are there exposed as prey, they are watched and spied upon; and it is apparent that the greatest preparations were made in unthinkable rage and cruelty, and that the obstinacy of wicked men against God is greater than ever. It is, then, well for us, while God gives us leisure, to think carefully about this, and to practice this account which we see: namely, since the Holy Spirit descended upon those who were of one accord, may we learn to assemble ourselves, and although we are far from the front lines, nevertheless may we be joined with those who do battle, and may we help them in combat by our prayers with mouth and heart; so that the Spirit of God may be in charge of everything, and that He may inflame us with such a zeal that we may be ardent to call upon our God, instead of being too cold. As for our brothers who need to be confirmed in such assaults as they have to sustain, may the good God show that it is He Who has worked in them, and that He leads and governs them.

Besides we must still note the word "consent"[11] or "accord," to lead us to the Head, Who is our Lord Jesus Christ. For it will be seen how the Gospel is preached today; but if a census is taken of the believers, the number will be found to be very small and obviously scattered; for there are hardly any places where the pure doctrine is preached, and even where there is Church, there are many despisers of God, dissolute and profane people, who are there to infect the remainder, if God did not preserve it by His power. Others will remain always in their brutishness. There are so many today who have not in twenty or twenty-five years advanced a single pace in the knowledge of God; they have no more idea of faith or reverence than beasts. Others, although they have intelligence enough, yet lose

10 This sermon was preached in 1549. On September 4, 1534, Calvin had written to Martin Bucer in behalf of a French refugee in Strasbourg. The systematic persecution of the Waldensians by Rome was also going on at this time. Calvin was urging a German prince to sponsor the removal of some of them to Germany, beyond the mountains, out of reach of Rome.

11 Fr. *Consentement*

courage and are entirely asleep, and no longer take account either of God or of His Word, so that the number of sheep and true lambs is very small. However, we see how through all Europe the devil is popular, that lies, snares, and delusions are received, and that the world is so bewitched that there is no means to reduce it. It is seen that men not only provoke God and knowingly blaspheme against Him, but they are so inflamed by madness that it seems that they ought to pull the sun out of the sky and to take away its brightness. When, then, we see that, we need to commit ourselves to our Head, our Lord Jesus Christ. For what cause is such scorn and impiety seen everywhere in the world, and so many rebellions and mockeries, unless that grace is not given to all to be led under the sovereign Shepherd Who was given for us by God His Father? We know that those who are in His keeping will never perish, as He has pronounced. Thus, then, let us take the side of our Lord Jesus Christ, if we wish to experience to our salvation the profit and the fulfilment of what is here narrated by St. Luke: namely, not only may God speak to our ears, and may His doctrine pierce our hearts, may we be inflamed, may we be remade and renewed, in such a way that the corruptions of this world may be put down, and, as we wish to be owned and acknowledged as His people, may we be able to claim in truth our God in the Name of our Lord Jesus Christ, to Whom we are joined in order that He may unite us in perfection to God His Father.

That is also why this Holy Table is now prepared for us. For, as I have already said, we cannot communicate any grace from the Holy Spirit without being members of our Lord Jesus Christ. How can we arrive at that condition unless He presents Himself to us and He lives with us in such a manner that everything that is His belongs to us, and we enjoy the benefits which have been given to Him in our name? It is said in the eleventh chapter of Isaiah[12] that the Spirit of God has rested upon Him, but not for any necessity He had of it, nor for His private use; it was for the profit of all of His body, that is to say, of all of the Church. So then, let us recognize,

---

12 Isaiah 11:2.

when now the Supper is offered to us, that our Lord Jesus wishes that we might find all our good in Him, He draws near to us through His goodness. It is true that He does not leave His heavenly glory, He need not descend here below (as the Papists imagine) to communicate to us His body and His blood, but although we are far away from Him, yet He does not cease to feed us with His body and His blood. Also we shall not cease to be united to Him, in entire perfection, indeed, as much as it will be needed. That is why I call that "perfection," although He comes to us little by little. For though that may be, we shall not cease to be joined to Him. Indeed, let us recognize that He did not wish to disappoint us when He declared that He is our Head and that we are His members, and that, if we let ourselves be governed by Him, we shall experience that He will be our good and sure Guide, and that the power of His Holy Spirit is infinite in order to sustain us. In the first place, then, when we come to this holy table, let us recognize that it is a secret which surpasses all our senses, and yet we must here give place to faith. Let us know that what cannot be conceived of by men is accomplished, nevertheless, by the secret and invisible grace of the Holy Spirit; for this is how we are made partakers of the body and of the blood of Jesus Christ.

Besides, when He dwells in us and we are truly His body, let us not doubt that all that is said in Isaiah of the gifts of the Spirit belong to us and are appropriated by us. It is true that we do not receive the Holy Spirit in complete perfection, for there is the measure of the gift, as St. Paul says, and we must believe more and more. Also it is not without cause that our Lord distributes them thus to us by certain portions and degrees; for His strength needs to be made perfect in our weakness, in order that we may depend always upon Him, that we may be solicitous to call upon Him; and also that we may be humbled, recognizing that there is still much to find fault with in us. That, then, is how we shall know that it is not in vain that Jesus Christ dwells in us, for He will give us testimony through the fact that His Holy Spirit will display His power to strengthen us in Him, to draw us toward Him, and to withdraw us from this world. It is said in this passage from Isaiah that the Spirit of wisdom rested upon Him, to show that there is only darkness in us, that we are poor blind people, and that to the extent that we presume to be clever and artful, we shall always pervert and falsify the truth of God, until He has enlightened us, and He has given us heavenly brightness, which we have not by birth nor by heritage. Then it is said that He has also the Spirit of fear of God, because our desires are so many rebellions against the will of God, until they are reformed, even entirely changed. Next it is said that He has as well the Spirit of power, in order that we may recognize our weakness, and that we cannot do otherwise than fail, unless we are strengthened from on high. We shall experience, then, all these things when we shall come to receive the testimony which is here given to us, and when we shall be persuaded that, as mortal men distribute the bread and the wine, our Lord Jesus Christ will work, since it is done by His authority and in His Name, and that it is not a thing which men have contrived in their brains, but that Jesus Christ is the author of it. That, then, is the purpose to which we must apply this account.

Besides, let us be so united under our Head, that we may adore God with one heart and with one mouth, and so may we be joined together. For it is not said that the Apostles were joined with everybody in one accord. They had all the city of Jerusalem for an enemy, and yet they did not cease, although they were small in number, although they were despised people, to persist and to be there united and gathered together under the sign of God in the Name of Jesus Christ. So now, seeing that so many mastiff dogs bark against us, seeing that the devil raises up so many troubles and in various manners, may we be all the more joined and in greater firmness, and may the cord of our agreement be unbreakable, so that we may defy Satan and all his minions by this means. It is true that we ought to seek peace in general with all without exception; we ought to love those who hate us and persecute us, we ought to desire their salvation, although they are not worthy of it; all the same we must be enemies to them, or else we would separate ourselves from Jesus Christ. Let us despise, then, all the world, and let us recognize even that we must leave our selves to be joined to the Son of God, and that we are not wicked because the rage of unbelievers is stirred up against us, when we try to agree together among ourselves and to be united in the Name of Jesus Christ. Let us recognize that He acknowledges our agreement, although we are only a handful of people, let us defy boldly all the world and all those who are governed by Satan and are at all rebels against God. Although then, we are nothing in comparison with them, let us not doubt that God acknowledges us, and that He dwells in our midst. At the time which St. Luke described here they offered sacrifices in the Temple as previously, and the Priest[13] was there with great dignity; he was there in his pontificate. There was as well the "common order"[14] which had luster, so that it seemed that God was attached to that people. Now the Holy Spirit was only over a house, indeed over a room where the disciples were inclosed, like poor frightened people, like poor trembling lambs, seeing themselves surrounded by wolves. It surely seemed that the condition of such people was miserable; however, the Holy Spirit appeared there to this little company. So then, today, although we are despised by the world, and though we are not a great crowd, yet let us not doubt: that the Son of God displays the power of His Holy Spirit over us, that He makes us to experience His gifts, according to our need; and let us content ourselves with this inestimable benefit, so that we may not be at all envious of the prosperity of wicked men and enemies of God; that it will do us no harm to be rejected by the world, and to be considered rotten members; that this is all one to us, by means of which we may remain joined together, indeed, in this union which we have by means of the Gospel, and by means of Jesus Christ, Who is the Fountain of every benefit and of life and Who has in Himself all perfection of joy.

Now let us bow in humble reverence before the majesty of our God.

---

13 Fr. *le sacrificateur*.
14 the order of worship.

SERMON 17

Third Sermon on Pentecost *

In which is expounded the first exhortation which St. Peter made after the Descent of the Holy Spirit upon him and the other apostles.

Others, mocking, said, "These men are full of new wine." But Peter, standing with the eleven, raised his voice and said to them, "Jewish men, and all who dwell in Jerusalem, may it be well-known[1] *among you, and give ear to my words; for these men are not drunken, as you suppose, seeing that it is the third hour of the day. But this is that which was spoken by the Prophet Joel: 'And it will happen in the last days,' says God, 'that I shall pour out My Spirit upon all flesh; and your sons and your daughters will prophesy, and your young men will see visions, and your old men will dream dreams.'"* — ACTS 2:13-17

That which St. Luke narrated at the beginning of this passage is a very noteworthy example of the malice and ingratitude of men. Behold the Apostles, who were surely known as country folk, and even of low condition, who speak the language of various people and distant regions, and discuss true religion in an excellent manner, proclaiming the salvation which is in Jesus Christ. This ought to astound with admiration even those who heard it told a long time afterwards; much more should those who contemplate the thing right there, and who hear the statements with their own ears, be moved to be led into proper obedience of the Word. Yet they do not recognize the works of God, to magnify and glorify Him in the same, but on the contrary they make fun of them. Now this vice was

---

* From: *Corpus Reformatorum, Calvini Opera,* volume 48, pp. 636-646. The sermon on Acts 2:5-12 has not been preserved.

1 Fr. *notoire,* notorious

not in the world only then; we still see it in our time. For God works every day with such power that it is impossible to comprehend it; however, we are not at all moved by it to give thanks to Him for it; and even for so great a benefit as His having called us into the knowledge of His Gospel. But on the contrary do we not see a crowd[2] of wastrels who make fun when God speaks, and take as much account of the preaching as if fables were spoken to them? And in so doing do they bear toward the Word of God such reverence as they ought? Certainly not. Although many such mockers are found, who profit neither by the Word of God nor by its miracles, yet we ought not to be at all scandalized, but remain firm, in order that we may not fall into the same condemnation by having despised the marvelous works of God, and by not having given Him the honor which belongs to Him.

That is what we ought to note in the first place. Now St. Luke adds that Peter, in the name of all the Apostles, showed that the mockers and despisers of God were greatly mistaken in that they took such a miracle, which they had seen before their eyes, in derision and mockery, and that it ought not to be attributed to such drunkenness of which they accused the Apostles. He said, *"Jewish men, and all who dwell in Jerusalem, may it be well-known among you, and give ear to my words; for these men are not drunken, as you suppose, seeing that it is the third hour of the day."* Now by this we must note firstly that the ancients had a manner of counting the hours different from ours; for they took the first hour at sunrise, and there were always twelve hours, until sunset, so that, according as the days were longer or shorter, the hours also were longer or shorter. Further, they divided the day still otherwise into four parts: namely, from the first hour until the end of the third hour, from the third to six, from six to nine, from nine to twelve. So the sixth hour of the day was at noon, and the third was about eight or nine o'clock in the morning as we count.

We come now to the reason which St. Peter brings forth to show that they were not drunk, as the Jews considered. It is as if he said, "We are now in the third hour of the day,"

2 Dutch, *tas*.

which is, (as I have said) between eight and nine o'clock in the morning; "it is not true to life that men get drunken at this hour; even those who do not attend to serving God." By this St. Peter denounces drunkenness, and shows that it is something to be ashamed of when a man begins in the morning to get drunken. However, more are found who do not care, though they are given to drunkenness, that they lose sensibility and reason. Some are not drunken from what they have imbibed in the morning, but they are so besotted with wine that when they hit the evening, it seems that even in the morning they had done nothing else but drinking. Others, for fear of refusing to drink begin so early in the morning that they do not get sober again all day: and wine then takes away all intelligence and reason, so that they know neither how to help nor to conduct themselves. St. Peter, then, says, "These men are not drunken," showing thereby that it is a thing displeasing to God. Now we must note here that the Jews held drunkenness in detestation, so that when any of them were subject to falling into drunkenness, they considered that it was by night, in shame that they had to be manifest to others. By that we see that men are more shameless now than they were at that time. For then they sought the darkness of night, and now they have no scruples against getting drunken at high noon; then they have to sleep and ferment the wine. Even while listening to the sermon they let it be seen in what condition they are; for they do not know how to stay an hour to hear the Word of God, without showing the effect of their drunkenness; they are so drowsy that they profit nothing. But no one should be too much astonished by this, for wine and meat which are not yet digested, because they are filled with them to the limit, worse than brute beasts, cause them to sleep so soundly. Sometimes they even sleep at the morning sermon, although it seems that they ought not yet to have drunk or eaten. But by that they show what taste they have for the Word of God, for they would not know how to excuse themselves, seeing that they arise from sleep at the same hour as other people.

To come, then, to the matter at hand, St. Peter speaks according to the custom of that time, saying, "It is not true to life that these men are drunken, seeing that it is the third hour of the day." Now he applies the miracles which had been done, by his teaching. For the Holy Spirit had not been given to the Apostles to be kept secret, when it would be a matter of magnifying the works of God; but they had to be firm to carry constantly the Word, and to publish the Gospel, inasmuch as our Lord gave them the means to do it. Also we see that God worked mightily, and that it did not proceed from men, that God should have been preached to the entire world[3] by such a small number of people. Now St. Peter in his preaching shows a holy boldness of the Spirit of God, and warns those who had not received it in reverence, that Jesus Christ does not manifest Himself to those who hold His works in derision and mockery. Besides, when he says, *"And all you who dwell in Jerusalem,"* he speaks in common to us; however, that did not include certain ones: namely, those who had made fun of the miracle. For there were many then in the company of the Apostles who were greatly astonished and who had come in reverence. Why is it, then, that St. Peter attributes to them all, that they had made fun of it? Now in reprehending their vice he wished to benefit the whole company, and by this occasion to confirm all the more, even to the hearts of others who were astonished, an admiration and reverence for the work of God, by casting far away the opinion and all other foolish fancies of these mockers. Today we still speak this way; for if there are mockers in a company, and we wish to reprehend this vice, we cry against all, although all are not charged of it. However, those who are blameworthy ought to be convicted in their consciences; for they have enough testimony of their misdeed, without having anyone's bringing an action against them, and making specific charges. Nevertheless, sometimes it is needful that someone speak to people more directly, and that they be charged by naming them, to recall them to memory, and to use the eye and the finger in pointing out to them their faults; for then they are more ashamed than if one merely rebuked them in public. But it is a marvel if anyone can bear a rebuke for some vice, even if it is in public; for they wish to cover themselves, saying that, although there may be many worthy of

3 Fr. *en l'universal monde,* to representatives of all the then-known world.

blame for the vice of which they are accused, they are among those who are innocent of it. Thus they murmur, "Why does anyone cry against us? If there are such, is it necessary to reprehend all others and speak thus in public?" That is how men always find occasion to murmur against doctrine, and yet we see that, although there may have been very few who made fun of the miracle of which is here spoken, nevertheless, St. Peter addresses his word to all when he says, "*All you who inhabit Jerusalem*, may it be well-known among you that these men are not drunken as you suppose." Yet when we see that St. Peter spoke thus, let us not be more wise than the Holy Spirit; when there is a vice which is not in all, let us not therefore quit speaking to all, and let those who are innocent of it, by this example, be advised not to murmur, knowing that if they are free of one vice, when anyone looks at them very closely he finds them worthy of blame a thousand times.

We come now to what St. Peter intends to do by this preaching; that is, by this means he intends to lead the people to the knowledge of Jesus Christ; as in fact, it is the purpose for which the Apostles received the gift of tongues. For diversity of languages was, as it were, an impediment which closed the door to the Gospel, so that without the knowledge of tongues it seemed impossible that the Gospel could be published throughout the world. St. Peter, then, says, "If you remember the prophecy of the Prophet Joel, the promise which is contained there has been fulfilled in the coming of Jesus Christ. For after the Prophet made some threats, he adds this promise: that *God will pour out His Spirit upon all flesh.*" By which he indicates that, when God punishes the iniquities of the world, it will not be to put the elect in despair, but to confirm them by the exercise of tribulations of this world, which are sent even sooner to the elect than to the reproved. This, then, is why our Lord does not slacken the reins on His vengeance, that He may not withhold it to pardon those who will have refuge in His goodness and mercy; for He is always near those who call upon Him in truth. Now the common style of the Prophets has always been such that, when they wish to console sinners, they lead them to the knowledge of Jesus Christ. And not without cause; for if Jesus Christ is taken away from us, what shall we find in God? We shall find in Him a highness, which is to cast down all creatures; on account of which, when we have come to the knowledge of ourselves, we find there only vice and sin, and to present ourselves before the majesty of such a great Judge, we are able to understand only the justice and rigor of His vengeance, which is prepared for us on account of our iniquities. In fact, what will happen to those of us who except ourselves from the number of sinners, by saying that there is no need at all of recourse to the knowledge of Jesus Christ? Nevertheless, we see the indifference which is in men in this regard. It is true that they will not declare openly that they do not wish to know Jesus Christ; but there are very few who do their duty by seeking Him in a manner proper to Him. Thus it is not at all to be wondered at if the Prophets always insist upon this point of leading us to the knowledge of Jesus Christ; For He is the only means of reconciling us with God, and wherein we must establish our foundation. We see now that, when the Holy Spirit was poured out so abundantly, it was not for any other purpose except that men, who were estranged from the knowledge of Jesus Christ, might be called, and we might all be converted together to be the people of God and to receive Him.

But to have a better understanding of this passage, we must expound what the Prophet said: *"It will happen in the last days that I shall pour out My Spirit upon all flesh, and your sons and your daughters will prophesy, and your young men will see visions, and your old men will dream dreams."* By that we must note that, although the Prophet says that the Holy Spirit will be poured out upon all flesh, nevertheless, all do not receive Him. As in fact we see that there are many who are deprived of Him. However, God calls us all, but we resist Him by our ingratitude and malice. It always remains true, that no one comes to Him but him whom He draws by His Holy Spirit. By that also it is signified to us that, if we come to Jesus Christ by faith, and we hold it in true humility, we shall receive gifts of His Spirit so abundantly that we shall be able to communicate them to our neighbors. That, then, is how Jesus Christ calls all of us in general; however, it is very necessary that we come to Him; for we refuse this benefit which is presented to us. Why? Inasmuch as we render ourselves unworthy of it, preferring to give ourselves to our vanities rather than to the fear of God. Now since it is true that many do not receive the gifts which are presented to them, although they are all called, one could ask why the Prophet speaks thus. But he wished to take such a generality to show that from all conditions and from all ages of people He will bring them into His knowledge; also, because now God makes no distinction between Jew and Gentile; for the Holy Spirit by His power works through all. We see that the Jewish people among all others were the first who had knowledge of the true God; and although the number of those among the Jews who believed, may have been very small, yet the Holy Spirit has been presented to them. Pagans also have been instructed by the preaching of the Gospel. That is how without marvels the Prophet said that God has poured out His Spirit upon all flesh. Now the doctrine which was proclaimed at the beginning of the preaching of the Gospel, came first from the Jews, in order that what was said by Exekiel might be fulfilled, "Rivers will flow to the ends of the earth from the fountain of Jerusalem."[4] By which the Prophet wishes to indicate that this diversity of tongues might never have been understood if the Holy Spirit had not been sent to the Apostles to make their doctrine trickle out into all the world. So, then, let us consider how God worked by His incomprehensible wisdom to cause His Gospel to be published. For although the Apostles had been sufficiently instructed by Jesus Christ, yet they do not cease to be gross until they receive the Holy Spirit. But when they receive Him, see them made from poor, ignorant men into great scholars, so that they have knowledge of the diversity of tongues, which were an impediment to the Gospel's being published. So, it is not without cause that the Prophet Joel says that God has poured out of His Spirit upon all flesh.

Besides, we must note well the passage where he says that *old and young will prophesy*. By that he indicates that old and young will all be partakers of the gift of the Holy Spirit. We must not now seek to gloss over knowing the exposition of the

4 A summary of Exekiel 47:1-12.

text, when the Prophet said, "all flesh"; for the text itself shows sufficiently the intention of the Prophet. Besides, when he says that young men will prophesy, he speaks according to the custom of his time; for God made use of these two means toward his servants: namely, (1) vision or (2) dream; as it is written in the twelfth chapter of Numbers, He will show Himself to the Prophets by vision, and He will speak to them in dreams, but concerning His servant Moses He says that He will speak with him mouth to mouth.[5] However, someone might allege that the doctrine was not under the Law as it is at present, and that, if God manifested Himself to the Prophets of the Old Testament, He does not show Himself to us in such a way. To answer we must note that, although the Prophet uses these terms, it is only to accommodate himself to his time, and not to say that we may not have a greater measure of knowledge. For the truth is not declared so openly in the Old Testament as it is now to us through Jesus Christ. For instead of the sacrifices which were ordained by God in the old Law to be types and shadows which He needed often to repeat to show how men have access to God only by means of the Mediator, we have now the Mediator in person, who once for all by His unique Sacrifice fulfilled everything. And we now do not have to make any sacrifice at all of expiation and satisfaction for our sins, but we have to render to God sacrifices of praise; and He is satisfied with them by means of our Lord Jesus Christ. And although it may be said in the Scripture, that at the coming of Jesus Christ altars will be prepared by all the world to make sacrifice to God, nevertheless we must leave the type and dwell on the truth. For inasmuch as the altar was the sign of the adoration which ought to be given to God, when it is said that He will make sacrifice throughout all the world, it is intended that God will be adored universally. It is true that the Pope and all of his own wish to conclude from this passage that sacrifices have to be. And when they wish to approve their mass, they bring forward this testimony of Scripture. But if what they make believe to be were so, we would have to conclude that Jesus Christ has not yet appeared, and that His

5 Numbers 12:6-8

Kingdom has not come at all. But the opposite is seen. And if the Prophets have thus spoken it is to indicate that God will be adored universally in spirit and in truth, without dwelling any longer on the types. Besides we must note that the word of Prophecy is not here taken by the Prophet to declare things to come, as it was taken in former times, but he intends that he who has the gift of Prophecy will be to teach and to apply the doctrine, in order that we may be led into the knowledge of the truth and that we may know how to profit by it. So, the promise which had been made of the coming of Jesus Christ contains this: that men might have a higher knowledge of things divine than they had had previously. In fact we see that St. Paul calls it a wisdom of God under which all things ought to be humbled. Now we must take from all these things a summary conclusion: that as our God, sending Jesus Christ His Son into the world, wished to assure us more expressly of our salvation, also sending His Holy Spirit, He made us partakers of His graces more than ever.

The Prophet Joel in this passage then adds, "*God will perform marvelous things in the sky above, and signs on earth below, blood and fire and vapor and smoke; the sun will be converted into darkness, and the moon into blood.*"[6] By these words he indicates that great and marvelous things must happen when Jesus Christ will manifest Himself. And why? Because the world undergoes a change. Also those who would follow Jesus Christ must change entirely from their natural selves. That is also why the time of the coming of Jesus Christ is called "the last days." Besides, this is not said of a day nor of a month, but the Prophet applies all that is said here to all the time between the coming of Jesus Christ and the Last Judgment; and we must enclose the wonders which will be done at the coming of Jesus Christ, between the time that He has come and the last day. In fact, the further we shall go, the more of it will be done, as we experience every day. Now since we have the sense of the Prophet, we must look to apply it to our use. In the first place, when it is said that God will pour out His Spirit upon all flesh, it must

6 Joel 2:30-31.

be noted that it is the greatest benefit that we can have to be partakers of the gifts of His Holy Spirit. And it is the most excellent gift that God offers to men, in comparison with which all the liberality which He shows through earthly things is nothing. For when we are deprived of this gift, Jesus Christ is taken away from us, and until we are clothed in Him all that we do is to our condemnation. Also God pronounces that we cannot be His children until we are washed by His Holy Spirit. Now if we are not His children, we are not partakers at all of the communication of Jesus Christ. For although God presents to us His gifts, nevertheless, Jesus Christ is nothing to us until we have received the Holy Spirit. Let us conclude then, by this, that until we are partakers of the Holy Spirit, we are lost and reprobate; for it is He Who sanctifies us and Who makes us to be saints before God. So then, until He has called us to Himself, through the knowledge of His Holy Scripture (which we cannot have except by gift of the Spirit) to raise our spirits on high, we are detained on earth as in a tomb. Thus says St. Paul, "Those who have received the Holy Spirit, and who conduct themselves according to this will of God which is declared to us through His Word, those, say I, are children of God; but those are children of the devil who following their carnal affections are given to nothing else than voluptuousness." That, then, is why the knowledge of the truth of God is necessary for us, if we wish to be of the number of His children.

Besides, we must not excuse ourselves if we do not receive His gifts; for He presents them to us; but we are so wretched that we refuse the gift which He is willing to offer. By this the goodness of God toward men is known, in fact, although they are always fighting against His will, He does not cease to present Himself to us; as it is here said by the Prophet, "*Young and old, men and women* will all receive of the same Spirit." It is in order that no one may argue like this: "Ah, I am no student, I cannot, then, understand what is in the Scripture, to receive the Holy Spirit." Indeed, has God promised only to scholars the gift of His Holy Spirit, without distributing Him to others? Now it is an abuse to bring forward such excuses. When, then, we see that God is so liberal that He wishes to exclude neither age nor sex from the reception of His Holy Spirit, are we not very wretched to draw back when He draws near to us? In fact, it is here spoken of the Prophecy which must be fulfilled at the coming of Jesus Christ. Since it is true, then, that He reigns today, it must be declared and we must know that what has been predicted in it is veritable. And woe upon us, since what has been said is so clearly opened to us, if we do otherwise than our duty of walking in the fear of God, and of receiving the gifts which are presented to us by Him. I have already said that there is no one excepted, but we are so wicked that we cannot accept what is given to us. And what is the cause of it? Our unfaithfulness. And yet it is an inexcusable vice, both in young and in old, when they do not wish to place themselves under the obedience of God, seeing that they are all called by Him. And we must not be astonished if it is seen that they profit so little by the teaching. For if one considers, old people will be obstinate and inveterate in their evil, and no one knows how to remonstrate profitably with them. Young people are carried away like devils, and if one remonstrates with them, they enter into such a fury that it seems they would ruin God, His Word, and those who bear it. Now Jesus Christ, Who is the Wisdom, the Sweetness and Gentleness of the Father, does not wish to have communication with such foxes and lions, and if one shows them that they must humble themselves under the strong hand of God, in order that they may know that they have a Father in heaven, Who will take care, not only of bodily nourishment, but also that He will preserve them and govern them by His Holy Spirit, they will not submit to it at all, but they wish to be at liberty, to have full license to do evil.

Now since time does not permit that we speak of it further, we shall reserve the rest until next Lord's Day. And since it is true that we shall not know ourselves acceptable to God, except by means of our Lord Jesus Christ, let us bow in humble reverence before His face in the Name of Christ.

SERMON 18

Fourth Sermon on Pentecost *

And surely in those days I shall pour out My Spirit upon My servants and upon My handmaids, and they will prophesy. And I shall perform wonders in heaven above and signs on earth below, blood and fire and vapor of smoke: The sun will be converted into darkness, and the moon into blood, before the great and notable day of the Lord come. And it will happen that whosoever will call upon the Name of the Lord will be saved. — ACTS 2:18-21

LAST LORD'S Day we showed how at the coming of Jesus Christ God had poured out His great treasures upon the world, so that men and women, both young and old, were partakers of His grace. Now the riches which have been shed abroad through the goodness of God were not earthly riches, which could perish and come to an end; but it is the Holy Spirit from Whom every richness of salvation proceeds. Further, we have shown that this was not just for one time only, but that God is ready to continue what He has said, and that even today we are enriched by His gifts, if He does not withhold them from us. But we are so wretched that we are stripped of them by our ingratitude; He is no less liberal today than He was at the time of the Apostle, to make us partakers of the same grace which He shed abroad upon them; but we are such unbelievers that we shut against Him the way by which He wishes to come to us. For when He calls us to Himself by His Word, to make us partakers of His Holy Spirit, we draw back; and it seems that we have conspired to set ourselves in defiance against Him. And instead of young and old, men and women, all being called to be partakers of His grace, and that they ought to strive to receive

* From: *Corpus Reformatorum, Calvini Opera,* volume 48, pp. 646-654.

the Holy Spirit, to persevere more and more in Him, we see that the old are more hardened and more obstinate than others, the young are overflowing with every evil; and if someone remonstrates with them, they become enraged, so that it seems that they ought to ruin everything. Men, instead of being, as they ought, full of virility and agility of mind, to be attentive to the Word of God, are blockheads like brute beasts. Women, instead of being, as they ought, humble, and walking in all modesty and honesty, are full of lewdness, pomp, vanity and every vain superfluity. So then, we see now that if men do not enjoy the gifts of the Holy Spirit which God here declares that He will send upon His men-servants and maid-servants, it is not because He has changed His purpose, but we will not allow Him to do us good, for when He draws near we draw away. He is not, then, the cause why we do not receive all of His gifts, for the Prophet says, *"God will pour out His Holy Spirit upon all flesh."*

He says especially, "Upon all flesh," namely, upon all peoples without exception. It is true that it is to the Jews that Jesus Christ was sent, not only to withdraw them from the captivity of the devil, but also to make them partakers of the gifts of the Holy Spirit. But now that we are all assembled in a self-same Church, nothing more remains but that we should show the effect of our Christianity and of the graces which God has performed in us; and then we must not doubt that we received the gifts of the Holy Spirit, since it is said that God has shed them abroad not upon one, nor upon two, but upon all in general. It is not enough to boast of being Christian, if the effect is not demonstrated, and unless it is known that it is not in vain that we attribute to ourselves this title of Christianity. We must not do like many, even like those who are in the Papacy, who care neither for God nor for His Word, but content themselves with only the title, "Christian," and the means by which they can bring it forward, to whom the rest does not matter at all. If they are asked if they are Christians, what response will they give? Now it seems to them that a great mistake is made in asking them such a thing. "How is this?" they say, "are we not Christians? have we not received Baptism?" "Yes, surely, but what faith have you on account of it?" They will say that they believe what the holy Church believes, and thus they have a faith wrapped up,[1] in which their teachers instructed them, saying that when they believe what the Church believes, it is enough for them. If they are asked how they must serve God: "We do not have to know that." And it is a true vengeance of God to punish the iniquity of men, when such poor, ignorant people are seen being led by such teachers of Satan to trap them in the same pit with them. We see, then, how Christianity has been plunged into every lie and false doctrine by the idol of Rome. And why so? Because men have closed the way to the Word of God and were willing to be plunged into falsehood.

Now, however, let us come to ourselves, and let us condemn neither the Papists nor anyone else without more fully applying this doctrine to our use. We have the Gospel which is the doctrine of all wisdom, and yet how deaf and blockheaded we are! We are preached to every day: yet what instruction do we receive? It is sufficiently perceived, it is well seen what fruit is brought back from it. It is true that we well say, "We have the Gospel." But unless we obey it, what testimony have we that we are servants of God? For, (as we discussed last Lord's day) we shall not know how to be servants of God, unless we are partakers of His Holy Spirit, Who is named not without cause "the Spirit of Wisdom." For by that it is shown to us that we shall not know how to have ever so little of the grace of the Holy Spirit, if we wish to persevere, unless God augment Him more and more in us. It is true that every one will not be able to have Him in equal measure, but that does not hinder us from profiting by our little talent. If a man has the gift of tongues, he will not have a grace which someone else will be able to have. And it is what St. Paul says, "God will give to each one according to the measure that we are members of Jesus Christ; as we see that the members of the body have not all the same office; for the feet will do what the hands would not know how to do, the eyes are applied to a use other than are the ears; and thus consequently all other parts of the body. So our Lord

1 *envelopée.* In an envelope?

will shed abroad His Holy Spirit upon some in a manner that He will not do upon others. Yet it is always the same Spirit, and if we wish to be recognized as Christians, we must have understanding of what is said; and that it is God Who leads us by His Holy Spirit, in order that we may not be as blind men who walk in unbelief." So much for the word which is said, "God will pour out His Holy Spirit upon all flesh."

Besides, when it is said that, "They will prophesy," by that the Prophet wished to indicate that, when God instructs us, it will be in such perfection that not only will the doctrine be profitable to us, but also we shall teach others. In fact, he who will have received more of the gifts of God than others will be all the more responsible to instruct the humble and the small, and to apply himself to teaching his neighbors.[2] So then, let us learn that it is our office, after we shall have been taught by God, to try to lead others into the knowledge of Him. That is what Isaiah says, "Let each one take the hand of his neighbor to help him to ascend into the holy mountain."[3] And it is one of the principal points by which God approves our Christianity, when we have this charity toward our neighbors of instructing them in the work of God. Now that is done by the doctrine which we have received from Him through the hand of His Apostles; which went out (as we alleged last Lord's day) from the fountain of Jerusalem, whose rivers overflowed through all the world, so that each one will be able to receive it not only for himself, but we shall distribute it to our neighbors. It is true that all are not doctors to teach; yet if we are Christians we have enough wherewith to exhort our neighbors.

Now we come to the other part of the prophecy of Joel, where it is said, "*God will send terrible and marvelous signs, blood and fire and vapors of smoke,*" by which the Prophet wished to indicate that, when God would visit His people at the coming of Jesus Christ, although a great bliss and blessing was promised, this was not to say that we would not see horrible and marvelous things. And it was very needful that we had this warning, in order that we might know that the

2 *ses prochains,* sometimes "those next akin."
3 Not the usual interpretation of Isaiah 2:3.

coming of Jesus Christ was not in order to put us in this world as in a paradise, and in order to live here at our ease; but that Jesus Christ was sent for another purpose: namely, to withdraw us from these things below and to raise us into heaven. In fact we see that there might never have been things so horrible and marvelous as at the coming of Jesus Christ. If anyone asks why such things happened even after Jesus Christ was revealed, it is because we are so wretched that we do not wish to receive the gifts which He wishes to give us. Now when our Lord presents Himself to us and we reject Him, must He not then raise His hand, strike with lightning and storm in such a way that we may be moved and troubled by such an ingratitude? That, then, is why it is said that, when God will have shed abroad His Holy Spirit, we shall have to see wondrous troubles, and that, when we shall have looked above into heaven, and here below upon the earth, we shall see such great troubles and wonders, that it will seem that the sky should cave in and the earth be mixed together; the sun will be darkened, the moon will be turned into blood, stars will fall from the sky, and other wonderful signs will appear. It is true that each of these is reserved for the last day; but the Prophet wished to speak of all the reign of Jesus Christ, until He comes at the last day as Judge. We must, then, apply to our time all the signs which are here declared. For if we shall consider the things which have happened since the Gospel was preached, we cannot think that the hairs on our heads are not numbered. It is true that if we should see what was done at the coming of Jesus Christ, we shall be very weighed down if we are not terrified by it; yet if we consider well what happens every day, we shall have still further cause to be astonished. So then, the Prophet did not wish to indicate for only one time the signs that he here says should appear at the coming of Jesus Christ. For although at His coming He displayed these great treasures to distribute them to all, yet we shall nevertheless see wondrous judgments, because of the ingratitude of men who did not receive what was presented to them. And it is even what Jesus Christ said when He spoke of the destruction of the Temple. There are the disciples who ask Him when these things will be, and what will be the sign of His coming and of the consummation of the world; for they had this foolish opinion with all the Jews, that it seemed to them that the Temple ought to remain until the consummation of the world, and that they might still reign in peace like earthly princes. That, then, is what makes them put this question, although Jesus Christ had not spoken of the last day. Now He responds to them, "You will see wondrous and terrible things; you reckon that you will remain here below in peace and that you will reign at your ease; but it is entirely to the contrary, for there will soon be seducers, then the devil will make his efforts that false doctrines will be spread everywhere, there will be pestilences, wars, famines, that it will seem that the whole world ought to heave itself upside down.[4] And when you will see these things, it will not yet be the end; for Jerusalem will be destroyed." And by that He indicates that, whereas the Jews had tranquility of life in this world, they will have to begin to experience the judgments of God coming upon the ingratitude of men, which afterwards would be poured out through the world at large. Consequently He alleges, "After the tribulation of those days the sun will become dark and the moon will not give its light and the stars will not shine from the sky, and the powers of heaven will be moved." Which is a sentence like that of the Prophet, as if he said, "Not only will great troubles be seen here below, but if anyone raises his eyes on high, he will see confusion everywhere." Yet we must not be left without comfort. For although we see above and below many troubles and divisions, so that, when we shall have circled the whole world, we shall see only all wretchedness, yet we must take cause for rejoicing in the Creator of all these things. That is the sum of what the Prophet intends to show.

And now it is to us that this is addressed. For when God visits us and He gives us His doctrine, it is not that we ought to live at our ease in this world, and that we may be exempt from wars, famines, and pestilences; but we must be advised, when such things happen to us, that when we are in such great confusion everywhere that we do not know what is to grow out of it; we must, I say, then prepare to bear patiently such

---

4 *renverser ce que dessus dessous,* that the face of the earth should be upset.

afflictions, which we ought not to find strange; for they come to us because of the ingratitude which is in us. Our Lord asks only to show Himself as a Father sweet and lovable, and if we could not bear it, it would show that it is not without cause that He calls us His delicate children; but since we are so crude, that we wish neither to receive nor recognize Him for Father, must He not punish us for such a misunderstanding? We must know that He will have no less authority over us than a Father, and yet, when He sends us afflictions, however great and trying they may be, we must not fall into despair; but we must know that they come to us for our ingratitude. That, in sum, is how we ought to consider the judgments of God, and that what the Prophets have predicted is fulfilled before our eyes.

We come now to the comfort which the Prophet offers: namely, *"Whosoever will call upon the name of God will be saved."* If he had said only what we have already mentioned, we might be entirely astonished; for that which is here recited would know how to cause us only discomfort; but here is the further comfort which he offers, that if we call upon the Name of God we shall have salvation; even in the midst of the greatest troubles and divisions which could possibly be; even when hell would be ready to swallow us, there is a refuge which is assured to us, provided that we put our confidence in God to call upon Him. When a man will be in tribulation and trial, the devil will have the craftiness to put him in defiance, so that he cannot have access to God. But here is a great comfort that we ought to have in that we see that God does not set any predetermined boundary for us to call upon Him; but that, when we were as in the depths, we can call upon Him boldly. For since the Prophet says that he who will call upon the Name of the Lord will be saved, also on the contrary he who will not call upon Him will be damned, even though he were as in a paradise. Even Angels without this invocation could be rejected by God, which yet could not be. But by that we see that it is impossible to be able to exist in this world a minute without calling upon God. So here is a lesson which we surely ought to record often; for the Prophet pronounces a sentence upon all those who do not call upon the Name of God, when he says, "He who will call upon the name of God will be saved." For from that it follows on the contrary that he who will not call upon Him will be damned. And inasmuch as we are so cold and so easily turned away from calling upon the Name of God, the Prophet wished to signify that we must not desist from calling upon God, in the midst of all the troubles which could come to us; even when heaven and earth would have conspired against us, it is then that we must address ourselves toward God with both heart and mouth, and all our faculties. But it is not everything that we have our mouths open to say a *Pater noster,* or perhaps to say in a known language, "Our Father, Who art in heaven;" unless there is a real affection of heart founded upon faith. Otherwise we could repeat this prayer ten, twenty, thirty times, and it would be nothing but words thrown into the air. I leave also those who mix in their *Ave Maria,* thinking by such bits of trash to really call upon God as He demands. But such people are very far from the true invocation of God; these are witches and sorcerers who cannot forget their old devilish superstitions. Now we must not be too much astonished by such relics of Satan; for they never had, nor have they yet at present any faith in Jesus Christ. And for this reason, (as says St. Paul) "How will they call upon Him in Whom they have not believed?" This is a passage which we must note well; for St. Paul declares to us that, when it is spoken to us of calling upon the name of God, we must seek Him as our Father; knowing that we have in Him every benefit and that He is ready to receive us as soon as we return to Him. Otherwise what courage would we have to request of Him if we had not this? We must, then, be entirely assured, that when we call upon the Lord God in truth He receives us. By this is seen what fancy the faith of the Papists is. They say that one need not in any wise presume to be heard by God when one calls upon Him, because no one knows whether or not he is in a state of grace, and that it would be too great a presumption to think that he is. What must he do, then? They say that he must pray doubting, and that provided one commits himself entirely to their holy Church it is enough: namely, that one always have this answer ready, "I believe what holy mother Church believes." That is how they always have a doubting and concealed[5] faith, and St. Paul declares that God disowns them. For the Gospel must be preached, not to put us in doubt, but to assure us of our salvation. It is, then, very easy to judge what is the faith of the Papists, in which we were from the time of our ignorance. We must know that God has worked in us a particular grace when He withdrew us from the shadows of error where we were, and gave us His Gospel to lead us into view of salvation. When we think of all these things we ought to gasp and groan, seeing the goodness of God to be so great upon us that among so many people He has elected us to give us the knowledge of His Word. Now there is this evil in the Papacy that they say that one cannot call upon God in firm confidence, and that it is presumption, but that in calling upon God we must doubt. And they are not the little or the common people who wish to maintain that, but they are the greatest teachers, and those who will be expected to have all the Holy Scriptures imprinted upon their hearts. They will not be so ardent to defend their grotesque images, although they take great enough pain to maintain them. But when it is a matter of coughing up such blasphemies, they will be animated in such a way that it will seem that they are enraged. And why so? Because the devil wishes to hinder through them our calling upon the Name of God as we ought.

So then, may all those who pray to God as in the Papacy be assured that God disowns them. For it is not thus at all that we ought to pray to God, by saying three or four times, "Our Father, Who art in heaven" and repeating it and muttering it often. All those who do it are like sorcerers and witches. It is true that we would not know how to be too long in saying our prayers; but that means from the heart. For when we pray we ought to go outside ourselves, and forget our own nature, the world and all its allurements, in order to have more easy access to our Lord. That is how we must do it. Besides, let us know that, not having the true invocation of the Name of God, we have nothing at all. And let us weigh well this word where it is said that we are damned unless we call upon God. It is written in the fourth chapter of

5 *envelopée.*

Genesis, when it is spoken of the wretched line of descendants of Cain, that they build cities, they erect towers, and yet they have not the true manner of calling upon God.[6] But after Adam begat Seth, it is said that the Name of God was called upon rightly. God, then, was served and honored; for after Seth was taught to serve God, he also then instructed his children. Now for all the service of God we see that it is only said, "The Name of God was called upon." It is, then, the principal thing that we ought to have. For although the name "Christian" now flits about among us, yet it is only an abuse if the Name of God is not called upon by us. And we shall not be able to call upon Him (as says St. Paul) unless we have believed in Him. It is true that far from the front line we shall not be too bold. Wastrels are seen, when they are under the shadow of a jug or a glass, who will make the best Christians in the world, and it will seem that they are the real champions of Jesus Christ, and that they have acquired for Him all that He has. Then others, upon coming, will promise that they will do wonders, and it will be thought (to hear them speak) that if Christianity were abolished, it would not be taken away from them; yet if they are looked at closely and their hearts are sounded, it will be found that they are far from what they promise. And they will be the first who will turn away from God. And why? Because they have not considered what they are; for when anyone takes a good look at himself, he will find a sea of sins, of which we shall not be able to be stripped unless, groaning, we have our recourse in God, to call upon Him in our necessity. Besides let us know that this sermon, which at another time was delivered by St. Peter in the city of Jerusalem, is now delivered among us, in order that we may profit by it; and let us note that it is not without cause that he brings forward the passage from the Prophet Joel. Therefore, let us have confidence in this promise, "Whosoever will call upon the Name of God will be saved."

Following this holy teaching let us bow in humble reverence.

6 Genesis 4:17, 26

SERMON 19

Fifth Sermon on Pentecost *

Men of Israel, hear these words: Jesus of Nazareth, a man approved by God among you through works of power, through marvels, and through signs, which God did in the midst of you, as also you know; Him (I say) being delivered through the definite counsel and foreknowledge of God, you have taken by the hands of wicked men and have crucified and slain Him, Whom God has raised up, having loosened the pains of death, because it was not possible that He should be held by it. — ACTS 2:22-24

AFTER St. Peter declared in his sermon that the promise contained in the prophecy of Joel had been fulfilled, in that the Holy Spirit was given to him and to his companions, as a testimony and as a pledge that God wished to communicate the Holy Spirit to His Church and to each believer, and that, however, great troubles must come, and that the faith of Christians must be proved; after all these things, I say, he calls the attention of the Jews to Jesus Christ. For since the Holy Spirit was given. they had to recognize the coming of Jesus Christ; because it said that this promise of Joel should be fulfilled only in the last time. So then, when we see the Holy Spirit thus poured out, it is a certain mark that God has sent Jesus Christ in order to accomplish the salvation of men. Now it is a beautiful manner of teaching and a very suitable order which we must especially note: namely, inasmuch as gifts which God gives us through His Holy Spirit are just so many means of leading and conducting us to Jesus Christ, in order to learn from Him all wisdom; for He is the fountain from which we must draw everything. In fact, firstly, since He was from all eternity the Word of God, He is the life and light of men, and because He has received all the gifts of the Holy

* From: *Corpus Reformatorum, Calvini Opera,* volume 48, pp. 654-664.

Spirit in perfection, since He was made man, it is of His fullness that we shall receive grace for grace. It is, then, by Him that we shall find grace before God, for if we wish to address ourselves to His majesty without availing ourselves of this means, we shall not be able to have access to Him. We must, then, come straight to Jesus Christ, since we know that He received in such perfection the gifts of the Holy Spirit, that through Him we shall all be able to be partakers of them. Thus St. Peter here uses a good reason to admonish the Jews that the Redeemer has come: namely, inasmuch as the Holy Spirit is poured out, we are in the last time.[1]

Then he adds: "*Men of Israel, hear these words: Jesus of Nazareth, a man approved by God among you through works of power, through miracles, and through signs, which God did through Him in the midst of you, as you also know; Him, I say, being delivered through the definite counsel and foreknowledge of God, you have taken by the hands of wicked men, and have crucified and slain Him.* It is He through Whom God has given Himself entirely to you, and nevertheless you have put Him to death. Yet you must know that it is He Who had been promised to you in the Law. He has come to be your Saviour, and you can recognize Him in that He has not remained in death, for God has rendered Him victorious over it, and He surmounted it." That is what St. Peter alleges in the first place to the Jews, to lead them to the knowledge of Jesus Christ. And we must note that he is not here still treating only of the death and resurrection of Jesus Christ. For, first of all, the Jews had to know that Jesus Christ was the Son of God. And that is what St. Peter wished to prove by what he here proposes. There are two things that we ought to know about Jesus Christ. The first is that we must believe that He is the Messiah, that is, the Anointed of the Lord promised in the Law, and of Whom the Prophets have written, and that it is He Who has endured death for our redemption, and that nevertheless He was not held by it, but that He was risen in glory, triumphing over all His enemies. So much for the first point. Then for the second, when we know that Jesus Christ has died for us, we must know Who He is and

1 The last dispensation, the age of the Church.

what benefit we are to receive from Him. There are two things which we must note well: for if we had now to teach a Jew, we would have to begin by this to instruct him in Christianity, by showing him that Jesus Christ, Who was born of the Virgin Mary, Whom those who took rank over Him delivered to death, is He Whom God has promised to them, and the way in which He has assigned to them the time He had to come into the world. Then how He bore witness to Him, that He was His Son, that He approved Him through signs and miracles which He did in the midst of them, and likewise that after He ascended into heaven He sent His Holy Spirit, following what had been predicted of Him. That, I say, is what we must tell a Jew to cause Him to know Jesus Christ. Then we would have to make him understand that, when it is spoken in Scripture of the reign of the Messiah, it is a spiritual reign, in order that he may not be mistaken by thinking that He is an earthly king, as all the Jews imagine. That is what has made them deny Jesus Christ, inasmuch as they have not seen Him ruling over the people as they considered that He ought to do. Now toward the Papists we do not have to insist upon the first point, but only upon the second. For they will confess with us that Jesus Christ is the Son of God, and He Who was promised in the Law, that He was put to death and that He was raised from the dead. There is where we agree without difficulty. But they must be taught why He came, for they do not recognize Him at all for what He is. We know that we must believe that in Jesus Christ alone and through the merit of His death and passion, we have salvation. The Papists on the contrary attribute it to their works and merits, and to their foolish inventions, and it seems to them that through this means they can be sanctified. They seek, then, in their works that which cannot be found except in Jesus Christ. That is how it would not be at all necessary to teach the Papists anything touching the person of Jesus Christ, but only to show them what His power is, why He came, and what profit we can receive from it.

St. Peter here needed to declare both of these articles: for the Jews did not know that Jesus Christ was the Messiah sent by God, and still less the power which was in Him, and why He had come. Therefore he shows them that He appeared as Son of God among them in that He was raised from the dead and that by this resurrection they could know that He was such; because He was delivered from death and was victorious over it, and therefore we must seek in Him life and salvation. That is what St. Peter wishes to show in the first place; then he will show what fruit we have of His resurrection, and that will be declared afterwards in its place. Now, since we know the intention of St. Peter, and what order he follows in his sermon, let us follow it, and let us learn to know that as soon as God has done us some good, it is inasmuch as we are members of Jesus Christ, and not that He is moved to do it through our works, nor for anything we can present to Him. Therefore, let us wander no longer in our imaginations, to persuade ourselves of this or that, but let us come straight to the knowledge of our sins to take no pleasure in them; as we see that St. Peter leads the Jews to this when he treats of the death of Jesus Christ.

He accuses them in the first place, saying *"You have murdered Him."* It is clearly seen that this is not to flatter them. In fact, St. Peter had to put that before them to prick them at the heart, and to wound them to the quick; as we shall see later that they had such compunction and bitterness of heart, that they were converted through it. By this means he had to catch the attention of the men to humble them and to lead them to the knowledge of their faults. For if one preaches to them always pleasant and delightful things, he will only make them gab about it,[2] and they will wish to be companions of God, and to enjoy Him like a mortal man. We see what happened to the Samaritan woman when she speaks to Jesus Christ and He offers her living water, of which if she drinks she will never thirst, she makes fun of him like the harlot that she is; but after He leads her to the knowledge of her sin, telling her to go and get her husband, and He declares to her all her iniquity, she speaks more humbly than she did at the beginning. When He put before her simply the gifts of God, she made fun of Him: "And whence the container to draw water, seeing that the well is so deep?" But when He said to her, "You are an

2 *s'en gaber,* one of Calvin's colloquialisms.

impure woman, you have had five husbands, and he whom you now have is not your husband," then she recognized her sin and calls Jesus Christ a holy Prophet. So then, until men are terrified by their sins, they will never give place to the Word of God. That is why St. Peter accuses the Jews of having crucified and slain Jesus Christ; not that he takes pleasure in casting upon them this reproach, but it is in order that they should know that their condemnation was at hand for their sins; and on the other hand the absolution for these through Jesus Christ if they will recognize Him and address themselves to Him. Now the ministers of the Word of God have here a norm: namely, that they ought to touch men to the quick, and show them their sins, in order that they may know that God is their Judge Who will not leave the obstinacy of sin unpunished; and by this means they will be drawn to Him in repentance, which they would not do at all unless they had been reprimanded and treated rudely. Therefore we must allow God to rule over us and to condemn us, in order to be absolved by Him. There are many who would surely wish that the Gospel might be preached, provided that it might draw them to their profit and fleshly desire, and that it might be for them a cover for their villanies. Now it is not to this end that we must preach; for our Lord Jesus Christ says that, when the Holy Spirit will come, He will rebuke the world of sin; He will be seated as a Judge on His throne and He will judge the world. So then, we shall not be able to treat faithfully the Gospel so that the world may not be led into this condemnation, unless each one knows what he is in order to rebuke himself. Therefore, may those who flatter themselves, groan; may those who are satisfied with themselves, be frightened; and may those who are persuaded that they are righteous in themselves, look at themselves more closely, in order that all may be led to this knowledge of sins by which we shall be led to repentance and consequently to the grace of God.

That is why St. Peter reprehends so rudely the Jews, saying that they have crucified and slain Jesus Christ. Then he adds, "*Being delivered through the definite counsel and foreknowledge*[3] *of God.*" As if he had said, "Although He has

3 *prévoyance,* strictly speaking "foresight."

been delivered by the hand of wicked men and you have put Him to death, yet that was not done without the will of God." Now it is not without cause that Peter adds this word, "Through the counsel and foreknowledge of God." For the Jews could at least reply, "If it is thus that Jesus Christ of Whom you speak to us is the Messiah, why has He suffered to be thus tormented and put to death?" And it is a very difficult thing to persuade them of, as we still see today that they mock and say, "If Jesus were the Son of God, why did He endure this opprobrium of the cross?" So wicked men disgorge this blasphemy because the cross is an object which seems to them to take away from the majesty of the Son of God. Yet St. Peter anticipates such fancies, which could hinder the Jews from giving credence to his teaching. And he says that not any of this has been done through chance (as they might have supposed) but through the will of God. Now when we shall fully consider the power of God, we shall escape all such fancies. We know that God is not at all disproved by sense and by reason, and that all that which He did was proper for the salvation of men. There is also the resurrection which we must diligently consider. For although the death of Jesus Christ could scandalize us, if we considered it all alone, because of the cruelty and shame of it, also we see in the resurrection a glory and an admirable power of God, which ought to turn us away from all the troubles and fancies which could scandalize us. It is not, then, without cause that St. Peter declares that what Jesus Christ endured was through the providence of God. Jesus Christ had to be the sacrifice offered to God His Father to blot out the sins of the world. When, then, we see such a purpose to the counsel of God, that we may know that all He does is for our benefit, we ought no longer to inquire why Jesus Christ suffered, because in that we see the infinite goodness of God, we see His love which appeared to us (as St. Paul says) in that He spared not His own Son, but has delivered Him to death for us.[4] We see on the other hand the

4 Romans 8:32.

obedience which Jesus Christ renders to God His Father. Yet let us not be so presumptuous as to enter into these foolish cogitations by saying, "Why has God done this or that?" We know that all that He has ordained is founded upon this fatherly love which He bore toward us. So then, in contemplating this, we see why Jesus Christ suffered. And that is the reason for which St. Peter said that God had determined this in His immutable counsel.

Besides, this was not just left to be done through the hands of wicked men. By which we see that the wicked may well be able to injure the good, but they will execute nothing unless God permits it. And even we have not any better mirror of all that than in the person of Jesus Christ. For we must know that all that He endured was predicted by the Prophets. It is said that He was put on the cross even as it was predicted. There are the brigands of Rome who crucify Him (that is, the officers who had been commissioned for the execution); it was thus prophesied. They give Him to drink a beverage very hard and bitter, they divide His clothing, and all that just as it was written. Briefly, nothing is done except what God had ordained. By this we see that wicked men can do nothing, except insofar as God unleashes the bridle upon them; as it is seen that these wicked men do not pass the limits which God has given them. Now what is said of Jesus Christ, we must also properly apply to our use. For He Himself testified that little sparrows will not fall without His ordaining it. If, then, the providence of God is such that it extends to these little beastlets,[5] it follows that nothing will happen unless God has ordained it. Then He adds that the hairs[6] of our heads are numbered. By which He indicates the care which He has for us, and since we are members of Jesus Christ and we are near enough to touch Him, He wishes that we may know that He holds us for His children. For although this world may be, as it were, the house of God, and though He may be to it the Father of a family, yet He has His Church

5 Neither good French nor good English, as far as I know, but one of Calvin's most descriptive colloquialisms.

6 Not good modern English but I follow the King James version, Mt. 10:30.

by special recommendation, and for her He has a special regard. So then, we see how we must think of the providence of God: namely, that St. Peter did not wish at all to put forward fantastic things and then to seek a thousand subtleties which do not serve for any edification. He did not wish to proceed in such a way, but He shows that God has so well proved our salvation, that we must not seek other means than Him Whom He has given us. Then he wishes to indicate that we are in such wise in the hand of God and in His refuge, that one can do nothing against us except what He has determined. Otherwise what would our lot be? If we were led through chance (as fanatics consider) our condition would be more wretched than that of brute beasts. But when we know that God governs everything, it ought to be a great comfort to us, and we can well lean upon it. We see, then, that it is a very necessary virtue[7] that we know the providence of God. Therefore we must consider that just as Jesus suffered nothing without Divine permission, so all that will happen to us comes from God. That is what we must note from this passage.

We must still further parse the word "*Counsel.*" It is true that some will speak well of the providence of God, but they will have only a foolish notion of it; for they think that He is resting high in the sky, and yet He leaves chance[8] or nature to rule here below. On the contrary it is here declared to us that God ordains everything and disposes of things just as it pleases Him. It is true that this is unfamiliar to us and we cannot comprehend it, but we must be content to know that He is the Governor of it, and we must not do at all like some dreamers who say, "And God knows what will happen, and we do not know how to put it in order; of what use to us, then, is His counsel and advice?" That, then, is the reason that such fanatics wish to give to their dreams, which are such great arrogancies that God will not leave them unpunished. For although God does not call us by His strict counsel, to declare to us His will, and what He

7 or source of strength.
8 *fortune.*

has deliberated to do, yet we must know that we are governed by His hand, and that the wicked will be able to do nothing against us, except insofar as God unleashes the bridle on them. Yet He does not cease, therefore, to have an order in nature; and that is not to say that, as for us, we must not make use of His counsel. For God has declared to us that He wishes that we should live by the bread which He gives us to eat, and that we should be cured of illness by medicine. It would then, be too great a presumption, if we wished to reject the means which God gives us to remedy our infirmities. And he who thinks he will get ahead by means of such presumption —it will be to his ruin and confounding. For when we say that the providence of God proved all things, it is not, therefore, that we must reject the means which He gives us.

St. Peter will say a little after this passage that it was impossible for the flesh of the body of Jesus Christ to change by putrefaction. And why? Only since it had been thus ordained by God, and not according to its nature. For when He was conceived in the womb of the virgin Mary, He took our own nature and was like us, sin excepted. Therefore His flesh would have been subject to corruption like ours, except that God had thus foreseen it. If one contemplates what the bones of Jesus Christ were, they might easily have been broken and fractured; however, we see that it was impossible for them to be, since God had thus ordained, and not at all according to their nature. This is what we must note touching what can be alleged from this passage; not at all that we should go speculate and invent a thousand sophisticated questions like the Papists know how to put forward; but in all humility let us consider that not only did God foresee things, but He disposes of them according to His will. Therefore let us learn to commend ourselves to Him when we shall endure great assaults of Satan and of the world, of which he is called the prince. And when it seems to us that the wicked ought to crush us, let us withdraw under the wings of our God, in order that He may give us wherewith to resist, and that being armed by His power we may be able to repulse all temptations which could happen to us. For when all the devils and all the wicked will have raised themselves against us, He will surely know how to bridle them and hold them tightly, provided that we have recourse to Him, putting ourselves in His safeguard. That is how we must contemplate the providence of God by faith, and not according to our senses. Now, concerning our having said that the wicked will execute nothing except what God has ordained, many would be able to reply. "Why? If that is so, we would have to say that God is the cause of evil, and that the wicked should be excused." Now to answer we must know in the first place what the will of God is, and even how He declares it to us in His Law. We know that He prohibits us from stealing. If I, then, go steal, for example, do I do His will? Certainly when the wicked are given to doing evil, it is not doing the will of God at all; for they well know that God reproves all that. When, then, they do evil, there is a resistance to the will of God. By which it follows that God does not wish at all that they do evil, but He permits them to do it, and they are not at all excused thereby, inasmuch as they do it against His commandment. We must not say that God is the cause of evil, for He does not commit the vices that we commit. As also we see that He checks the devil by punishing those who are deserving of it. The devil commits evil and has no other regard but to do evil, and yet God does not let him serve any other different purpose. God will permit a thief or a brigand to rob a good man of something, even though he will be faithful and living well. Why so? To prove the patience of the latter, and in order that it may be known. We see what Job said in all his persecutions, "God had given it to me, God has taken it away from me, His name be blessed." And always he was pillaged by brigands. How does he understand that, then? Does Job accuse God of robbery? No. We must not understand it thus; for we know that the brigands are wicked men, and they come not only against the will of God, and in the intention of doing evil; but he looks higher, that this is not done without the providence of God. So then, Job does not attribute the evil deed to God, but he knows the condition of the men. He sees that the Chaldeans and the Sabeans are as it were, the scourges of God. They pillage him, they rob him, they kill his servants, they lead away his beasts; briefly, they completely impoverish him, and nevertheless he always praises God, knowing well that this would not be done without His ordaining it. Thus we must do; for if the wicked persecute us, we must not regard them alone, but our faith must fly higher: namely, to know that the providence of God is over them. That is how we must judge the matter, and not enter into frivolous speculations about it.

Now we see that Jesus Christ was surely crucified by wicked men, and yet it was not done at all without God's having ordained it. But God surely used it for another purpose. The wicked men wished to destroy Jesus Christ, and God wished that His blood and His death should be a perpetual sacrifice, and that our redemption should be fulfilled and accomplished. So then, when we contemplate that, we have occasion to glorify God, and he who will come to a contrary conclusion is rebuked in his own conscience. Now St. Peter says that Jesus was raised from the dead, to show that we must always join the resurrection of Jesus Christ with His death. For if we contemplate Him only in His death we shall see Him there entirely full of shame and opprobrium, and disfigured like a leper; but when we come to the resurrection, we see how He was exalted by the hand of God, Who has given Him all power in heaven and on earth. So then, as soon as we have said, "Jesus Christ has died," let us know also that He is raised. He is dead according to the weakness of the flesh, but in that He is raised, He appeared Son of God. That is what St. Peter wished to indicate by saying, *"Whom God raised up, having loosened the pains of death."* Now in that he says the pains of death, he does not intend the pains of physical death which Jesus Christ suffered; but the horrible anguishes in which He was, because He had to be our Pledge, and to bear the pain of all our sins. So then, He endured not only in the body, but also in the Spirit; yet it was not to be conquered by it. But we shall not be able now to deduce what is needful to declare the meaning of the pains of death; therefore we shall reserve it for another time.

Following this holy teaching let us bow in humble reverence.

SERMON 20

On the Final Advent of Our Lord Jesus Christ *

God is just in giving affliction to those who afflict you, and rest with us to you who are afflicted, on that day when the Lord Jesus will manifest Himself from heaven with the Angels of his power, and in flame of fire, working vengeance against those who know not God, and do not obey the Gospel of our Lord Jesus Christ, who will suffer punishment: namely, eternal perdition before the face of the Lord, and by the glory of His power, when He shall come to be glorified in His saints and to be admired by all believers, because our testimony to you was believed.

— 2 THESSALONIANS 1:6-10

OUR LORD Jesus Christ must appear from heaven. It is one of the principle articles of our faith. His coming must not be useless. Then, we should look for it, waiting for our redemption and salvation. We need not doubt it. For that would violate all that our Lord Jesus Christ did and suffered. For why did He descend into this world? Why was He clothed in human flesh? Why was He exposed to death? Why was He raised from the dead and lifted into heaven? It was to gather us into His Kingdom when He shall appear. Thus this coming of our Lord is to seal and ratify everything He did and endured for our salvation. Now that should fully suffice to brace us up to resist all the temptations of this world.

But since we are so frail that we cannot place faith in what God says to us, St. Paul now uses a new argument to better confirm us in this hope, to which he had exhorted us in the person of the Thessalonians. God will not allow Himself to be thus despised by those who hold the Gospel in contempt, who do not take account of His celestial majesty. He is not

* *From Corpus Reformatorum, Calvini Opera*, volume 52, pp. 225-238.

willing to permit His creatures to rise against Him and to resist Him. That is why we ought to be all the more confirmed in the hope of our salvation, since God is interested in it as His own cause. This point we should note well.

Although God amply assures us of His concern for our salvation, our nature is so full of distrust that we are always in doubt. But when the teaching is set before us that God will maintain His right and that He will not permit His majesty to be trodden underfoot by men, it should fill us with assurance. Then it is certain that God gives us this grace of joining His glory with our salvation so that there is an inseparable bond between the two. Since God cannot do otherwise than maintain His majesty against the pride and rebellion of men, is it not infallibly certain that our Lord Jesus will come to give us release and rest?

Let us note, then, that Jesus Christ cannot maintain the glory of His Father unless He declares Himself to be our Redeemer. These things cannot be separated. We see the infinite love of God for His faithful ones, when He joins Himself in such a way to them that just as He cannot forget His glory, so He cannot forget our salvation. When He employs His power to take vengeance on those who resist Him, He will all the more punish those who have afflicted unjustly His own. That is the intention of St. Paul when he brings out here that Jesus Christ will come even to take vengeance upon those who have not known God and obeyed His Gospel. It is as if he said, "Here are your enemies who persecute you. Now will you question whether God regards your afflictions to pity you and apply the remedy? Do you think that God does not take account of His glory and that He is not willing to maintain it? Although adversaries afflict you because you adhere to the Gospel, God also in maintaining His cause will show Himself to be your protector."

However, St. Paul here gives us other admonitions which are very useful to us. For when he speaks of the vengeance which is prepared for our enemies, he says, "Jesus Christ will come, even with the Angels of His power and in flame of fire." And to what purpose? It is to confirm what he goes on to say: namely, that the enemies of the truth will suffer their punishment before God and before the face of His majesty. It is as if he said that we can never understand what will be the torment of unbelievers, just as also we do not see the glory of God, for when we speak of the glory of God we know that it is infinite. We cannot measure it, but we must be rapt in astonishment. Such is the horrible punishment prepared for all unbelievers, since God unleashes His power against them. For since His majesty is inestimable, their torment must also be incomprehensible to us. So much for item one.

Besides, when St. Paul speaks of infidels and enemies of God, he says, "They have not known Him," and that they have not obeyed the Gospel, or that they have been rebels. This manner of speaking implies a very useful doctrine. For when one asks men, although they may be very wicked, if they wish to wage war against God they will say no. However, they do everything contrary to what they profess, since they are not willing to be fully subject to the Gospel. How can that be? It is said that we cannot obey God except by faith. So says St. Paul in both the Epistle to the Romans and in the book of Acts. Since faith is true obedience and such as God requires and approves, it follows that all those who do not wish to believe the Gospel are rebels against Him and as much as they are able they rise against Him. If they protest that such is not their intention, the deed is such, all the same. By this we are taught that we cannot serve God acceptably unless in the first place we believe the Gospel and accept all that is contained there to humble us. In short, faith is the principal service which God asks of men. It is true, however, that we must note that faith is not simple assent of the mind to what we are taught, but also we must bring the heart and the affections. For not only by mouth or by imagination must we accept what is said to us, but it must be impressed upon the heart and we must know that we are not permitted to set ourselves against our God. But with true desire we ask to adhere to the doctrine offered to us. Faith, then, is from the heart where it has its root and is not knowledge pure and simple. For if we were only convinced that the Gospel is a reasonable doctrine and meanwhile we did not at all relish it and perhaps it even displeased and angered us, would that be obedience? Certainly not.

Let us learn, then, in order to obey God, not only to regard the doctrine of the Gospel as good and holy, but to love it, and also to join reverence with love according to what David says of the Law, that he finds it more sweet than honey and more precious than gold or silver. We must, then, prize and hold in high esteem and take the doctrine of the Gospel above all that may be sweet and lovable to us. When we do that, then God will approve our obedience. That is the peculiar service He asks of us. On the contrary it will be in vain for us to do this or that, everything that we can attempt will be an abomination before God, until we have believed the Gospel.

In that see how miserable is the condition of the Papists. They torment themselves more and more with their so-called devotions. It seems to them as if they have a good grip on God. When they joke as they do, when they babble their paternosters, hear many masses, trot on pilgrimage, pay their money to do their abomination, it seems to them that God must allow that much good to their credit. And why then? They lack the principal thing, which is faith. For even if those things were not evil, nor against God, yet they will become frivolous before God when they are offered without faith on the part of men. Then we see that although the Papists work confidently to serve God, they only add to their condemnation and bring down His wrath still more upon their heads. So much so that they are here named rebels against God, since they do not wish to be subject to the doctrine of the Gospel. To be sure they will say, "Look, our intention is to serve God, and we do this and that to this end."

Very well. But here is God who invites you to Himself. He shows you that your only good rests in His pure grace and mercy, that you must look for salvation only in Jesus Christ. He declares to you that He has sent His Son so that you might experience the result of His passion, that in His Name and through Him all your debts will be receipted and remitted, that you ought not to seek any other advocate than Him to find access to His majesty, that you should ask to be renewed by His Holy Spirit. Behold our Lord, Who speaks in this way. You Papists, what are you doing? There is nothing but pride and presumption in you. You charge like a bull against all the promises God gives you and claim to have gotten by yourselves what only Christ can give you. You place confidence in your works and in your merits. You go to seek such patrons and advocates as seem good to you. Meanwhile Jesus Christ is left behind. There is no faith in you. What is worse, you are rebels against God, you wage mortal war against Him instead of serving and honoring Him, as you think you do.

So then we surely have to magnify our God, because He has drawn us out of such depths and has shown us what is the true entrance into His service: namely, that He joins us purely to the doctrine of the Gospel and that we receive the promises He gives us. Besides, if we perceive that men are humbled, that is a true preparation to bring them to the service of God, even the full and perfect obedience which God approves. That then is a point, that all unbelief is rebellion against God, since there is no obedience unless it begins by faith.

St. Paul says that those who do not obey the Gospel do not know God at all. By which we see that ignorance is no excuse for men, as much as they trust in it as a shield. It seems to them enough if they are not openly convicted of having sinned knowingly. They reckon that God must forgive them everything. Really? But St. Paul says particularly that Jesus Christ will come to destroy those who have not known God. Let us realize then, that we are bewildered and lost unless we know Him Who has created us and Him Who has redeemed us. In fact, that is very reasonable. For why has God given us sense and spirit, unless that knowing Him we may adore Him, and that we may render to Him the honor which belongs to Him? Men would like to be highly esteemed and honored, no matter what becomes of their Creator. Is that proper? Is it not against nature?

However, note that the ignorance of unbelievers does not proceed from pure simplicity, but there are malice, pride, and hypocrisy, which cause them not to have discretion and sense. How so? For if we could know God, it is certain that we would come to humble ourselves before Him. For it is impossible for men to think of what God really is, without being touched to the quick by some fear so as to bow under Him. Thus, when we are rebels against Him, it is a sign that we have never known Him. For this knowledge of God is a thing too much alive for us to say we see it and then be obstinate and rebels like unbelievers.

If one alleges that they are ignorant, it is true. But so are they also evil-doers and hypocrites. For have we not all of us enough things to render us inexcusable? Even though there were only the seed that God put in us by nature, that contemplating the sky and the earth we ought to think there is a Creator from which everything proceeds, God reveals to us as in a mirror His majesty and His glory, and there is no one who is not convinced by that. The most wicked, even though they have mocked God, if they find themselves in any distress, will have recourse to Him without thinking of it. For God drives them to it in order to take away from them every excuse so that unbelievers are not so ignorant that they have no hypocrisy in them. They wish to cover themselves, but they close their eyes knowingly. There is also pride and malice in it. For if we would bring honor to God such as belongs to Him, we should have a great anxiety to inquire about Him and His will. When, then, we are so cowardly and cold it is a sign that we scorn Him. Then we do not ask for anything but to be left in darkness. How can that be? For when we approach God and He reprimands us for our faults, we ought to learn to be grieved for our vices and to correct ourselves. We are content to be asleep in our rags. That is how we avoid the piercing rays of God.

Note well, then, that not without cause men are punished, notwithstanding their ignorance. For they cannot allege that it was simple ignorance, but rather hypocrisy, pride and malice are mixed up in it. That is why St. Paul, when he says that those who have sinned without the Law (that is, those who have no knowledge of the Word of God) shall be lost nevertheless, he adds that God has engraved a law upon the hearts of all. While we may not have Scripture nor preaching, yet we have our conscience which ought to serve us as a law, and that will be enough to condemn in the last day. We may well have many subterfuges before men, and we will think that we ought to be acquitted, but our accounting will be found to be very faulty when we appear before the celestial Judge. There we shall find that all our excuses are frivolous. Let us note well this passage where it is said that our Lord will come to execute His vengeance upon all those who have not known God and who have not obeyed the Gospel, that is, all unbelievers. Thereby we see that faith is the only door to salvation and life, since Jesus Christ must come to confuse those who have not believed.

Besides, let us observe that until God has enlightened men they are entirely ignorant and blind. And why so? For we may well comprehend everything in heaven or upon earth, but until we have known God, what is all the rest worth? We shall not know Him until He enlightens us by His Holy Spirit. So we see that we shall not be excused on account of our ignorance, so let no one flatter himself or go to sleep. However, let us note also that when we have known God it is only reasonable that we should be subject to Him, and that He should hold us in check, and that His will should guide our thoughts and affections, and that we should have such faith in the Gospel that we can profess like David that this doctrine is sweeter to us than honey and more precious than gold or silver. So much for this point.

Besides, we see here how God wishes to assure us of our salvation. For if Jesus Christ is to come to take vengeance upon all those who have not believed the Gospel, but have resisted it, we can and we must conclude that the world will be judged only according to the Gospel. Now it is said to us that when we have received in true faith the promises of God we must not doubt His goodness nor His love toward us, nor doubt that Jesus Christ will make good what He has offered for us and our redemption. All those, then, who believe in the Gospel can pride themselves without any doubt, that Jesus Christ will come as their Redeemer. God gives us this certainty, provided we do not refuse such a gift.

As for what St. Paul here says of the power and glory of Jesus Christ, it is so that His coming may be more terrible to all unbelievers and rebels. Is it a small thing when it is said that Jesus Christ will come in the company of Angels, that He will come with flame of fire, that He will come with an incomprehensible majesty, indeed to strike down with lightening against all His enemies? So, we see that St. Paul here wished to admonish unbelievers, in case there was any remedy for them, that they be warned not to remain always incorrigible. However, when we see that all those who are drawn by Satan and hardened only mock all the threats of God, may we take a lesson from that. And when we hear that Jesus Christ will come in such a terrible fashion, may we be held in fear and in check in such a way that, when Satan comes to sting or tickle us to turn away from obeying the Gospel, we may think to say to ourselves, "Where are we going? into what perdition? are we provoking against ourselves Him to Whom all majesty, dominion and glory is given so as to cast into the abyss those who oppose Him?" If we thought of this, certainly we would be held back in such a way that all the lusts of our flesh and all the temptations of the world could do nothing against us.

Now, however, St. Paul has also wished to compare the first coming of our Lord Jesus Christ with the second. Why do the wicked and the despisers of the Gospel rise so boldly so that we see them enraged and uncontrolled? It is because they hear that Jesus, while here in this world, took the condition of a servant, even that He emptied Himself of everything, as St. Paul says, even to this death which was shameful and full of disgrace. Although the enemies of God do not know Jesus Christ apart from this weakness, they take it as an opportunity to blaspheme against Him with such fury. To be sure, but they do not consider that, as He suffered according to the weakness of the flesh, so also He was raised by the power of His Spirit. He unfolded, then, a glory under which we all, both great and small, should tremble. But again, if unbelievers do not know what the Power was that appeared in the resurrection of our Lord Jesus Christ, may they listen to what is here said: namely, that He is not coming to be held in contempt.

He appeared thus, then, to be made obedient in our name, as was necessary to satisfy for our sins. But now He will come to be Judge. He has been judged and condemned so that we might be delivered before the judgment seat of God, and that we might be absolved of all our sins. It will no longer be a matter of coming in such humility. He will come then with the Angels of His glory. That is what St. Paul meant by saying that the coming of our Lord Jesus Christ will be dreadful.

Further, let us note that he adds still more. "He will come to be admired in His saints" and to be glorified in them. Not without cause St. Paul adds this sentence. For who are we to endure the presence of the Son of God, when He comes in burning fire and flames? When He comes with strength beyond understanding, alas! shall we not melt before Him like snow in the sun, and shall we not be reduced to nothing? Even the mention of this Divine glory of Jesus Christ would be enough to sink us into the depths. But St. Paul shows us that if we are of the number of the faithful, and we believe today the Gospel, we need not fear when Jesus Christ appears, nor be frightened by the majesty that will then be shining in Him. And how is this?

For He will come (says he) to be glorified in His saints and to be admired in them. As if he said that, what he said above of fire and flame, what he spoke of terror and dread, is not to discourage believers, that they should not desire the coming of our Lord Jesus Christ and raise their heads every time it is spoken to them. For He will come for their redemption. The doctrine that our Lord joins together these two things is common enough in Holy Scripture. He will come to take vengeance on His enemies, and He will come to deliver His own. He will come to be Savior of those who have served and honored Him, and to cast down and confound those who have hardened themselves against Him and His Word. Let us remember well then that this terrible description which is put here is not to frighten us but rather to make us glad that such is the love and grace of God toward us. Our Lord Jesus will come, indeed, with a dreadful power. And what for? To cast into the abyss all

His enemies, to avenge the injuries, insults, and afflictions that we shall have endured.

How are we worthy that the Son of God should thus unfold His majesty and show Himself with such terror against those who are His creatures? We certainly are not, but He wills to do it because He loves us. As I have already mentioned, we should be consoled when he says that the Son of God will come, even with such a fright and such dreadful majesty. For in this He effectively declares the infinite love which He bears and shows toward us, since He spares not His power and His majesty to do vengeance for all the injuries which we have endured. But we would not be able to take any pleasure in it unless what St. Paul says here is observed: namely, that our Lord Jesus Christ will come not only for revenge against His enemies and those who have been rebels against His Gospel, but also to be glorified and to be admired in His saints and those who have believed.

When St. Paul adds this, it is as if he said, "He will come to make us sharers in His glory, that everything worthy to be honored and revered in Him will then be communicated to us." Briefly, St. Paul declares that our Lord Jesus is not coming to keep His glory to Himself alone, but that it may be poured out upon all the members of His body. This is why he says to the Colossians, "Now our life is hidden, but it will be shown at the coming of our Lord Jesus Christ." He is not coming, then, to have anything peculiar to Himself and of which we are deprived, but rather that His glory may be communicated to us, not that He had not always preeminence over His own, which is the reason why He is the Head of His Church. In fact, the glory which He has communicated to us is neither to detract from nor obscure His own but rather that we must be transformed, as says St. Paul to the Philippians. Instead of being pitiably full of infirmities as we are now, we must be conformed to the heavenly life of our Lord Jesus Christ.

So St. Paul in speaking thus has paid special attention to the condition of believers as it is in this life. For we are marked men, they point fingers at us; they shoot out the tongue: we see the evil-doers mock the children of God. We must be thus rendered contemptible so that we may learn not to seek our glory in this world. God could surely make us to be esteemed by all if it pleased Him, but He wills that we bear such infamies so that we may look on high to seek our triumph there. And besides, would it be proper that we should be glorified and applauded here while God were dishonored? Evil-doers fully mock God and if it were possible they would even spit in His face. Would we still wish to be honored by them? If we desire it, must it not be said that we are too cowardly? Continuing what I began to say, although the faithful are now despised and rejected, some mock them, others oppress them, they are eaten out of house and home, and they are trodden under foot; for this reason the Apostle reminds us of the last day, saying that then we shall be admired, even as the Son of God is. However, let us not fear that the glory which He places upon us will fail to frighten our enemies, so they will be made our footstool, as Scripture says.

But St. Paul shows here especially who ought to hope to share the glory of the Son of God, and he describes the character of those who have believed when he calls them "the Saints". For he shows (1) that those who are given to the pollutions of this world must not expect to have any part or portion in this inheritance, nor to have anything in common with the Son of God. However when he adds "those who have believed" he shows (2) that faith is the true source and origin of all holiness. And thirdly he shows (3) that if we have pure and upright faith we cannot help becoming more and more sanctified. Those are the three points we have to remember.

The first is that if now we are going to defile ourselves and wallow in our filthiness and pollutions we are cut off from the Son of God and we need not expect that His coming will be of any profit to us, but let us remember what the Prophet said. "Desire not that the Day of the Lord come, for it will be to us (sic) a day of terror and astonishment and not a day of salvation and joy. It will be a day of cruelty and confusion. It will be a day of darkness and shadows." Since at that time there were many hyprocrites who shielded themselves with the Name of God, the Prophet shows them that it will cost them very dear. Likewise today we see the most wicked people making confession with full mouth and voice. How is that? Do they think we do not fear God and we do not also wish to be as good Christians as others? True enough. Yet they are people debauched and full of all impiety who have as much religion as dogs and swine. When they are finally examined on their life, it will be seen that they are full of disloyalty, that they have no more faith or loyalty in them than foxes; that they are full of treachery and perjuries, full of cruelty, full of bitterness against their neighbors; that they are given to every nuisance and outrage, that whoever will offer them the most will win their vote; they open a shop to grab with both hands so that they sell not only their faith but their honor before men; they open a fair and a market to lay themselves open to every evil. In short, they are seen to be extremely impudent and contemptible, although they never stop boasting that they are some of the most advanced in the Church of God, and God will help them, so it seems to them, as if He were most obliged to them. As we see today, the Prophet speaking to those of his own time says, "How is that? Why do you boast? of the Day of the Lord? Do you think His coming will get you anything? No, not at all. But it will be to you an appalling day, a terrible and fearful day. There will be nothing but fright and astonishment for you." So we must remember from this passage of St. Paul that if we wish that the coming of our Lord Jesus Christ may profit us, and that He may appear to us as Redeemer for our salvation, we must learn well to dedicate ourselves to holiness and we must be separated from the pollutions of this world and of the flesh. So much for the first point.

But to succeed in it let us note that we must begin by faith, which also follows what we have already discussed considerably. In fact, faith is the source of all holiness, as is mentioned in Acts 15, where St. Peter says that God purifies the hearts of men by faith. That is said to show that, however beautiful men may appear, they will always be polluted and infected before God until He purifies them by faith.

Now by the third proposition we are admonished that, if we have true faith, we cannot help becoming more and more sanctified. That is, *we are reformed for the service of God only* and we are dedicated *to honor Him alone.* How is that? As soon as by faith we embrace Jesus Christ, He will dwell in us, as all the Scripture says, as St. Paul especially says. Jesus Christ (says he) dwells in your hearts by faith. I pray you is it not incompatible that Jesus Christ dwells in us and we are still given to all villainies and filthy things? Do we think that He wishes to dwell in a pig-sty? We must, then, be consecrated to Him.

Besides, He cannot be with us except by His Spirit. And is He not the Spirit of holiness, justice and uprightness? Would it not, then, be a strange mixture if men were to boast of having faith in Jesus and at the same time lived lives dissolute, wicked, and polluted by all the infections of the world? That would be to say "I accept the sun, but not its brightness." That would reverse the whole order of nature. For the sun without its brightness would come sooner than Jesus Christ without His justice. Note well, then, we must not take this covering of hyprocrisy to say that we have faith in the Gospel and believe it with a sure knowledge, unless our life corresponds, we show that we have received Jesus Christ, and by the grace of His Spirit He dedicates and sanctifies us to the obedience of God His Father.

Thus we shall not rely upon false tokens to usurp this title of faith, as it is such a sacred thing. Let us beware then, lest we profane it. But if we believe in the Son of God, let us show by the result that we have believed in Him. It is also certain that He will cause us to experience His power. He will give us grace to wait with patience for His coming. Although we must suffer in this world many injuries for His Name, in the end we shall be reclothed with His glory and His righteousness. He has given us the promise, the force of which He will cause us to feel provided we receive it without any doubt.

Let us bow in humble reverence before our God.

Other Related Titles from Solid Ground

In addition to the book in your hands Solid Ground has published more than 300 titles since 2001. Some as follows:

Covenant Theology: A Reformed and Baptistic Perspective by Greg Nichols

The Complete Works of Thomas Manton

Deluxe Leather Edition of the *1689 Baptist Confession of Faith*

Deluxe Leather Edition of the *Three Forms of Unity*

Robert Hawker's *Poor Man's Commentaries*

Scriptural Exposition of the Baptist Catechism by Benjamin Beddome

The Marrow of True Justification by Benjamin Keach

The Travels of True Godliness by Benjamin Keach

Gospel Sonnets by Ralph Erskine

A Body of Divinity by Archbishop James Ussher

Heaven Upon Earth by James Janeway

A Short Explanation of Hebrews by David Dickson

Commentary on Hebrews by William Gouge

Commentary on Jude by Thomas Jenkyn

Commentary on Second Peter by Thomas Adams

Commentary on the New Testament by John Trapp

The Christian Warfare by John Downame

An Exposition of the Ten Commandments by Ezekiel Hopkins

The Harmony of the Divine Attributes by William Bates

The Communicant's Companion by Matthew Henry

The Secret of Communion with God by Matthew Henry

The Redeemer's Tears Wept Over Lost Souls by John Howe

Call 205-443-0311 for a Free Catalogue

CPSIA information can be obtained at www.ICGtesting.com
Printed in the USA
LVOW062038180113

316354LV00001B/5/P